P9-DMH-256

Computer Crime

Computer Crime

August Bequai

Lexington Books
D.C. Heath and Company
Lexington, Massachusetts
Toronto

Library of Congress Cataloging in Publication Data

Bequai, August.
  Computer crime.

  Includes index.
  1. Computer crimes. 2. Computers—Access control. 3. Criminal investigation. 4. Criminal law. 5. Criminal justice, Administration of. I. Title.
HV6773.B46   364.1'62   77-3857
ISBN 0-669-01728-0

Copyright © 1978 by D.C. Heath and Company.

All rights reserved. No part of this publication may be reproduced or
transmitted in any form or by any means, electronic or mechanical,
including photocopy, recording, or any information storage or retrieval
system, without permission in writing from the publisher.

Second printing, December 1978.

Published simultaneously in Canada.

Printed in the United States of America.

International Standard Book Number: 0-669-01728-0

Library of Congress Catalog Card Number: 77-3857

364.162
B481c

For my mother and father

34658

Contents

Preface

The development of gunpowder had a great impact on European society and law. It allowed monarchs to end the power and autonomy of their nobles. It also changed the nature of crime and gave rise to new forms of antisocial behavior. The "highwayman" entered the scene; gangsters would later use this new tool to dominate and terrorize America's cities.

Like gunpowder, the computer is here to stay. Its positive impact has been immense, and will continue to grow with time. However, on the negative side of the ledger, the computer enables a small group of individuals to steal sums of money that would have made the gangsters of the 1920s blush. Computer technology has enabled groups of political zealots or criminals to terrorize cities at the push of the button. A product of the electronic revolution, the computer criminal strikes anywhere and everywhere. He is not a product of our slums; his clothing is usually the best; and his schooling, the finest. He represents the criminal of the future. Our laws are challenged by him, and our jurists are left stunned. What makes this criminal more dangerous than any before him is that, should our system of laws fail to meet his threat, he may, in fact, ring the death knell of our entire system of justice. The stakes are high indeed.

Acknowledgments

The impetus for this book grew out of my interest in law and technology. After studying the field for a number of years, it became apparent to me that computer technology poses a serious challenge to our justice system. The ability of our lawmakers, jurists, scholars, and attorneys to meet this challenge may make the difference between a future under an "Orwellian" regime or a democratic one.

A project is never the product of one individual. Every author needs adequate support if he is to succeed. I am grateful to many individuals. Principally, I would like to thank both Phillip Manuel and Fred Asselin, staff members of the U.S. Senate Committee on Government Operations, for their assistance. Our working relationship culminated not only in this book, but also in the drafting of the Federal Computer Systems Protection Act of 1977, which hopefully will remedy some of the problems associated with computer crime. I would also like to thank Joe Kalet, my legal assistant and a student at George Washington National Law Center, for assisting me in the research. In addition, I am grateful to Kathleen M. Ferguson, for typing the manuscript, and also to Maureen McNamara for assisting her. I am also grateful to Waverly Yates, and to my sister, Teuta Bequai, for their comments and insights.

Suffice to say that there were many others; a book is the product of one individual, made possible by the assistance of many.

Introduction

In 1969, the U.S. Justice Department filed suit against the nation's largest computer manufacturer. Involved in this litigation were more than 150 million pages of documents, thousands of witnesses, and hundreds of attorneys for both sides. Four years later, during a pretrial conference, the judge assigned to the case was asked if he thought the suit would prove "too much" for the courts to handle. "No," replied the judge, "our system is sophisticated enough to handle any case." Presently, legal observers estimate that the trial may run into the 1990s. The case illustrates the sophistication and complexity of highly technical litigation.

In 1976, alone, more than 100,000 cases were filed in our federal courts. Many of our tribunals have serious case backlogs. Our investigatory and prosecutorial capabilities are presently overtaxed. The legal system in many of our large urban centers has ceased to be effective. This is the environment in which the computer felon operates. At present, he steals more than $100 million annually from our citizenry. Experts estimate that this is only the tip of the iceberg. Fewer than 1 percent of all computer crimes are uncovered. When finally discovered, the felon escapes justice by simply taking advantage of the legal maze we have created.

This book addresses the history and present dilemma posed by this felon. Chapter 1 deals with the criminology of computer crime. Chapters 2 and 3 deal with the problem of computer vulnerability and recommendations for improved security. Chapters 4 and 5 address the issue of present laws, both federal and local, to deal with the problem. Chapter 6 reviews the prosecutorial machinery and its shortcomings. Chapters 7 and 8 deal with the available investigatory machinery, both at the local and federal level. Without an adequate prosecutorial and investigatory apparatus, even the best of laws have their limitations.

Chapters 9 through 13 deal with evidentiary problems in the prosecution and conviction of computer felons. At present, both the prosecutor and litigant in computer-related litigation face serious obstacles. Chapters 14 and 15 deal with presently litigated cases involving computers; chapter 16, the last chapter, deals with the Electronic Funds Transfer System (EFTS) to adapt our legal system to the needs of an ever-growing technology, we and the problems it will bring about.

The computer is a marvel in its own right. It is the workhorse of the twentieth century, found in all facets of our economy. However, we must learn to safeguard it. If it is to be our "magic Genie," we must learn to harness it properly. This book is meant to offend no one, other than the computer felon, but it is meant to awaken us to a serious and growing problem, a problem aggravated by an antiquated and overbureaucraticized legal apparatus. At stake is our very form of government, for if we fail to adapt our legal system to the needs of an ever-growing technology, we will lose.

The Criminology of Computer Crime

In 1971 the New York-Penn Central Railroad disclosed that more than 200 of its boxcars had been rerouted from its Philadelphia yards to an obscure railroad yard in the Chicago area.[1] The original markings had been painted out and changed. A federal grand jury was told that this practice was common, and that more than 200 other boxcars were also missing from the Philadelphia yards— some of the cars cost an average of $60,000 each. The chief of the Federal Organized Crime Strike Force hinted that the Penn Central Company's computer may have been manipulated and instructed to misroute the cars to another location.[2] Organized crime elements were believed to have been involved.

In 1972 California authorities arrested a student of engineering on charges of stealing more than $1 million in electronic equipment from the state's largest telephone company.[3] Using only a telephone and the computer's secret entry code, he placed orders with the firm's computer. He was finally discovered when a fellow conspirator "blew the whistle." He was found guilty of grand theft and sentenced to 60 days in jail and 3 years probation. He later went into the consulting business to advise firms how to avoid attacks on their computers.

These two cases illustrate what has become, at least in this country, a growing problem—crime by computer. The United States Chamber of Commerce has estimated that the annual cost of this new form of technological crime may be in the area of $100 million.[4] Others put the figure even higher. There can be no doubt that the computer offers organized criminal groups that possess the requisite funding and sophistication the ability to threaten society with mass frauds. The threat of the computer challenges not only our economic well-being, not to mention our privacy, but it also raises fundamental questions regarding our very system of governance. For if the present legal apparatus proves unable to cope with this problem, then its legitimacy and its very existence may in turn be challenged. Historically, a legal system's survival, at least in part, has been based on its ability to meet societal challenges.

Computer crime is part of a larger form of criminal activity—white collar crime. White collar crime has been defined as any illegal act characterized by deceit and concealment and not dependent on the direct application of physical force. Its annual cost exceeds $40 billion.[5] The annual cost of computer crime exceeds $100 million. Computer criminals know that prosecution is rare and, even if convicted, that sentencing is extremely lenient—a "slap on the wrist," as the notorious Equity Funding fraud amply demonstrates. They also know that firms are reluctant to inform the authorities that they have just been "taken" for several million dollars, for stockholders and creditors will lose their confidence in management. In addition, they know that detection, investigation, and prosecution are ineffective against computer crime because criminologists have concentrated their efforts and studies on other areas, leaving this type of crime largely unstudied. Ignorance is the computer felon's first line of defense.

The Failure of Criminology

Throughout the evolution of criminology, its students have concentrated their efforts and studies in the areas known as "traditional crimes." These are usually associated with the more serious commonlaw crimes, such as rape, burglary, larceny, and murder. As a result, a legal structure has evolved that addresses essentially only these types of offenses.

However, with the rise of modern technology, nontraditional crimes have increased in currency and attention. The electronic revolution has given the criminal a new tool. With the aid of modern technology, he can steal millions of dollars. Computer crime is the product of this new era. It not only merits our study, but tests our society's ability to adapt its underlying legal philosophy to the challenges of a changing technology.

One of the fathers of modern criminology was Cesare Beccaria (1738-1794).[6] He was a reformer more than a scholar. He studied the inequities of his own society and proposed reforms to assist the poor and weak. Beccaria, as well as others who followed him, viewed crime in terms of the "poor." There was no effort to study or address the problem of crimes by the better-educated and more-affluent members of society. These were viewed as moral perversions, and no serious attempt was made to develop a police science that could effectively deal with crimes by the better-educated, crimes of deceit and concealment.

Jeremy Bentham (1748-1832) spoke of sanctions against criminals, designed to bring them into conformance with the dictates of society.[7] However, Bentham's sanctions were also aimed at the poor and ignorant. There was no attempt to evolve a legal system to deal with the problem of technological crime. In America, Edward Livingston (1764-1836) proposed a novel approach to deal with criminals, a quasi-religious concept.[8] Livingston had been heavily influenced by the Quakers and believed that it was necessary to reeducate the criminal through religious and secular teachings. However, just as his predecessors had done, Livingston associated the criminal with the poor and ill-educated.

Issac Ray (1807-1881), another noted American criminologist and scientist, suggested that criminal behavior might be the product of mental illness.[9] He was instrumental in developing a legal approach to crime as an illness, thus the rise of the "medical model" in later years. Henry Maudsely (1835-1918) followed this same path and suggested epilepsy and other physical and environmental causes to explain criminal behavior.[10] The Italian, Enrico Ferri (1856-1929) stressed the role and influence of anthropological factors.[11] The legal structures that evolved, both in this country and abroad, were an outgrowth of concern with crimes of the poor. Technological crimes were not studied.

However, by the turn of the century, this pattern began to change. American criminologists began to examine the problems of crime by the nonpoor—the educated and the sophisticated of society. In the 1940s, Edwin H. Sutherland began a vigorous attack on traditional criminology. He pointed out that:

... crime is in fact not closely correlated with poverty or with the psychopathic and sociopathic conditions associated with poverty, and an adequate explanation ... must proceed quite along different lines.[12]

Sutherland's attack was timely and important. Technology and the communications revolution of his time had enabled a few well-educated and sophisticated felons with the requisite training and organizational support to defraud the public of millions of dollars. He pointed to the new danger made possible by modern technology. For more than two centuries, criminologists had neglected to consider the power technology gave the sophisticated felon.

Sutherland suggested that criminologists should turn their attention to the crimes of technology and intellect. His observations, at first strongly attacked, eventually began to develop a following. In the 1950s and 1960s, the controversy continued; some people still dismiss Sutherland. Many law schools, as well as colleges of criminology, make little, if any, mention of his name and works.

However, Sutherland's contribution must be viewed as a key step in the study and analysis of crimes made possible by intellect in combination with the tools of modern technology. He viewed these crimes as even more serious than those committed by the poor and ill-educated. The computer had not come into its own in Sutherland's lifetime. However, today crime by computer is a serious corollary matter. It is not a "game," as some recent authors portray it; it is a matter for serious study by criminologists.

The Computer Criminal

There is no widely accepted definition of computer crime. Some authorities define it as making use of the computer to steal large sums of money. Others include theft of services within this definition, as well as invasions of privacy. Some take an open approach to the problem, viewing it as the use of a computer to perpetrate any scheme to defraud others of funds, services, and property.

However, a more sophisticated and encompassing definition must be developed to take into consideration the advances in the economic sector.

Computers can easily be employed to create false assets, to manipulate the price of stock, to provide "insiders" with material information on a company, thus enabling them to make millions of dollars. The computer can provide a small group of terrorists with the ability to manipulate the arsenals of large armies; it can make possible a $2 billion fraud. The computer is a giant calculator that enables individuals to obtain large amounts of data at the press of a button. It also enables felons to hide their crime as though it were a "needle in the haystack." By simply destroying a computer's program, felons erase their tracks.

An adequate definition of computer crime should encompass the use of a computer to perpetrate acts of deceit, concealment, and guile that have as their objective the obtaining of property, money, services, and political and business advantages. Computer crime may also take the form of threats or force directed against the computer itself. These crimes are usually "sabotage" or "ransom" cases. Computer crime cases have one commonality: the computer is either the tool or the target of the felon.

The computer felon is also a product of this new technology. He may be allied with organized crime, or to white collar felons, or even to foreign intelligence services. At present, there are over 2 million men and women who operate approximately 90,000 computers in this country. They constitute a large and growing army in both business and in government in all the developed nations, as well as in many developing ones. Today, there is no large firm that does not use computers. There is no one individual whose life is not affected by computers. Even more important has been the development of the technology for a "cashless society," also known as the Electronic Funds Transfer System. This new technology seeks to replace paper currency with "electronic impulses." Evidently, the computer is here to stay.

Studies of computer criminals usually portray them as young, educated, technically competent, and usually aggressive. Some steal for personal gain, others for the challenge, and still others because they are pawns in a larger scheme. This latter group has not been properly studied, since attention has generally been focused on the former groups. One study found that more than a dozen computer felons saw themselves as being pitted against the computer. Another study of several hundred felons showed that, on the average, each felon stole about $400,000.[1] Still other studies typically portray computer criminals as technicians, managers, and programmers. They are usually perceived as jovially challenging the machine, and discovery occurs only through inadvertence. Computer criminals attack large firms and take them for millions. They have victimized firms in West Germany, Norway, Denmark, England, Japan, and South Korea. The theft usually involves money, services, or trade secrets. However, when caught, the computer criminal's sentence is light compared to that of traditional property-crime felons, who usually receive harsh sentences for crimes involving much less property or money.

The studies tend to minimize the real impact and threat of computer crime.

Gary Library
Vermont College
Montpelier, Vermont 05602

Little or no attention is made of infiltration by organized crime in this area. The police chief of a large urban area has called it a serious threat. A former federal prosecutor has referred to it as a "picture of things to come." Further, the present studies are limited to the problem of security. Admittedly, security is extremely lax, and many computer systems are open to attack. However, more stringent security measures will not guarantee an attack-free system. This will only mean that the better-organized and more-sophisticated criminal groups will attack the system rather than those operating in the present "relaxed" form of computer crime. The teller, programmer, and manager may find their activities prevented by security systems that are unable to keep out the organized crime man, the Wall Street fraud-artist, and others.

Current studies also leave the erroneous impression that security measures alone will solve the problem. This is far from the truth. Security measures may mean that felons who now go unapprehended and undeterred will instead be brought before the law. The studies fail to state, however, that even if arrested, the felon must be brought to trial; that at present, our courts are congested; that computer felons would only add to this congestion; and that unless the factors that contribute to the congestion are also remedied, security measures alone will not solve the problem. For example, states such as New York and California lead the country in computer crimes. These states also lead the country in congested calendars.

Gary Library
Vermont College
Montpelier, Vermont 05602

Lack of Deterrence

The objective of every justice system is to dissuade individuals or groups from engaging in antisocial behavior. Unlike the felon of nineteenth century criminology, the computer felon is neither driven to theft because of hunger nor because of ignorance. On the contrary, he is fully conscious and well-versed in the criteria that society demands of its members. Deterrence may play no role with the mentally ill and ignorant, but it has a role in the world of the white collar felon.

However, white collar felons have had little to worry about from the justice system in this country. For example, a study of 82 white collar felons sentenced in the District of Columbia found that, of these, 50 percent received suspended sentences or probation.[14] About 8 percent received sentences ranging from 1 week to 6 months in prison; about 10 percent received sentences ranging from 6 months to 3 years in prison; and only about 20 percent received sentences exceeding 3 years in prison.

In another study of 207 convicted white collar felons, only one-third received prison terms.[15] The prison terms ranged as follows: 26 percent stole an average of $21.6 million and received only fines, suspended sentences, or probation; 16.7 percent received sentences of 1 year or less for offenses involving an average of $23.6 million; and only about 30 percent received sentences of up to 3 years in jail for crimes averaging $16 million.

Another study of sentencing in white collar crime cases found that sentences meted out to white collar felons were much more lenient than those meted out to traditional felons. For example, the likelihood of going to prison for securities fraud in the federal system is 21.5 percent, and most sentences average only 20.5 months;[16] it is only 19.5 percent for embezzlement, the average prison sentence being only 21.3 months;[17] for postal embezzlement (mail fraud), the likelihood of going to prison is only 19 percent, the average sentence being 11.6 months.[18] However, the likelihood of going to prison for crime classified as the "every-day type" by the government is 47.3 percent, the average prison sentence being 50.5 months.[19]

There are numerous cases that substantiate the "slap on the wrist" given white collar felons. In a recent example of this, an individual involved in a $2 million nursing home scandal received only a 6-month prison term. A felon convicted of falsifying records in a major commodity fraud, received only a $15,000 fine and probation.[20] In another case—the now classic Bank of Sark fraud, which involved the issuance of more than $500 million in phony letters of credit, certificates of deposits, and checks—the mastermind received only an 18-month prison term.[21] He also went on to serve as a consultant to the federal government. Perhaps the problem of white collar crime can best be summarized as follows: I recently asked a white collar felon who was serving a short prison sentence, "What do you plan to do when you get out of here?" He smiled and, in a low voice, said, "Do what I did before they put me here, steal."

Not only is there no penal deterrent for white collar felons, but the very prison system has been geared—and badly at that—to handle only traditional crime offenders. For example, the training programs, the counseling, and even the rating systems for parole are geared toward traditional criminals. In addition, a Presidential Task Force concluded that, for many, the penal system has little or no deterrent effect since endless appeals to the courts damage prison efficacy. White collar felons who are well educated and have large sums of money behind them can easily tie up the government in endless appeals.

At present, the computer felons who have been arrested and prosecuted have proven to be "small fries" in the overall corporate scheme of things. Yet white collar crime continues to grow, and there is little or no deterrence in this area. Prosecutors are ill-equipped and poorly trained to handle this new type of crime. Computer felons—who are also white collar criminals—will probably fare even better since their technology makes detection all the more difficult, makes prosecution more expensive and elaborate, and makes sentencing in its present form illusory. The computer felon challenges not only our imagination, but also our system of justice.

References

1. Gerald McKnight, *Computer Crime* (New York: Walker, 1973), pp. 152-153.

2. Ibid.

3. W. Thomas Porter, Jr., "Computer Raped by Telephone," *New York Times Magazine*, September 8, 1974, p. 33.

4. Chamber of Commerce of the United States, *White Collar Crime* (Washington, D.C.: Chamber of Commerce of the United States, 1974), p. 6.

5. Ibid.

6. Hermann Mannheim, *Pioneers in Criminology* 2d ed. (Montclair, N.J.: Patterson Smith, 1972), pp. 36-39.

7. Ibid., pp. 51-53.

8. Ibid., pp. 69-71.

9. Ibid., pp. 171-175.

10. Ibid., pp. 208-211.

11. Ibid., pp. 361-365.

12. Ibid., p. 26; see also 61, 84, 285, 288, 491.

13. Donn B. Parker, "A Look At Computer Fraud and Embezzlement in Banking," *The Magazine of Bank Administration* (May 1976):21-22.

14. August Bequai, "The Growing Problem of White Collar Crime," *Police Law Quarterly* VI (April 1977):14.

15. Ibid.

16. Ibid.

17. Ibid.

18. Ibid.

19. John A. Jenkins and Robert H. Rhode, "White Collar Justice," *Bureau of National Affairs*, April 13, 1976, p. 11.

20. Bequai, "The Growing Problem of White Collar Crime," pp. 13-14.

21. Jenkins and Rhode, "White Collar Justice," p. 13.

2

Why Computers Are Easily Attacked

Computers have come a long way since their unveiling at the University of Pennsylvania more than 30 years ago.[1] ENIAC (Electronic Numerical Integrator and Computer) consisted of more than 19,000 vacuum tubes and weighed 30 tons.[2] It could perform 5000 additions or subtractions a second and took only days to solve complex problems that took the human brain years.[3] The modern computer, however, has progressed; it can handle 400,000 calculations a second and has decreased substantially in size.[4]

The computer revolution has been startling. Its development is as important as, if not more important than, the steam revolution of the nineteenth century, touching every facet of our lives. For example, a computerized system has been developed to assist in the preparation of court transcripts.[5] It can cut the time in the preparation of a court transcript from 37 days to 18.[6] A new line of computers has been introduced recently in the business market, and their cost has been lowered to the point where most small firms can afford them. At present, there are more than 100,000 computers in use in this country, and experts estimate that their number will grow to 500,000 within the next several years.[7] The growth of the computer in our daily lives has also brought a rise in crime. The head of the Illinois Bureau of Investigation has said that there is strong evidence to suggest that organized crime has entered the computer crime field. Yet the computer, although growing more sophisticated and complex, remains a simple tool—it is easy prey for the criminal elements in our society. The problem demands critical and expeditious attention.

Why the System is Vulnerable

Although the average computer contains millions of storage devices, it continues to retain its simplicity. The operation of the system can usually be divided into five key components. Each of these lend itself to attack by the criminal.

The first stage of a computer operation is the *input*. At this point, data are translated into a language the computer understands. Several devices are employed to translate data into computer language: optical scanners, remote terminals, card readers, and magnetic tape units, to name a few. It is at this stage that error can be introduced into the computer. The error can be "planned" or "unplanned."

Data can also be altered and key input documents removed. Criminals have

9

frequently been able to feed false and misleading information into computer systems. For example, the system can be manipulated to make payments for nonexistent services; the computer can be fed false data concerning nonexistent purchases; fictitious companies can be set up, and the computer can be ordered to forward checks to them for services that were never performed. The felon can then easily take the checks and deposit them in bank accounts he may have. In one such case, the vice president of one company defrauded his firm of more than one million dollars.[8]

Unplanned errors are also common at this stage. For example, a federal government computer sent checks to more than 15,000 individuals at the wrong addresses.[9] In another instance, more than $600 million in erroneous payments were made by the Social Security System's computers.[10] The errors have cost both the state and federal governments millions of dollars. In 15 percent of the cases no explanation could be given for the errors.[11]

The second stage of the system is the *programming*. At this phase, the computer is given step-by-step instructions for the solution of problems it encounters. Programs are usually written in four language levels. The first level is the *absolute binary* and is intelligible only to the machine. The second level is *symbolic logic*, which consists of symbolic instructions translated into a machine language. The third level is *symbolic language*, which makes use of macroinstructions. These are coded instructions for performing a series of instructions. The fourth level is the *procedure-oriented language*. In this case, English words are usually employed.

The program controls and dictates the operation of a computer. The system can only operate on data and instructions in the program. If the program has errors or has been altered, manipulated, or falsified, this will show in the system's operations. The instructions the computer receives from the program will thus be erroneous. As programs become more complex, the ease with which they may be manipulated also increases because detection is more difficult. Testing of the program to ensure reliability also becomes more difficult.

Manipulation is not the only means by which programs can be changed. A felon can also patch programs to hide his fraud. A *patch* is a program that is extremely difficult to detect. In one case, a 21-year-old programmer put a patch on his company's computer that ensured that the felon's accounts would not be overdrawn.[12] If the account was overdrawn, the computer was instructed to ignore it when a computer overdraft was prepared.[13]

Programs are also open to theft. Valuable programs can be sold to a firm's competitors, to a foreign government, or even to other criminals who may then hold them for ransom. The destruction of a program can be costly to a firm, and place its operations behind schedule unless duplicates are maintained.

The third stage to the operation of the system is the *Central Processing Unit* (CPU). This is the central nervous system of the computer, without which a computer cannot function. The CPU contains the control units of the system. It guides the system, retrieves the required data, and directs the computer to perform. Within the CPU are also found the memory devices of the system. A firm, heavily dependent upon computer systems for its everyday business affairs, can be crippled if the CPUs of those systems are destroyed. Political extremists have been known to attempt to destroy a system's CPU. Assassination can take on a new meaning in a computerized environment. For example, since many machines employed in hospitals are controlled by computers, the destruction of the CPU or program could result in the death of an important political figure in that hospital.

Both criminal and radical groups could hold systems as "hostages" simply by threatening to blow up the CPU. The development of the so-called smart weapons further enhances the capability of small groups to inflict large and direct destruction on computer systems unless they are well protected.[14] Smart weapons are extremely dangerous because of their high rate of accuracy and their small size. For example, during the Israeli-Arab war of 1973, small groups of Arab soldiers were able to inflict heavy casualties on Israeli tanks with the aid of smart weapons. These same weapons can easily be employed against computer centers.

The fourth stage is the *output*. At this phase, data are received from the CPU and translated into intelligible language. This stage, however, presents the least likely target for criminal attack. However, output data can be stolen and sold to competitors, foreign governments, or the black market. For example, the mailing list of a large publishing firm was sold to its competitor by some of its own employees.

The final stage, and one of the most important, is the *communication process*. Data are translated back and forth from a computer to a terminal, or a computer to a computer. This process permits interception. Damage can be inflicted if a key component of this communication process is destroyed. Codes can be employed with some success, but even these can be stolen and sold to either competitors or criminals. In addition, should the government have access to these codes, it can easily listen in.

Security measures aimed at protecting a system should take into consideration all these various stages. For example, a competitor can engage, either directly or indirectly, in sabotage, espionage, or theft of valuable data at any of these stages. Extremist groups, as well as foreign powers, can also engage in sabotage and espionage. Valuable data may also be stolen by them or their agents. The system lends itself to such activities, and these elements, armed and well organized, can inflict serious damage on a system. It is not enough to protect the various stages alone. The entire system must be secured, especially where that system is employed in military or secret industrial matters.

Clerks and their supervisors have been known to falsify data, working alone or with others. They may even be pawns of organized crime. Programmers have also been known to attack systems. Some have held programs for ransom; others have stolen programs and sold them to competitors. Engineers have been known to engage in attacks against computers. They can easily gain access to a system, sabotage it, or install "bugs" in it. Operators have also engaged in computer crime. Many can easily copy files, destroy them, or sell them to the black market or a competitor.

These individuals have often been found to be involved in computer crimes. Foreign intelligence services and organized crime people have long been suspected of engaging in such ventures, although to date few provable cases are available to illustrate this threat. However, these last two groups can easily manipulate, directly or indirectly, the former ones. For example, programmers, operators, and others have proven easy targets for criminal elements. It is not sufficient to know the weaknesses of the system; many other factors must be considered in formulating a policy of computer security.

Electronic Penetration

The computer is not only vulnerable to direct human attack, but also to electronic attack. One of the most common methods of attack could easily be that of the wiretap.[15] This usually involves connecting a tap directly to the telephone or teleprinter of the computer in order to intercept and record messages. This mode of attack is most effective during the communication stage of a computer operation.

Valuable information can be intercepted and recorded, since tapping is extremely easy and common. Various proposals, including use of secret codes, have been presented. The National Bureau of Standards has proposed one such code system. Under this plan, all participating computers would employ a common cipher, and each participant would be given a key. Outgoing messages would be put into cipher, and incoming ones would be deciphered with the assistance of this key. Nonparticipating members would not have access to the key. The secret code would be too expensive for the private sector to crack. These keys would sell to members for a nominal fee. This system would permit communication between these computers and yet preserve the privacy of the data. However, the problem with this system is twofold: (1) insiders could easily sell the key to interested outside parties; and (2) government agencies could easily break the code. There are also those who charge that no foolproof code exists or can be devised.

Computer centers can also be bugged, and this is difficult to detect.[16] Consequently, such buggings are quite common. Computer personnel can be employed to place them, and since security measures in many centers are extremely lax, bugging can be an effective pipeline to the system's center.

"Browsing" is also an effective form of interception. It involves the introduction of an unauthorized terminal into the system, but the system must be one that does not authenticate terminal entry. Through this method, the interceptor gains access to the computer. However, verification of terminal entries could easily negate this method of electronic interception.

"Piggyback entry" is another method of electronic interception. It is achieved by intercepting messages from the computer to the user of the system. Data may be added or deleted, and the user then receives this altered information. By modifying the data, the felon has, in fact, affected the user's decisionmaking.

"Electromagnetic pickup" is yet another means of penetration. This involves the use of sophisticated devices that intercept the radiation generated by the computer, central processor, telephone, and teleprinter lines. These devices need not be connected directly to the system.

A more common mode of penetration is the "between-the-lines entry." This involves the unauthorized connection of a terminal to a valid private line. The penetrator enters the system whenever the legal user is inactive, but still holding the communication channel. This is one of the more common methods of penetration, and as with the others, is difficult to uncover, since users tend to be lax in security measures. It is this laxity that is responsible in large part for many penetrations of the system.

Categories of Crimes

Computer crimes may involve various violations of law, among them larceny, embezzlement, theft of property and services. In addition, they may involve violations of federal law. However, most computer crimes can be classified into one of several categories.

Sabotage is common and easily perpetrated against a computer system. It may involve an attack against the entire system or against its subcomponents, and may be the product of foreign power involvement or perpetration by a competitor. In addition, during labor disputes, systems are open to attack from irate workers. Criminals may also sabotage systems so as not to leave trails behind.

Sabotage may take various forms. It may involve the use of explosives, fire, or even destruction by water, and may be committed by an insider or from the outside. In one case, an irate employee destroyed hundreds of computer reels belonging to his employer. Irate employees have been known to steal programs and later destroy them. Some employees have discharged firearms at computers, and some have even poured gasoline over them and set them on fire. The electronic power source to the system can also be sabotaged, causing the system to malfunction.

Theft of services is also a common type of computer crime. This usually involves using a firm's computer at someone else's expense. For example, politicians have been known to use a city's computers for their political campaign mailings. A member of organized crime used a university computer to run his illegal ventures. Employees of a computer center may use it for their own benefit, at the expense of the company.

Property crimes are another category of computer crime. These usually involve the theft of merchandise and other property, either belonging to a private firm or to the government, by and through the use of a computer. For example, one can use a firm's computer to place orders for various merchandise and have that property delivered to selected locations. One can also use a firm's computer to order check payments for nonexistent services.

Data crimes involve the theft of information. This may take two forms: (1) theft of output data; and (2) theft by interception. The former may involve the copying of mailing lists, printouts, theft of programs, and other computer-related data. The latter may involve the interception of valuable and confidential data while in the transmission or reception stage.

Financial crimes are probably the most serious, although not the most common. The computer is usually manipulated to aid the felon in perpetrating complex and sophisticated financial swindles. False assets may be created to mislead creditors and stockholders into believing that the firm is doing well financially, when in fact it is not. The computer may be employed to provide insiders with confidential data on the firm for investment purposes. A company may also make use of their computer when acquiring another company to mislead the management of the new company through manipulated computerized data. For example, for many years, the management of the Equity Funding Company was able to acquire other firms by misleading them about its financial health through the use of computerized data.

As computer crime progresses, new and more flamboyant types of crime will come into being. It may be that with the influx and infiltration of organized crime into this area, a new category, devoted solely to that influx, will have to be established. Computers have the potential for sophisticated and complex crimes. Double sets of books can be maintained with computer assistance. Although much has been written about progammers stealing and copying valuable data, the area of financial crimes and organized crime in computer frauds has only been addressed superficially.

Lack of Vigilance

Unreviewed bills totaling in the billions of dollars are issued annually by automated decisionmaking computers. Yet a government study has found that government computers—as well as those in the private sector—have extremely lax security programs to ensure their integrity. More than 80 percent of the thefts that occurred at one large military installation may have been computer related.[17] Many of the computer crime cases that have been studied by government investigators were relatively unsophisticated and could have easily been prevented had proper security measures been employed.

An array of indicators exists that should make even the most uninformed take notice of the problem. For example, when the computer-generated data for a firm indicates record sales, and yet the industry is extremely depressed, one should be wary.[18] It may be that the firm's computer is being manipulated either by management or someone else within the firm. An increase in employee complaints about overwithholding by the computer or about inaccuracies in year-end earnings statements should also lead to further inquiry into computer manipulation.[19]

Absence of built-in checks and tests should also be remedied. Computer reports should not be thrown in an outside trash bin, and anything of major importance should be destroyed immediately, before others have an opportunity to use it for criminal activities. In the Pacific Telephone and Telegraph case, felons found some key documents in trash bins and used them to break into the computer's system. Computer operations are too often open to the general public. Most employees have access to the systems, although they have no business with them. For both investigatory and prosecutorial ends, this poses problems.

Another serious problem is personnel screening. Personnel departments are lax in hiring individuals for key computer operations, and many firms take no steps to secure data preparation equipment. In a number of instances, this equipment is readily available to most employees. Increases in customer complaints are, unfortunately, too often dismissed as cranks, and not given the serious consideration they deserve. An indepth inquiry should be the answer to such increases, especially where they are related to a computerized operation. Many times payments are sent to new suppliers who are not listed in the directory. This may be an indication that insiders are manipulating the system, and providing payments for nonexistent services. For example, the vice president of a major credit card firm acted in this manner and took his company for more than $100,000 before someone finally "blew the whistle" on him. In addition, firms that share computer time should keep an eye on their bills. Unusually high charges may be an indication that someone is using the service for noncompany business.

Americans, by nature, are lax in matters of security. However, present technology demands a philosophy that is mature and logical in matters relating to technological security. Computers, which control so many vast areas of society, should not be treated with such laxity. Privacy, security, and even the welfare of our society may be at stake.

Statutory Attempts to Preserve Security

At present, there is legislation aimed at preserving the confidentiality of computerized data. The Trade Secrets Act provides for fines of up to $1000 and imprisonment of up to one year for any federal official who discloses to unauthorized parties any confidential information that pertains to any individual or firm and that comes to his attention in the scope of his duties.[20]

The Privacy Act of 1974 also provides safeguards aimed at protecting the privacy of the individual from the government by regulating the manner in which information is collected, stored, or disseminated.[21] The act provides an individual with access to records containing personal information on him that are maintained by federal agencies. It also allows the individual to control the transfer of such information from one federal agency to another. It provides access to an individual's records only to those officials who have a reason to know, and requires agencies to establish rules by which an individual can gain access to his own records. Finally, records must be kept accurately. The act also provides penalties: up to $5000 in fines for agency individuals who make these records available to unauthorized parties.

However, the act also provides exceptions. For example, investigatory material, evaluation material used solely for promotion purposes in the military, and material regarding protection of the President of the United States can all be withheld.

The two statutes have as their objective the regulation of information in the possession of the federal government, and attempt to prevent abuse of such data. Information about an individual or firm stored in federal government computers would fall under both the Trade Secrets Act and the Privacy Act, which are intended to ensure the security of the data and their confidentiality. They do not address the security measures of the computer system, but proper control of the information requires effective security measures.

The Fair Credit Reporting Act (FCRA) has as its objective the requirement that consumer reporting agencies adopt reasonable procedures with regard to the confidentiality and use of personal data they possess.[22] Such data can only be released under certain circumstances: a court may order its release; the consumer himself may order its release if he provides written instructions; an employer, insurer, or any other firm with a legitimate objective may demand access to it. The reporting of obsolete information is prohibited. Thus credit bureaus are instructed to maintain up-to-date information. There are civil liabilities provided in the FCRA for any agency that misuses the data and fails to abide by the act. There are also criminal penalties for those who obtain the data under false pretenses. Further, the act provides that the Federal Trade Commission (FTC) will police the act to ensure compliance.

Computerized data maintained by credit bureaus would fall under the provisions of the FCRA. The act is a further step in the direction of preserving the integrity of the data stored in computer systems. Obviously, to preserve the integrity of the data and prevent their misuse, there must be provisions to secure the system from manipulation, the feeding of false data, and the alteration of existing data. However, the FTC has shown itself lax in enforcing the act.

Legislation is needed not only to ensure the safety of the data, and prevent tampering with it, but also to ensure the security of the system and to order firms to comply with rules and regulations in that area.

References

1. "Computers: A New Wave," *Newsweek Magazine*, February 23, 1976, p. 73.

2. Ibid.

3. Ibid.

4. "Minicomputers Challenge the Big Machines," *Businessweek Magazine*, April 26, 1976, p. 58.

5. "System Being Developed to Speed Court Transcripts," *Washington Post*, May 16, 1977, p. A-7.

6. Ibid.

7. Donn B. Parker, "The Increasingly Binary Nature of Crime," *New York Times*, July 11, 1976, p. 12F.

8. W. Thomas Porter, Jr., "Computer Rape by Telephone," *New York Times Magazine*, September 8, 1970, pp. 33-36.

9. "Computer Sends Checks to Wrong Addresses," *Washington Post*, May 9, 1977, p. A-4.

10. John Fialka, "More SSI Program Errors Suspected," *Washington Star*, June 17, 1976, p. A-4.

11. Ibid.

12. Porter, "Computer Rape by Telephone," p. 35.

13. Ibid.

14. Arthur T. Hadley, "Smart Weapons," *Washington Post*, January 30, 1977, p. C-1.

15. Stephen W. Leibholtz and Louis D. Wilson, *User's Guide to Computer Crime* (Radnor, Pa.: Chilton, 1974), p. 41.

16. Ibid., p. 44.

17. U.S. Senate, Committee On Government Operations, *Problems Associated with Computer Technology in Federal Programs and Private Industry* (Washington, D.C.: U.S. Government Printing Office, 1976), p. 2.

18. Chamber of Commerce of the United States, *White Collar Crime* (Washington, D.C.: Chamber of Commerce of the United States, 1974), p. 24.

19. Ibid., p. 25.

20. 18 U.S.C. sec. 1905 (1970).

21. 5 U.S.C. sec. 552.

22. 15 U.S.C. sec. 1681 (1970).

3

Securing the Computer

In 1972 the Federal Bureau of Prisons (FBP) began a program to train more than 100 inmates in computer technology.[1] Of this group, about 27 percent had been involved in white collar crimes before being confined.[2] Eventually, some 48 of these inmates were released from custody. Six were again rearrested for other crimes, and at least one of these individuals had been involved in a computer-related crime.[3] In a federal government study of computers, the investigators found that out of 69 computer fraud cases reviewed, about 50 involved computer personnel.[4] These two examples highlight the major problem related to computer integrity. Security is a key in the battle against computer crime; without security, there can be no containment. Security is the first line of defense.

Need for Personnel Security

At present there is no process whereby key personnel in sensitive computer jobs can be screened. Some firms require fingerprinting, and others administer lie detector tests. But some form of licensing may eventually be necessary. The computer is too important and the impact of computer abuse is too great for us to allow the present chaos to persist. Applicants for sensitive jobs should be screened through a series of indepth interviews. Technical qualifications, alone, are not sufficient. Background checks should be conducted. Some personnel may have organized crime links. Others may have been involved in non-computer-related crimes. Computer abuse can be too destructive to be treated lightly. Contacts with former employees should also be made to determine not only the applicant's suitability and skills, but also his integrity and character. Too often stress is placed on technical skills rather than moral character. With more than 2 million individuals employed in computer centers in both business and government, it is difficult, if not impossible, to conduct indepth background checks on all applicants. Neither is it necessary that such checks be conducted for all applicants. However, in sensitive areas, background studies should be conducted to ensure that key personnel have the professional integrity necessary for such positions.

It is also necessary that personnel employed at computer centers be educated in the areas of personnel security. Security should be taught in the classroom and stressed at the computer center. Many employees often discuss confidential matters with outsiders, without realizing that in the process they are compromising the security of the computer system. Further, they may be revealing confidential data stored in the computer regarding individuals and firms; especially in federal computer systems, this could constitute a violation of both the Privacy and Trade Secret Acts.

Another method of enhancing security would be to institute programs that include separations of responsibilities. A programmer should not act concurrently as a computer operator; personnel rotation should be instituted. Dissemination of information on the operations of the system should be strictly limited. Personnel should also be instructed to log any suspicious interruptions in the day-to-day operations of the system. Access by personnel should be on a need-to-know basis. Instructions to personnel should be in writing, and responsibilities for running the system should be separated, whenever possible. For example, no one individual should have authority to both modify and run programs. Program responsibilities should be divided between two or more individuals.

Functions assigned to personnel should also be divided. No one individual should have access to more than one area of the business. Thus, in a large firm, production, accounting, marketing, and financial responsibilities, even at the higher managerial level, should not be entrusted to one individual. Of equal importance, and greater implication for the future, is the development and implementation of a code of ethics for the members of this industry. For example, the British Computer Society has developed certain tenets for its members which are designed to assist, at least in part, in imbuing the industry with a greater sense of professional integrity. Among these precepts are the following: (1) each member will accept full responsibility for his or her work; (2) members will behave ethically; (3) members will protect the confidentiality of data entrusted to them; and (4) members will act impartially.[5]

Further, some form of certification is needed to ensure, at least in the sensitive areas of a computer operation, that personnel are not only qualified, but ethical as well. A code of ethics is sorely needed; and if the industry fails to develop one, the government will inevitably take the initiative and impose its standards upon the industry.

Physical Security

The complement of personnel security is physical security. The latter encompasses the construction, location, storage, and entrances of a computer center. Since the center may come under both criminal and terrorist attack, the construction of a secure center is extremely important. In constructing the site of such a system, the architect must be security-conscious, and must take into consideration the possibility of attack from both inside and outside the system.

Initially, the center should be isolated from other divisions of a firm. It should be constructed with resistance to fire in mind, wood being used sparingly, and only when absolutely necessary. Windows should be shatterproof and few in number. The facility should not be located near an airport, since radar waves can have a damaging effect on computer operations. The building should be constructed with flood-control devices, since water has caused serious damage to centers in the past. Alternate power sources should also be constructed, so that sabotage of the power source will not incapacitate the system.

Whenever possible, a center should be located in an unpopulated region. Only authorized personnel should have access, and control of the access points should be rigid. Staff should be given identification badges. All visitors should identify themselves and sign a log; the time of entering and departing should also be logged. Visitors should be escorted through the center, unless they are members of the permanent staff, and should not be allowed to bring in overcoats, luggage, or briefcases. Staff who bring in briefcases should have these checked at the entrance and exit points. Only authorized individuals should be allowed to remove objects from the center. The authorization should be in writing, with an explanation for the removal.

Safe storage must be available for computer records and data. The storage should be fireproof, and access should be limited and logged. Magnetic tapes, drums, and cassettes may be stored, and alternative safes should be available. Storage areas should be built to withstand not only fire, flood, and magnetic interference, but also criminal and terrorist attacks.

Emergency procedures should be developed well in advance. These should take into consideration the immediate securing of computer records and data, and alternate exits should be available. Communications within the facility should be protected from sabotage and should be designed to reach all center personnel. Audit trails should also be guarded and preserved. Replacement personnel must be available at a short notice. Further requirements are disaster plans and contingency plans for all eventualities. Negotiable items, such as checks, are to be numbered sequentially, and source records should be retained for a period of time. However, knowledge of the actual time period must be restricted to a small group of individuals within the center. Errors in processed data spotted by user departments should be reported promptly. A periodic physical count of all disks, tapes, programs, and other records is also important. Managerial personnel should maintain tight control over the operations, but periodic rotation of these individuals will prevent any one person from developing a workable scheme to defraud the firm through use of its computer.

Physical security measures can go a long way in safeguarding a computer from criminal attack, industrial sabotage, or espionage. All the laws in the world will not suffice as long as the computer center remains an easy and inviting prey.

Electronic Countermeasures

Electronic penetration of a computer center is a serious threat. However, electronic countermeasures can also be employed to defend a system. For example, closed-circuit television will make it more difficult to implant bugs in computer complexes. Security areas should be inspected for listening and other interception devices. Electronic equipment for the detection and neutralization of surveillance devices is available and should be employed to secure centers from electronic penetration. Sweeping is a valuable technique and should be employed periodically. Laser devices are also available and can enhance the security of a center.

Security codes and passwords may be employed to screen out unauthorized users of a system, but they must be changed periodically. Scramblers and cryptographic devices can be used where highly confidential data are being transmitted between two locations. The computer can be programmed to disconnect inactive terminals for certain periods of time in order to prevent unauthorized entry. The system should also be programmed to record any attempts to make unauthorized entries or to modify or alter its data.[6]

Electronic penetration of a system and its communications is a serious matter. The system is open to this mode of attack from criminals, competitors of the firm, foreign governments, as well as government agencies. Firms interested in the confidential data stored in a system may attempt to penetrate it through bugging, tapping, electromagnetic pickups, or other means. Blackmailers and political groups may seek confidential data stored in a system for still other purposes. Future political candidates may find their opponents burglarizing a computer system for "sensitive data" stored in its files. Electronic counter-measures should and must be employed to protect the integrity of computer systems.

Investigating Security Breaches

Penetrations and alterations of the data stored in the computer system should be investigated and traced to their ultimate sources whenever possible. Of the two, alterations of data are perhaps the more difficult to trace and reconstruct. Penetration can be dealt with through the employment of electronic counter-measures, which can trace, as well as neutralize, the source of such penetration. In investigating alterations, three key factors should be kept in mind: (1) the processed data; (2) processing instructions; and (3) those responsible for the instructions. The investigator should first bear in mind the source of the data. Original records should be compiled, whenever possible, and should be reviewed to see if any fabrication or alteration has occurred. In addition, such review can determine if false records were mingled with the originals and then fed into the system. The investigator should also review records and logs, and interview witnesses to determine who handled the records and their infusion into the system. The greater the number of persons involved, the more difficult the task, since background studies of the suspects must be conducted. The probability of error must also be considered. For example, could the altered data have been a product of human error rather than human design? It should be emphasized that if an individual is accused, and the alteration was actually a result of error, the firm could be open to civil suit.

The procedures employed must also be reviewed. For greater clarity, a review should be made of the collection and verification stages, as well as system safeguards. Did they fail? If the system fails, it is important to determine whether the failure resulted from sabotage or incompetence. The investigator should also review the history of the suspect employees in order to detect any past examples of similar behavior.

Review should be extended to the assembly stage and the input devices used at this stage. The matters to be dealt with at this point involve the identity of the actors and the time within which they fed the data into the system. The investigator should also review what procedures and safeguards were employed to ensure that false data would not be introduced into the system. The investigator should review all the input steps, determining not only the procedures through which the data were processed, but also who did the actual processing, and under whose directions.

It is important to determine who was directing the operation at the time the falsification was fed into the system, what instructions were given by this individual, and what his policies and attitudes were in relation to plant security. A background check of this suspect may be necessary. For example, has his standard of living improved dramatically? Have any behavior modifications occurred? What role did he and others play in the processing instructions? These are all key factors in ascertaining the likelihood of criminal activity.

Security is an ever-growing and important area in the war against computer crime. It takes on different shades and dimensions, and may differ in emphasis from system to system. Security measures applied in a computer system employed in secret governmental work need not be applied as rigidly in other areas of work. However, the laxity that has persisted cannot be tolerated in the near future. The computer can either serve or enslave us. Security measures can help ensure that it will serve.

References

1. U.S. Senate, Committee on Government Operations, *Problems Associated With Computer Technology in Federal Programs and Private Industry* (Washington, D.C.: Government Printing Office, 1976), p. 78.

2. Ibid.

3. Ibid.

4. Rebecca Leet, "Two GAO Studies Criticize Lack of Controls on Computers," *Washington Star*, May 10, 1976, pp. A-1, A-6.

5. Peter Hamilton, *Computer Security* (Philadelphia, Pa.: Auebach, 1973), pp. 55-56.

6. Stephen W. Leibholtz and Louis D. Wilson, *Users' Guide to Computer Crime* (Radnor, Pa.: Chilton, 1974), pp. 70-78.

The State Arsenal to Combat Computer Crime

At the local level, Rhode Island is one of the few states that has attempted, through legislation, to address the problem of computer crime. The majority of our local jurisdictions rely on traditional concepts to deal with this new and growing area of crime. These traditional concepts fall into two main categories: (1) laws dealing with crimes involving habitation and occupancy, and (2) laws dealing with offenses involving property.

Offenses Involving Habitation

One of the oldest of offenses is *arson*. Under the common law, arson was defined as the malicious burning of the dwelling of another. The common-law judges made no distinction between arson committed during the day and that committed during the night. From the earliest days of English law, the offense was classified as a felony, and, in most cases, punishment was death by burning. Under modern statutes, arson is still defined as a felony, the definition including not only the act, but also the attempt to commit the act. The definition of *dwelling* has been expanded to include any store, barn, outhouse, steamboat, vessel, canal boat, railroad car, schoolhouse, public building, church, and the property, in whole or part, of any individual.[1] The burning, however, must involve *malice*, as defined as an intent to burn the dwelling of another. Thus, in common-law jurisdictions, the burning of one's own home is not arson. This has been modified somewhat by statutes in most local jurisdictions that make it a felony to burn one's own house for insurance purposes.

The mere fact that the burning results from another unlawful act will not make it arson. For example, if an individual lights a match while burglarizing a house and ignites some flammable fluid which causes the dwelling to burn, he will not be charged with arson. There must be a specific intent to burn the dwelling.

In addition, there must be a burning. There need not be a total destruction of the dwelling, or even considerable damage, and it is not necessary that there be a blaze.[2] The slightest ignition of a building is sufficient. If the material is charred, the test is met. However, there needs to be some structural damage by the fire.[3] A blackening or discoloration is not enough.[4]

Computers, both in government and industry, are open to attack by arson. Felons, in an attempt to hide their tracks, may ignite a dwelling which houses a computer or the software. Explosives may also be used to conceal a computer crime, and these, in turn, may cause the burning of the structure which houses the system. A partial charring may be sufficient to enable the local authorities to charge the felons with arson. For instance, at least one jurisdiction found a prisoner, already in jail, guilty of arson when he burned a hole in the building for the purpose of escaping.[5]

Fire poses a serious threat to computers. For example, one recent government study found that 14 federal installations had magnetic tapes and paper supplies within the computer room that were easily combustible.[6] Twelve other installations maintained conditions that were conducive to fire.[7] In one installation, the investigators did not find any portable fire extinguishers.[8] Fire is a serious threat, and apparently, one that has not been taken seriously. Sabotage, either for political or industrial objectives, could easily take the form of arson.

In 1959 a fire at the Pentagon destroyed three computer systems valued at over $6 million.[9] In 1973 a major fire broke out at the Military Personnel Records Centers in St. Louis, Missouri.[10] The center had been the repository for some 52 million personnel records, stored there since 1912. The fire started on the sixth floor, and before it was brought under control, some 16 million personnel records were destroyed. The building was not equipped with smoke detectors, sprinkler systems, or fire walls. About this same time, a bomb exploded at the Pentagon's computer facility and caused extensive damage.[11] The facility was made inoperable for about 29 hours.

Arson is a serious and growing problem in the area of computers. The systems are vulnerable to sabotage, and security measures in many centers are poor or nonexistent. The arson laws, with penalties ranging from 1 to 10 years imprisonment, can easily be used to prosecute sabotage by fire. Whether or not the computer system itself is damaged is a secondary matter. Of primary importance is whether the building is partially damaged or completely destroyed.

The crime of *burglary* has been traditionally classified as a felony. Penalties usually range from 2 to 15 years imprisonment. Under the common law, burglary was defined as the breaking and entering of a dwelling of another in the "nighttime" with the intent to commit a felony.[12] There are six elements associated with this crime: (1) a breaking, (2) an entering, (3) of a dwelling, (4) of another person, (5) in the nighttime, (6) with a felonious intent. A felony must be the object of the burglar.

A dwelling includes any house, apartment, or even one-room shack. It may also include, in some jurisdictions, a bank, store, warehouse, shop, stable, or other building.[13] It makes no difference if the breaking occurs during the night or day under most modern statutes.[14] For the breaking requirement to be satisfied, damage to or destruction of the building is not necessary; but entering through an open door or window is not a breaking. The door or window need not be locked, but there must be an entry into a part of the building that is closed. One who has authority to open the door or window cannot be charged with burglary. Thus, in a computer crime case, an employee who has authority to enter the building cannot be charged with this offense, even if he enters with the intent to commit a felony.

Although a breaking is required, it will not suffice if there is not also an entry. The felon need not enter entirely within the building. Even if a part of him enters it will meet the criteria of the offense. Many jurisdictions have held that if the felon puts his hand inside the house while opening a window, he will have met the entry requirement.[15]

Under the common law, only dwellings used as places of habitation were covered by this offense. The building had to be one where an individual slept. Using it for business, or even meals, would not be enough to qualify it for the offense of burglary. Even the fact that the owner may sleep in the building on some occasions does not convert it into a dwelling for purposes of the common-law test for burglary. However, many jurisdictions have passed statutes covering banks, stores, and many other buildings not covered under the common law.

The law of burglary was intended to protect the owner of the dwelling who also dwelt there. Mere ownership was not enough to meet the dwelling-of-another-person test. An owner who leases a house to a tenant can commit burglary if he enters the leased house with an intent to commit a felony, and does so at night. However, a dweller cannot burglarize his own dwelling. He has a right to open the door or window of his dwelling and then enter it. Modern jurisdictions, however, have modified the dwelling-of-another-person concept to include even a hotel.

Although common-law burglary had to be committed at night, modern statutes have been changed to include daytime. The common law defined *nighttime* as including that period from sunset until sunrise. However, in jurisdictions adopting a modern definition of burglary, the offense can occur during the daylight hours as well as the nighttime hours.

There must also be a felonious intent. Under the common law this was interpreted as an intent to commit a larceny. An intent to commit a simple trespass was not enough. However, if there was a felonious intent, the fact that it did not achieve its end matters little. The attempt was sufficient. There must be an intent to commit a felony within the dwelling. Under the common law, there is no burglary unless there is this felonious intent. Many jurisdictions, however, have modified this by statute, and some will only require that there be an intent to commit "any crime."[16]

Burglaries in the computer crime area are common. Felons have been known to break and enter into a corporation's offices and destroy valuable programs. It is irrelevant that some of these individuals may have been employed by the burglarized firm. In order to be culpable, they must, however, have made an unauthorized breaking and entering. If they fail in their attempt once inside the dwelling, it matters little. The intent criteria is met solely by the attempt, regardless of whether the burglary takes place during the day or night. Modern statutes have broadened the common-law definition of burglary. Today, the law of burglary can frequently be employed to prosecute many facets of computer crime.

Offenses Involving Property

There are about a dozen theft crimes that relate in one form or other to computer crimes. The better known of these is *larceny*. The offense is one of the oldest of all common-law crimes, resulting essentially from the outgrowth of judicial interpretation rather than legislative action. Larceny was a felony under the common law, but most American jurisdictions have modified it by classifying the crime according to the value of the property involved: (1) grand larceny usually involves property valued at $100 or more; and (2) petit larceny involves property valued at less than $100. Petit larceny is a misdemeanor in the majority of the jurisdictions. Grand larceny, however, can result in a sentence of 1 to 10 years imprisonment.[17]

Under the common law, and most state statutes, six elements must be satisfied before an individual can be convicted of this charge: (1) personal property must be involved, (2) it must belong to another, (3) it must have been taken, (4) by trespass, and (5) it must be carried away, (6) with the intent to steal it. In some jurisdictions it is sufficient simply to allege that the defendant stole the property involved.

At common law, larceny was limited only to personal property. Although one could not be charged with larceny for taking and carrying away real property, stealing domesticated animals was held to be larceny. However, stealing wild animals was not larceny. The modern trend is to include any type of valuable property that can be moved. Many jurisdictions hold—some by statutes and others through court decisions—that the stealing of gas or electricity is larceny. The argument could then be made that the stealing of electronic impulses from a computer system is also larceny.

Some modern statutes make it a theft to steal services. New York classifies, by statute, a theft of services as a misdemeanor. The statute lists seven areas over which it has control: (1) use of stolen credit cards; (2) dodging restaurant or lodging charges; (3) dodging metered charges; (4) obtaining utilities without the supplier's authorization; (5) using someone else's equipment or labor; (6) dodging transportation charges; and (7) dodging telecommunication charges. Theft of computer services would probably fall within this statute, although it was not the intent of the legislators to deal with such theft in this way.

Intangibles are also property within the ambit of the law of larceny. For example, many statutes make it larceny to steal an airplane ticket or to secure a railroad ride without paying for it.[18] The property involved must have some value, even if it costs only 1 cent. The taking of articles that have no value is not larceny, but any value to the owner is usually sufficient to meet this requirement. Modern statutes have been extended to include virtually anything of value that can be taken and moved away. The taking of software, or even hardware, would constitute larceny. The taking of a printout, even if it is worth only a nominal fee, would constitute larceny.

The property must belong to another. One cannot steal from himself, because stealing is an offense against possession. Since only the possessor can be dispossessed, a lawful possessor cannot commit larceny. Thus an individual who is given lawful possession over some programs and in turn takes them and uses them for his own benefit is not guilty of larceny but rather embezzlement. The latter is a statutory crime, passed in England and adopted in the American colonies to deal with crimes involving one who has lawful possession of another's personal property. Larceny involves the act of wrongful dispossession. Consequently, one who has legal possession cannot be charged with it. However, one who does not have such possession can be so charged.

The owner of the property can himself be guilty of larceny. However, he must first have given lawful possession of the property to another, and must then take this property from the possessor, wrongfully and with the intent to deprive him of it. For example, X, the owner of some computer programs, delivers them to Y, who in turn is asked to store them for X until some later date. If X should at a later date steal these from Y, he can be charged with larceny. What matters is not ownership, but rather *possession.*

However, an employee holding the property of his employer usually has mere custody and not possession. This is an important distinction, for if an employee is charged with the custody of a computer system, he does not have possession. Thus should he take and carry away any property that is part of that system, he may be charged with larceny. For example, if a client merely examines a computer component, and later runs off with it, he has committed larceny, since he only had temporary custody over the property. In cases involving co-ownership, under the common law, a co-owner could not be charged with larceny for taking the property of the other co-owner because a partner cannot steal from his other partners what they hold in their partnership. The modern trend has been to make such acts illegal by legislation.

Taking for purposes of larceny means the taking of possession of the property at issue. The taking may be direct or indirect. For example, if X were to sell Y a stolen program and Y were to carry it away rather than X, it is still larceny. The fact that X may not have touched it does not exonerate him from the charge. Whether X or someone else takes possession of the property at his instigation is irrelevant, a larceny can be charged against X.

The taking need not be done by human hands. It can be affected by a mechanical device; another individual acting under the directions of the felon;[19] or even by a trained animal, such as a monkey, acting under the felon's directions and training. What matters is that the wrongdoer has set in motion any agency, either animate or inanimate, with the design of effecting an illegal transfer of the possession of some property of another to him.[20] The taking can also be in successive acts.[21] A series of acts has been held to constitute one single larceny regardless of the time between each act, provided however, that the successive takings be pursuant to: (1) a single intent and design, and (2) in execution of a common fraudulent scheme.[22] Thus, for example, if a physician files a dozen false claims with a medical insurance company, and that firm's computer has a dozen payments made to him, the dozen payments will constitute one act of larceny, provided there is a single intent and design, and provided that the acts were done in execution of a common fraudulent scheme. The significance of this distinction becomes apparent where prosecutors have to decide whether to charge the defendant with grand or petit larceny.

There is no larceny unless there is also a carrying away. The slightest carrying away may meet the test. The moving of an object even several inches may constitute a sufficient carrying away.[23] The object in question need not be moved out of a building. For example, a shoplifter can be charged with larceny and convicted if he simply moves an object from a counter, and never leaves the store.[24] Thus a felon need not carry the software or hardware away, but there must be some carrying away even if only for several inches.

There must, however, be intent to steal. If X takes away property belonging to Y under the mistaken belief that it is his, the taking is not larceny. For example, if a computer programmer were to carry away a program under the mistaken belief that he has authority to do so, it is not larceny. There is an absence of the requisite intent to steal. The intent itself must be to deprive the rightful owner *permanently* of his property.[25] An intent to take the property only for temporary use, as is the case in "joy ride" car cases, will not suffice. It is not larceny. Some states have specific statutes to address such problems. For example, many states have unauthorized-use-of-a-vehicle statutes. Others have statutes that make it a misdemeanor to misapply another's property—misapplication of property. For example, someone who pawns another's goods with the intent of returning them in the near future cannot be charged with larceny.

In New York, copying secret industrial material is a misdemeanor. There is no intent to permanently appropriate the chattel, merely an intent to appropriate its use. It is not larceny. Cases, for example, in the computer crime area that involve the copying of programs, rather than the taking and carrying away of them, may in fact be prosecuted under "use" statutes rather than under larceny statutes.

To take the property with the intent to sell it back to the owner for ransom is larceny. For example, several years ago a young programmer took several programs from his employer and went into hiding. He informed his employer that he wanted a ransom of $100,000 for their return.[26] Charges were never formally brought against him, a situation not uncommon in computer crime cases. Had he been charged, he could have been indicted for larceny. In another case, a programmer stole several million dollars worth of programs. He was later convicted and received 5 years in prison. If a person were to take some property with the intent of holding it until a ransom were offered by the owner, and then collecting the reward, it may be that he could not be charged with larceny since there is no intent to permanently deprive the owner of his property. However, some states have been able to overcome this common-law obstacle by statute.

Larceny statutes can and should be employed in simple computer crime cases where there is a taking and carrying away of the property of another. Both computer software and hardware would qualify as property under these statutes. However, there are problems. For example, a case could be made that the program, although valuable to the firm from which it is stolen, may not be valuable to the general public. The question is how does one ascribe value to such programs, tapes, or punch cards. The data on such may be valuable, but the article may cost only several cents. Case law will eventually work out such problems. The courts, as they come to understand and handle more and more computer-related cases, will also be able to determine value.

Embezzlement, unlike larceny, is not a common-law crime. It is a statutory crime that was enacted to close the gap created by the law of larceny. There are five general elements to embezzlement: (1) a fraudulent, (2) conversion, (3) of the property, (4) of another, (5) by a person to whom it is entrusted. Under the early English law it was a misdemeanor. Presently, modern state statutes make it either a felony or a misdemeanor, depending upon the value of the property.[27] The property itself may be any security, stock, loan, or other form of property. The owner may be an individual, a corporation, or an association, among others.

Unlike larceny, which is an offense against possession, embezzlement is an offense against ownership. The embezzler has lawful possession and may even have title to the property. For example, he may be a trustee. One who converts property given to him for an illegal purpose can be charged with embezzlement, provided the property has some value. The purpose for which the property is given to the embezzler is a secondary factor. The mere failure of an individual to pay his debts is not embezzlement.

However, depositing someone else's funds into one's own account is embezzlement. For example, for several years the vice president of a large New York bank ran a float fraud between two banks, with the assistance of the manager of the second bank. Deposit records were altered in the bank's computer system. The pair embezzled more than $500,000. Embezzlement crimes are common in the computer area.

The crime of *false pretenses* was unknown under the common law. It is a statutory crime. There are five key elements to the offense: (1) there must be a false representation of a material (present or past) fact, (2) it causes the victim,

(3) to pass title, (4) of his property to a wrongdoer, (5) who knows his representations are false and who intends to defraud the victim. In essence, the crime of false pretenses is one in which the wrongdoer obtains the property of another by means of untrue representations. This law, like that of embezzlement, was a legislative attempt to fill the gaps left by the law of larceny.

The statute has been expanded in most jurisdictions to include the obtaining of food, lodging, or other accommodations at a hotel, inn, or motel with intent to defraud. It also includes the wearing of uniforms with intent to deceive; use of slugs in slot machines; the falsification of corporate records; fraudulent advertising; circulation of false information as regards a company's stock; and many other areas.

The representation or representations must be untrue. For example, X represents (falsely) that his company's sales are on the rise, and even produces falsified records to substantiate his representation, and then uses that misrepresentation to encourage people to buy his company's stock. It should be noted that a company's computerized records can easily be manipulated to create a false view of that company's financial health. However, if the statements, false when made, later become true and the firm does in fact increase its earnings and attain a healthy financial position, false pretenses have not occurred.

A representation may be either oral or written, but it must be a representation of "fact." An expression or opinion does not fall within the statute. If, for example, a broker expresses his opinion to a client that, "I think it might be a good investment," this is an expression of his opinion. However, if he says, "I think this is a good investment because sales have gone up 300 percent," when in fact they have not and he knew this to be false but expressed it to induce his client to buy the stock, then he would be open to charges under the statute. Similarly, if he pulled out a computer printout to substantiate his recommendation, knowing that it was false, he would be open to charges under the statute.

A more subtle, and perhaps more dangerous, situation is the case in which a group of individuals makes recommendations on certain company stock and bases those recommendations on computerized data—knowing that the data fed the computer are false and misleading. Yet, this area has never been explored. Another example is the situation in which an investment advisor has only programmed his computer with half-truths and makes recommendations based on them. Further, if he receives a kickback for stock in certain companies that he recommends, he will not only be open to attack under the securities antifraud provisions, but also under a charge of false pretenses. In this instance, title to the property is passed to associates of the advisor.

However, representations must deal with present or past facts. If they deal with predictions, this will not suffice. A conviction for false pretenses cannot be based on predictions. A promise of future conduct will also not suffice. These may, however, be the basis for prosecution under the mail fraud statutes if the postal service is used.

There must be an intent not to perform the act from the first. Further, the defendant must know at the time of his representations that he cannot perform the act and that, in fact, his representations are false. However, if he truly believes at the time of his representations that they are true, even if they are not, he is not guilty of false pretenses.

The offense of false pretenses is perpetrated by obtaining the property. The wrongdoer must obtain possession over the property. If he does not, even though he made numerous false representations, he will not be guilty of this offense. It is not a defense that title to the property did not pass to the wrongdoer himself, but rather to a company owned by him or with which he is connected.

The victim must be deceived. If he is not deceived, the offense is not applicable. Further, the wrongdoer must knowingly have made the false representations with an intent to defraud. The offense itself can take various forms: false advertising, confidence games, and other related offenses. Some states have separate statutes for these related offenses. However, the law of false pretenses is one law that can be utilized in computer fraud instances.

Extortion has its roots in the common law. Historically, it dealt with the corrupt collection of unlawful fees by an officer of the law, under the color of the law. However, many states have passed extortion statutes. Under these, it is unlawful to: (1) extract money or other things of value, (2) by means of threat, (3) not sufficient for robbery, or (4) a communication for the purpose of such extraction. Generally, the offense is classified as a felony under the blackmail statutes, as they are known.

In most cases, it suffices if the wrongdoer obtains the victim's property merely by threats. In some states, the threats must be in writing. All statutes cover the demand for money, but some include chattels, property, or even pecuniary advantage. Threats to injure the victim, his family, or even his business—economic threats—are also included within some statutes, as well as the threat to publish defamatory material.

The computer falls under the protection of these blackmail statutes. Threats against the computer center, in lieu of money, are covered by these statutes. Threats to publish material stolen from a computer—sensitive data—may also be covered by the blackmail statutes. Threats to damage the economic welfare of a business or an individual, either through the use of a computer or by directing threats at the computer system, may also be covered. There are also federal extortion statutes which address this problem. Such statutes can often be used effectively in instances of computer crime.

Malicious mischief may also be relevant here. Malicious mischief statutes usually apply where there is malicious damage or destruction to the property of another. Under most statutes, the offense is a misdemeanor. For a finding of guilty under this statute, there must be some physical injury to the property of another. The injury, in turn, must impair the utility or diminish the value of the property.[28] The property must either be destroyed or have suffered some substantial injury.[29] For example, shooting a rifle at a computer would constitute an offense under this statute. Destroying programs or pouring paint over the computer—as was the case during the Vietnam war demonstrations—would also constitute a violation of the statute. Throwing things, such as a bottle, at the computer are violations as well.

The damage, however, must be done to the property of another and must have been inflicted with malice. For example, if one's rifle goes off and accidently strikes a computer in a building across the street, the statute will not be applied because there was no malice. Computers have become, more and more, the targets of attack by both politically and nonpolitically motivated groups. The malicious mischief statutes may prove of considerable assistance for local law enforcement.

Forgery statutes are also common in local jurisdictions. Forgery involves the making of a false writing and is generally held to be a felony. The elements of the offense are: (1) a writing, (2) which is false, and (3) was made false with the intent to defraud another. Forgeries may involve negotiable instruments, wills, contracts, receipts, governmental documents, and many other writings. The writing itself must be a lie.[30]

As in the case of false pretenses, forgery must include an intent to defraud. However, there is no requirement that another's property actually be obtained. It may be that the forgery is detected before the plan succeeds. The wrongdoer can still be charged, despite the failure of his plan. If he does succeed in passing the document, and does receive the money or property, he can be charged not only with forgery, but also with false pretenses. If the wrongdoer intends to make reparations at a future date, this is no defense. He is still guilty of forgery.

Although forgery covers writings per se, it has been suggested that it could as easily accommodate computer entry codes.[31] Whether this is true, remains to be seen. Many jurisdictions still retain the requirement that the writing be a paper.[32] However, there can be little doubt that if forged documents are used to gain entrance to a secure computer center, or if forged data are fed into a computer, the statute could be applied. In the latter case, the writings fed into the computer must be false and must also have been made with the intent to defraud. In another case, it was held that checks issued by a computer—based on false data fed the computer—were forgeries since the computer acted as the agent of the felons.[33]

Many states have statutes pertaining to *receiving stolen property*. In most jurisdictions, this crime has been made a felony. There are four elements to the offense: (1) the property must be received, (2) it must have been stolen, (3) the wrongdoer must have knowledge, and (4) it must be done with the intent to deprive the owner. Actual possession of the property is not necessary. One may have received the property if he or she solely exercises control over it. For example, an agent, employee, or coconspirator may have handled it, and this would be sufficient to constitute receipt.

The statute will not, however, apply to the perpetrator of the crime. One who steals cannot also be guilty of receiving stolen property. The statute is aimed at the buyer or receiver—the so-called fence. However, if the stolen property is restored to the owner, it ceases to be stolen. For purposes of this statute, the receiver must be aware that the property is stolen; he must have "knowledge." He may know that the property is stolen, or he may suspect that it is stolen. In some instances, he may not know with certainty, but the circumstances of the case may be such that his curiosity should have been aroused. If he refuses to investigate for fear that he might discover the truth, he is still guilty.

There must also be intent to deprive the owner of the property. Thus, if his purpose is not to enrich himself, but only to assist the thief, who may be a friend or associate, it is no defense. He will still be guilty under the statute. If he destroys the property or holds it up for reward, he still has displayed the requisite intent to deprive the rightful owner of the property.

In the area of computer crime, one who receives or buys computer software or hardware can be prosecuted under this statute if he knew at the time that the property was stolen and he had the intent to deprive the owner of it. The statute would cover all facets of the computer system—theft of any part. For example, if several employees of a company stole and sold its most valuable customer list to a competitor who knew, at the time, that the list had been stolen, and who bought it with the intent to deprive the owner of his property, the buyer could be prosecuted under the receiving-stolen-property statute.

Local jurisdictions have various other statutes at their disposal. However, the major tools have already been discussed. Much will also depend on how the courts translate these statutes and laws when applying them to computer crime. The term *property* may lose its present meaning in some instances. In others, it may vary in definition from jurisdiction to jurisdiction. States would be wise to pass some legislation specifically aimed at this area rather than attempting to impose outdated laws on the disposition of modern technological crimes. It is as if someone entered a store, shot the owner dead, and was charged with trespass. Statutes that specifically address themselves to the problem of computer crime are needed at the state, as well as at the federal, level.

References

1. D.C. Criminal Law and Procedure, Title 22, sec. 401.
2. *People* v. *Oliff*, 197 N.E. 777 (1935).
3. Ibid.
4. Ibid.
5. *Smith* v. *State*, 357 S.W. 219 (1887).
6. U.S. Senate, Committee on Government Operations, *Problems Associated with Computer Technology in Federal Programs and Private Industry* (Washington, D.C.: U.S. Government Printing Office, 1976), p. 7.

7. Ibid.

8. Ibid.

9. Ibid., p. 9.

10. Ibid.

11. Ibid., p. 8.

12. *Reagan* v. *State* 234 A.2d 278 (Md. App. 1967).

13. D.C. Criminal Law and Procedure, Title 22, sec. 1801.

14. Ibid.

15. *People* v. *Roldan*, 241 N.E.2d 591 (App. Ct. 1968).

16. N.Y. Penal Law, secs. 140.20, 140.25, and 140.30; also, Miss. Code Ann., sec. 2036.

17. D.C. Criminal Law and Procedure, Title 22, sec. 2201.

18. *Miller* v. *State*, 83 Tenn. 179 (1885).

19. *Commonwealth* v. *Metcalf*, 212 S.W. 434 (1919).

20. *Woods* v. *People*, 78 N.E. 608 (1906).

21. *People* v. *Cox*, 286 N.Y. 137 (1936).

22. Ibid.

23. *Blakley* v. *State*, 292 P. 878 (1930).

24. *Dougherty* v. *State*, 48 N.W.2d 76 (1951).

25. *State* v. *Wood*, 435 P.2d 857 (1968).

26. U.S. Senate, Committee on Government Operations, *Problems Associated with Computer Technology in Federal Programs*, p. 377.

27. *United States* v. *Bryant*, 454 F.2d 248 (4th Cir. 1972).

28. *Kerby* v. *State*, 342 S.W.2d 412 (1961).

29. *State* v. *Watts*, 48 Ark. 56 (1886).

30. *State* v. *Young*, 46 N.H. 266 (1865).

31. U.S. Senate, Committee on Government Operations, *Staff Study of Computer Security in Federal Programs* (Washington, D.C.: U.S. Government Printing Office, 1977), p. 206.

32. D.C. Criminal Law and Procedure, Title 22, sec. 1401.

33. *United States* v. *Jones*, 414 F.Supp. 963 (1976).

5

The Federal Arsenal

In July 1977 the United States Attorney's office for the District of Columbia announced that four individuals, including the former teller of a local savings and loan association, had participated in a computer fraud scheme in which thousands of dollars were illegally withdrawn from the savings accounts of customers at the financial institution. The group used the financial institution's computer terminal to locate savings accounts that had been inactive for long periods of time. The funds were then transferred from these accounts to a number of fictitious accounts the group had set up under other names, and then they withdrew from these latter accounts. Prosecutors suspected that at least one other person within the financial institution may have been involved in the fraud.

At the federal level, no less than at the local level, computer crime is on the rise. To deter criminals from preying on our vast network of computers, prosecutors need the requisite legal armament. The best prosecutorial machinery in the world is of little value if it lacks the legal "muscle" to perform its assigned task. Federal laws are statutory, and numerous.

At present, there are no federal statutes that specifically address themselves to the problem of computer crime. U.S. Senator Abraham Ribicoff recently introduced a bill that would create such a statute. Having personally worked on this proposed legislation, I am well familiar with it and will discuss it in greater detail in the latter part of this chapter. There is also talk of reforming the present federal criminal code. The proposed new code (S.1437), however, does not differ radically from the present code and has no provisions for computer crime. Whether these proposed changes of the federal criminal laws are passed or not will not discharge the prosecutor of his responsibility to bring computer felons to justice. There are a number of present federal laws that can be employed, either by themselves or in conjunction with the proposed legislative changes, with some success against computer felons.

Present Federal Laws

The key weapon in a federal prosecutor's arsenal has been, historically, the *mail fraud statute.*[1] The statute has two key elements that must be met: (1) use of the mails for the purpose of executing, or attempting to execute, (2) a fraud or scheme to obtain money or property under false pretenses. The federal judiciary has also been liberal in its interpretation of what constitutes a fraud under this section. If a felon were to employ the mails to perpetrate a computer crime, the prosecutor could easily fall back on this statute if necessary. The problem, however, is that the felon must make use of the mails. Sophisticated criminals can easily evade the statute simply by not using the U.S. Postal Service. At present, however, there are many alternate options available to criminals. For example, they can make use of telephones, telegraph, and even private couriers. These options make the statute of limited value.

Our modern society makes wide use of the telephone and other wire services. Here, the *wire fraud statute* can be of great assistance in prosecuting felons who make use of the wires or air to perpetrate their frauds. The statute provides for fines of up to $1000, or up to five years of imprisonment, or both, for anyone who:

... devise(s) any scheme or artifice to defraud, or for obtaining money or property by means of false or fraudulent pretenses, representations, or promises, transmits or causes to be transmitted by means of wire, radio or television communication, in interstate or foreign commerce, any writings, signs, signals, pictures, or sounds for the purpose of executing such scheme or artifice. ...[2]

To be in violation of this statute, a felon must not only use the wires, but must also cross the state lines or engage in foreign commerce, or both.

To illustrate the limitations of the wire fraud statute, we can refer to the *Bertram Seidlitz* case, prosecuted in 1976 in federal court in Baltimore, Maryland.[3] In that case, Seidlitz had gained unauthorized access to the computer of Optimum Systems, Inc. (OSI), a Maryland firm that provides computer services to the Federal Energy Administration. OSI had developed a software package known as Wylbur, which had been used to obtain various government contracts. The program was one of the most sophisticated yet developed.

Seidlitz had at one time been employed by OSI. While with that firm, he had worked on a federal project. In that capacity, he had learned the secret access codes to the firm's computer system. Seidlitz later left OSI, retaining the knowledge he had acquired there. With the aid of the telephone and a computer terminal, he dialed the computer's telephone number and gained access to the system. Through the use of various codes, he requested and obtained various portions of the Wylbur software package. Over a period of 4 months, Seidlitz penetrated the system more than 40 times. The data had been transmitted, by telephone wires, from the OSI offices in Maryland to Seidlitz's Virginia office. Seidlitz had engaged in interstate commerce. This was to be his undoing, and also, fortunately for the prosecutors, it enabled them to make use of the wire fraud statute.

Seidlitz was discovered (by accident, as is the case with most computer crimes) and prosecuted. He was charged with two counts of wire fraud[4] and one count of interstate transportation of stolen property.[5] The prosecutors were fortunate, for had Seidlitz operated only within the state of Maryland and made his telephone calls to the OSI computer from his Maryland home rather than his Virginia office, the wire fraud statute would have been inoperative and of no assistance to the prosecutors.

However, the Maryland United States attorney's office faced other obstacles in the prosecution of Seidlitz. The wire fraud statute requires that the scheme to defraud be for purposes of "obtaining money or property." The question that had lurked in the legal community for some time was whether computer programs and software packages were property. Some legal experts had argued that they were not. If that were the case, they did not fall within the statute. The federal district judge, however, ruled in favor of the government. He noted that the Wylbur program had been developed by OSI and had been used by the firm to obtain government contracts. It was a trade secret, and thus was property. The court relied on a 1967 decision involving the fifth circuit, the case of *Hancock* v. *Decker*, for its reasoning.[6]

In the *Hancock* case, the defendant, an employee of the Texas Instruments Automatic Computer Corporation (TIACC), photocopied 49 computer programs belonging to the company.[7] He attempted to sell these to Texaco, one of the company's clients, for $5 million. The matter was brought to the attention of the authorities, and the defendant was brought to trial. During his trial, the defendant argued that since he had photocopied the programs, no original documents had been stolen and thus no property had been taken. The defendant, however, was found guilty, and the court held that the programs were in fact property. The U.S. Court of Appeals upheld the conviction.

Seidlitz had also been charged with violating the interstate transportation of stolen property statute.[8] His attorney filed a motion for a judgment of acquittal as to that charge. The court agreed with the defendant as to this count and noted that Seidlitz could not be found guilty of transporting stolen property in interstate commerce since this was not the case of a photocopy being transported in interstate commerce, but rather the only thing that did cross state lines was a series of electronic impulses over telephone wires. The valuable information never left the physical structure of the computer. No property was thus stolen. The court was not willing to define electronic impulses as property within the requirements of the stolen property statute.

On August 3, 1976, Bertram E. Seidlitz was sentenced to be confined in a jail-type or treatment institution for a period of 3 months, and placed on probation for a period of 33 months.

The federal *embezzlement and theft statute* can also be of some assistance. The statute makes the embezzlement or theft of public money a crime, punishable by a fine of up to $10,000, or imprisonment not to exceed 10 years, or both.[9] The statute, however, covers only agencies of the federal government and corporations in which the federal government has a proprietary interest.

Further, the felon must "knowingly convert" public property. It is no defense that he attempted to return it; nor is it a defense that the defendant did not perpetrate the act himself but is only the receiver of the stolen property.

The courts have given this statute a broad interpretation. Theft of services and/or labor have been held to be a conversion of public property when those services or labor came from federal government employees.[10] The question, however, remains whether software being developed for the federal government is property within the meaning of this statute. To date, the federal courts have not dealt fully with this issue.

It may be that courts in the near future will interpret the federal embezzlement and theft statute as applying to computer software. To date, they have not. However, the statute does have its limitations. The federal government must have a proprietary interest in the property. In addition, in cases where the property is in the custody or possession of the federal government but is not held by legal title, the application of the statute remains dubious. The felon can also easily circumvent the statute by simply not stealing property in which the federal government or any of its agencies have a proprietary right.

The federal *banking statutes* provide for penalties of up to 5 years imprisonment, or fines of up to $5000, or both, for anyone involved in the embezzlement or theft of funds from a federally insured bank.[11] The offender, however, must be either an employee, officer, or agent of the federally insured financial institution. The bank statutes only cover insiders. The statute applies only in cases where there is an unlawful taking or concealing of funds, money, bonds, or securities from federally insured financial institutions. Felons, however, who are not employees, agents, or officers of these institutions would not be covered. Computers not owned by federally insured financial institutions would also not be covered. Again, therefore, unless the defendant in a computer fraud is an insider, the statutes would not apply.

False entries in the records, reports, and transactions of banks and federal credit institutions are violations of federal law and carry fines of up to $10,000, or up to 5 years imprisonment, or both.[12] The objective of these statutes is to protect the integrity of bank records. Omissions are also covered. False entries or alterations of bank computer records would probably be covered. It is the intent of these statutes to protect the integrity of bank records. The statutes, however, are limited only to the officers, agents, and employees of any Federal Reserve Bank, member bank, national bank, or insured bank; and also to any officer, agent, or employee connected with the Reconstruction Finance Corporation, the Federal Deposit Insurance Corporation, the Home Owners' Loan Corporation, the Farm Credit Administration, the Department of Housing and Urban Development, the Federal Crop Insurance Corporation, the Farmers' Home Corporation, the Department of Agriculture (acting through the Farmers' Home Administration), or any land bank.

The objective of these statutes is to ensure the authenticity of the records of these institutions. A teller's failure to file a deposit slip has been held to be equivalent to making a false entry. Even the minutes of meetings of the board of directors of these institutions have been held to be bank records. To date, these statutes have not been applied to computer crime cases. However, there can be little doubt that these statutes can play a role in cases involving the use of the computer to alter or falsify records of federally insured or connected financial institutions.

Title III of the Omnibus Crime Control and Safe Streets Act of 1968 makes it a federal crime to willfully intercept any wire or oral communication.[13] The 1968 act defines *intercept* as the acquisition of the contents of any wire communications through the use of any electronic, mechanical, or other device. The objective of the 1968 act was to protect the privacy of the wire and oral communications, not to protect financial institutions. If computer communications were intercepted, the data would be in code. Since the 1968 act contemplates only "aural communications," it is doubtful whether it would apply to cases involving the electronic interception of coded data being transmitted between computers. To date, the 1968 act remains untested in this area.

There are also federal statutes that protect federal property from *malicious destruction*. These would probably apply if the property in question were a federal computer. The malicious injury statute provides for up to 10 years imprisonment, or up to $10,000 in fines, or both, for those who are convicted under it.[14] However, if the property damage does not exceed $100, then the punishment cannot exceed 1 year imprisonment, or more than $1000 in fines. The statute was widely employed during the Vietnam war against antiwar demonstrators who damaged federal property.[15] Malicious injury to nonfederal computers would not be covered by the statute. Damage must be to federal property to qualify.

Arson within a federal enclave is covered by federal law. The *arson statute* makes it a felony, punishable by up to 5 years imprisonment, or up to $1000 in fines, or both.[16] The question, however, is whether the definition of *machinery, building materials, or supplies* would include computer software and hardware. It probably would. Several other federal statutes also address themselves to the destruction of various federal properties. Willful injury to war or national defense material during wartime or national emergency can be punishable by imprisonment of up to 30 years, or up to $10,000 in fines, or both.[17] However, unless there is a national emergency, the likelihood of that statute being applicable in computer crimes is remote.

The *conspiracy statute* can be employed where two or more persons conspire to defraud the federal government. It provides for fines of up to $10,000, or imprisonment of up to 5 years, or both.[18] However, the shortcoming of this statute is obvious—it applies only when two or more felons are involved. If a computer crime is committed by a sole felon, the statute would not apply.

The federal *bank robbery statute* provides for severe penalties when a felon takes by "force and violence" money or property belonging to, or in the custody or possession of, any bank or savings and loan association insured by the federal government.[19] Computer crimes usually involve no force or violence, and thus this statute would be of little value.

There are several federal statutes that cover a compromise or breach of national security. These might be applied in a situation involving data of national security importance that are stored in federal computers. For example, gathering and transmitting defense information to aid a foreign government is a felony,[20] as is the delivery of defense data to a foreign agent or power.[21] However, there are some drawbacks to these *national defense statutes*. They do not apply if a felon were to sell the data to a ring of criminals. They also might have no applicability when a ring or group of political zealots is involved rather than a foreign power. The now classic case of *New York Times Company* v. *United States* made it clear that the "mere classification" of data as secret does not in itself make it so. Lack of "substantial injury" to national security could be a defense.[22]

The federal *disclosure statute* might also have some applicability where federal software is involved.[23] For example, if a federal officer were to disclose data retained in a federal computer, it might be a violation of the law. However, to date, few federal officials have ever been prosecuted under this statute. Further, the statute is limited in that it does not apply to the states, nor to private data, unless these data are in the custody of the federal government. Only federal officials are covered; state officials and private parties can evade it.

It is a felony to transport stolen goods, securities, money, fraudulent state tax stamps, or articles used in counterfeiting in interstate or foreign commerce.[24] The statute provides for penalties of up to $10,000 in fines, or up to 10 years in imprisonment, or both. There are limitations on the application of the statute—the property *must* cross state or national lines. It is not sufficient for it to merely be introduced into interstate or foreign commerce.

The statute faces additional problems when applied to computer crimes. For example, in the case of *United States* v. *Jones*, prosecuted by the U.S. Attorney's office in Baltimore, the defendant was charged with violating Section 2314, for being involved in the transport of stolen goods in interstate and foreign commerce.[25] The defendant's brother had been employed by a Canadian appliance firm, affiliated with the Whirlpool Company, an American firm. Defendant's brother instructed a keypunch operator at his firm to open a new account for his sister, assigning her a new vendor code name. On several occasions, he substituted the Whirlpool Company vendor number with that of his sister on the accounts payable distribution slip. He then passed this information to the keypunch operator who in turn would place it on data processing cards. The data were then programmed into the computer. They remained there for about two weeks. During this period, the defendant retrieved the accounts payable distribution slips from the keypunch operator and returned the correct vendor code to them to avoid detection. The company's computer, acting under these instructions, issued the checks, as programmed, to the defendant, a resident of Maryland. They defrauded the company of more than $130,000. The scheme was one of the simpler forms of computer crime.

The defendant was prosecuted in Baltimore for allegedly violating Section 2314 ("interstate transportations of securities in excess of $5000 which were stolen, converted and taken by fraud, knowing the same to have been so taken"). She was also charged with violating Section 2315 ("receiving stolen securities, which had traveled in interstate commerce"). The defendant argued that the charges were faulty, and that they should be thrown out. The federal district court agreed. The judge held that the issued checks were forgeries and that Sections 2314 and 2315 did not apply to falsely made or forged securities issued by banks or corporations of a foreign company. The indictment was held invalid.

The decision was a blow to the prosecutors, and they immediately appealed it. The U.S. Court of Appeals for the Fourth Circuit heard the case, and on April 12, 1977, handed down its decision.[26] The court held that the crime was not in fact a forgery, as the lower court had held, but rather a fraud. It reversed the lower tribunal's decision. The court referred to the case of *Lemke* v. *United States*, heard by the Ninth Federal Circuit.[27] In the *Lemke* case, the Ninth Circuit faced a similar situation. However, this one did not involve a computer. Here, the manager of a cafeteria, who had previously purchased vegetables from a farmer, attempted to have the farmer falsify some of these vouchers so as to show payments for nonexistent sales. The manager then attempted to present these bogus slips for payment. The court held that he was guilty of false pretenses. The Fourth Circuit was heavily influenced by the *Lemke* decision. The *Jones* case raises serious questions, and the matter is far from closed.

A Need for Computer Legislation

On June 9, 1977, federal indictments were returned against two Philadelphia computer programming managers employed by Sperry-Univac. The programmers had used the company's computer to run a music-arranging business. The two alleged felons had, with the aid of the computer, developed a program to turn out sophisticated musical arrangements. They also employed the firm's computer to maintain a record of their business transactions. The two men were charged with mail fraud.[28] Prosecutors complained that they had no computer crime statute at their disposal.

In another recent case, the employee of one firm had his company's computer print out a list of 290,000 customers, which he attempted to sell to a competitor firm.[29] Prosecutors are aware of the shortcomings of our present criminal codes. Many of the statutes that have been discussed are useful and can prove valuable in some cases. However, more direct legislation is needed. This is not to say that the other statutes will then be cast aside. On the contrary, rather, they can be employed to supplement and give greater "muscle" to federal attorneys. For example, a felon engaged in a massive securities fraud will be charged with violating these statutes. However, he can also be charged with violating the mail fraud and wire fraud statutes. These latter statutes are not a substitute for the securities laws, but rather are employed to supplement them. Present laws can play a similar role when combined with a statute that specifically addresses itself to the problem of computer crime. Such a statute may be forthcoming.

In late 1976 I met with Phil Manuel and Fred Asselin, both staff members of the U.S. Senate Committee on Government Operations, to discuss the need for legislation in the area of computer crime. We soon began work on a proposed statute. On February 2, 1977, Senator Abraham Ribicoff, after having been briefed by these two staffers, informed the U.S. Senate of the need to enact legislation in this area. Phil and I then met with Ken Feinberg, an advisor to Senator Edward Kennedy in matters dealing with criminal law. Ken is also an ex-prosecutor, and thus needs no persuading; he understood immediately the need for legislation in the area of computer crime.

Phil and I continued work on the proposed bill. Several drafts were prepared. Phil also consulted with the Justice Department, and they agreed to support the legislation if it ever came to the floor of the Congress. In late June, 1977 Senator Ribicoff introduced the Federal Computer Systems Protection Act of 1977 in the U.S. Senate.

The proposed statute was not meant to replace the other federal laws. On the contrary, it was meant to work in conjunction with them, to facilitate the task of federal prosecutors in the area of computer crime. The mail fraud and wire fraud statutes, as well as dozens of other statutes found in the federal criminal code, could be employed to supplement it. However, the act does one thing that other statutes do not: it addresses itself specifically to the problem of computer crime. The act makes it a felony, punishable by up to 15 years in prison, or up to $50,000 in fines, or both, for anyone who:

... directly or indirectly accesses or causes to be accessed any computer, computer system, computer network, part thereof which, in whole or in part, operates in interstate commerce or is owned by, under contract to, or operated for, on behalf of, or in conjunction with, any financial institution, the United States Government, or any branch ... or agency thereof ... for the purpose of (1) devising or executing any scheme or artifice to defraud, or (2) obtaining money, property, or services by means of false or fraudulent pretenses, representations, or promises.

In drafting this proposed statute, we were careful to make it as broad as possible, to be effective against the many types of computer crime. We tested it against many computer crime cases that have come to our attention. What we wanted was a simple and yet effective statute.

The legislation would cover all intentional alterations or destruction of any kind of any part of a computer system or network. It would cover both software and hardware. Further, we defined *network* to include all communication links with a computer. Our definition of what constituted *property* was made sufficiently broad to include all "electronically produced data."

The Federal Computer Systems Protection Act of 1977 may eventually be passed. It could become a model for states to review and possibly adopt for their own criminal codes. At present, such legislation is badly needed. Our present laws are not enough. Sophisticated computer felons can easily evade them. Prosecution, both at the federal and local level, is difficult and, at times, unsuccessful. One federal agent has called this the "crime of the future." It is only a matter of time before organized crime becomes heavily involved in the area of computer crime. At present, we are dealing with a group of felons who are well educated, sophisticated, and constitute the cream of our technological world. Present laws are not enough. New legislation is needed, not to replace but rather to supplement the present arsenal.

References

1. 18 U.S.C., sec. 1341 (1970 ed.).
2. Ibid., sec. 1343.
3. *United States* v. *Bertram E. Seidlitz,* U.S. District Court for the District of Maryland, Criminal No. 76-079H.
4. 18 U.S.C., sec. 1343 (1970 ed.).
5. Ibid., sec. 1343.
6. 379 F.2d 552 (1967).
7. Ibid., pp. 552-553.
8. 18 U.S.C., sec. 2314 (1970 ed.).
9. Ibid., sec. 641.
10. *Burnett* v. *United States*, 222 F.2d 416 (1955).
11. 18 U.S.C., secs. 656, 657 (1970 ed.).
12. Ibid., secs. 1005, 1006.
13. Ibid., sec. 2511.
14. Ibid., sec. 1361.
15. *United States* v. *Eberhardt*, 417 F.2d 1009 (1969).
16. 18 U.S.C., sec. 81 (1970 ed.).
17. Ibid., sec. 2153.
18. Ibid., sec. 371.
19. Ibid., sec. 2113.
20. Ibid., sec. 793.

46

21. Ibid., sec. 794.
22. 403 U.S. 713 (1971).
23. 18 U.S.C., sec. 1905 (1970 ed.).
24. Ibid., sec. 2314.
25. 414 F.Supp. 964 (1976).
26. *United States* v. *Jones*, U.S. Court of Appeals (4th Cir.), App. No. 76-1815.
27. 211 F.2d 73 (9th Cir.), cert. denied, 347 U.S. 1013 (1954).
28. "Crash Course in Computer Science Enables FBI to Nab Brainy Crooks," *Crime Control Digest*, June 27, 1977, p. 5.
29. Ibid.

6   # The Prosecutors

The best of laws and courts will not suffice if the prosecutorial machinery is lacking. It is the prosecutor who ensures that the laws of the country are properly enforced.[1] When the most effective security measures fail to stop the criminal, the prosecutorial machinery must assume control. Prosecutors rely on several investigatory agencies and an array of laws. However, if the prosecutorial machinery itself is unable to handle challenges to the criminal justice system, even the best of laws and investigators will not succeed. An attack against computer crime needs good security measures, investigatory agencies capable of dealing with computer felons, and prosecutors who can bring these felons to justice.

Local Prosecutors

Unlike many European countries, which have a highly centralized prosecutorial machinery, the American system is fragmented and has given rise to various prosecutorial entities. These usually take one of three forms: (1) local prosecutors, such as a district attorney, who have jurisdiction over a city or county; (2) state prosecutors, such as a state attorney general, who have jurisdiction over an entire state; and (3) federal prosecutors, such as United States attorneys, who prosecute only violations of federal laws. The prosecutorial machinery, in general, is divided into two categories: (1) the nonfederal, which includes local and state offices, and (2) the federal, which includes an array of local federal offices, such as the United States attorney, to the more specialized units found in the divisions of the United States Justice Department. Both categories of prosecutors have had limited experience with computer crime, and both must ultimately devise effective approaches.

At the local level, city and county prosecutors have been trained, historically, to handle traditional common-law crimes. These are the common, everyday crimes familiar to the community, such as robbery, burglary, murder, and others. These crimes are usually simple in nature and present no serious problems to the prosecutor. In addition, both judges and juries have little or no difficulty in understanding them. However, in the realm of computer crime, prosecutors find that such cases are difficult to present to juries, and difficult to fully grasp by most juries.

Not only are prosecutors faced with the problem of getting a jury of average citizens to understand a sophisticated crime, but they also face internal problems of their own. At the local level, citizens are more concerned with crimes of violence. Few are concerned with crimes that are neither easily understood, nor relevant to their everyday lives. It is difficult to convince a concerned citizenry that computer crime may, in the long run, affect their lives more than the thousands of daily burglaries. Computer crimes, like other forms of white collar crime, suffer from a "lack of understanding" by the public at large. This ignorance is many times also shared by prosecutors. Lawyers are not trained to deal with technological crimes; law schools teach only the common-law categories of crime. Many facets of white collar crimes, including computer crime, are handled as civil matters.

Faced with an ignorant citizenry and an ill-trained legal body, local prosecutors tend to devote their resources to the areas of common-law crime. For example, at the local district attorney level, a study by the National District Attorneys Association found that only a small number of local prosecutors devoted much of their resources to white collar crime cases. In large part, this was due to public apathy, and also a shortage of funds.[2] A study of 41 such offices found that collectively they received more than 150,000 inquiries annually,[3] and more than 40,000 of these were in the form of complaints.[4]

At the state prosecutorial level, the situation is no better. Typically, local prosecutors are limited in resources, manpower, and jurisdiction. The state prosecutors, however, are also limited. For example, only 34 states appropriate more than $1 million annually to their attorney generals.[5] Three states appropriate less than $500,000 annually for their offices.[6] Since the cost of prosecuting a computer crime can require large amounts of staff time and large sums of money, many state attorney generals are limited in their prosecutorial ability. Only 8 states employ more than 100 attorneys in their attorney general's offices.[7] The majority of state prosecutors have no white collar crime sections, and few offer any training in this area. There are no computer crime branches in any of these offices. The state prosecutor, like his local district attorney counterpart, is limited by resources, training, and an antiquated concept of crime. At present, the effectiveness of local prosecutors in the war against computer crime is minimal. This is particularly unfortunate because local prosecutors can play a most influential part in the enforcement of our laws. These offices must be upgraded through funding and training programs to deal effectively with computer crime.

Federal Prosecutors

The United States Attorney General is the chief prosecutor in this country. He heads the United States Department of Justice, the largest prosecutorial machinery in the Western world. The Department had its origins in the early days of the Republic.[8] In 1789 Congress created the office of the Attorney General,[9] who was assigned the responsibility of advising the President and the heads of other governmental departments on matters of law.[10] Congress also established the offices of United States attorneys—the local federal prosecutors— to prosecute both criminal and civil matters affecting federal laws.[11]

In 1870 Congress formally established the Department of Justice.[12] The early Attorney Generals were only part-time employees of the federal government. Many of them had to pay office expenses out of their own income.[13] The office, from its inception, was a political institution. The idea of a professional prosecutorial office never took hold in the Republic. Consequently, office-holders were politicians first and prosecutors second.[14] At present, the federal prosecutorial system is manned by a large number of political appointees. Nevertheless, that machinery must, of necessity, direct the war against computer crime. Only the federal prosecutor has the resources, manpower, and jurisdiction necessary to carry on the struggle successfully. Local and state prosecutors, even if trained and funded, are still limited jurisdictionally in instances where the felons are in another state. However, with a staff of 50,000 employees (of whom some 9000 provide legal services) and a budget of $2 billion annually, the Justice Department must lead in the battle against computer crime.[15] Skeptics have, with good cause, raised serious questions about its ability to do so.

The Justice Department is divided into various divisions. Under its jurisdiction also fall the 94 United States attorney offices.[16] These are situated in the 94 Federal judicial districts found in the 50 states, Guam, Puerto Rico, the Virgin Islands, and the Canal Zone.[17] The United States attorney is the chief local federal prosecutor. Each attorney is selected by the President and confirmed by the Senate, for a four-year term.[18] The office fulfills, among others, a political function. The President usually selects people who are professionally acceptable, and who usually have the political support of the local power establishment. The local federal prosecutor is chosen for his political ties rather than his legal wisdom. Consequently, the local federal apparatus remains highly politicized, and the prosecutor maintains an appropriate public image. An innovative local federal prosecutor may find that, at the end of his four-year term, the succeeding prosecutor decides to discontinue his programs. It is difficult to develop and initiate a program to combat computer crime in such an environment.

The federal prosecutor usually selects his own staff. At present, there are more than 1400 assistant United States attorneys employed in the 94 offices.[19] However, the offices themselves are generally small; few have large staffs. The District of Columbia office has a staff of 154 attorneys, but this office is unique.[20] Much of the staff's time is devoted to prosecuting local common-law-type cases. The fraud section, which prosecutes white collar crimes and would thus prosecute computer crimes, employs about six attorneys and to date has prosecuted only one computer-related case. The smallest local federal prosecutor's office is located in Guam, and has a staff of two attorneys. More than half these offices, however, have staffs of 4 to 10 attorneys.[21] A computer fraud case could easily tie up the entire staff of some of the smaller offices.

In addition, these local offices handle the great bulk of federal litigation, both civil and criminal. Although the other federal agencies and departments—as will be seen in the following chapters—employ large staffs of attorneys, they must rely for their prosecutions on the Justice Department. Thus the local United States attorney offices are forced to handle not only the bulk of federal cases that fall within the jurisdiction of the Justice Department, but also the many cases brought to their attention by the federal investigatory agencies and departments. The number of criminal cases filed annually by the Justice Department averages more than 40,000.[22] Thus the Department, although it has a large staff and budget, may find itself unable to keep abreast of computer felons because of its many other commitments.

United States attorneys enjoy great autonomy from the Justice Department. They are not required to obtain approval from the Justice Department prior to deciding whether or not to prosecute a case. Their cases, with the exception of instances wherein the local federal prosecutor seeks to dismiss an indictment, are not reviewed by the Justice Department.[23] The local offices need not inform their superiors when they decline to prosecute a case.[24] Further, the local offices, like the local state prosecutors, tend to be more responsive to the needs of local groups than to the national policy of the Justice Department. This fragmented prosecutorial structure may well be incapable of combatting technological crimes.

The local offices are very sensitive to any jurisdictional challenges. They litigate the majority of cases referred to the Justice Department by other federal agencies and departments. However, the local offices must also be responsive to their own constituents. Crimes that affect their locality will take priority over those of a national dimension. Unfortunately, very few of these local offices have any expertise in the areas of white collar crime. Few, if any, have ever prosecuted a computer fraud case. Even the key urban centers of this country have small local offices. For example, Philadelphia has a staff of about 12 attorneys;[25] Baltimore, about the same; and San Diego, only slightly larger.[26] Many of the local offices that have the capability to prosecute such complex fraud cases as computer crimes are located in jurisdictions with backlogged court calendars. Thus the computer felon may profit from this backlog and be able, if he chooses, to work out a better plea bargain than he normally could.

The Justice Department also has several specialized divisions that could, if given the appropriate training, play a role in the area of prosecuting computer crime. They should also be allowed to litigate many of the cases presently handled by local federal prosecutors. At present, many attorneys in these divisions do little more than shuffle paper. Both the Department and the public are denied the litigating talents of these attorneys. Computer crime cannot be beaten by shuffling paper.

One of the more important units at the Justice Department is the Tax Division. The Division's central office is located in the Justice Department's headquarters in Washington, D.C.[27] The unit handles both criminal and civil cases,[28] and assists Internal Revenue attorneys in complex civil tax cases.[29] The Division processes a variety of tax-related cases, including suits brought by the federal government to collect unpaid taxes.[30] The local federal prosecutors, however, handle the bulk of the criminal tax cases.[31] The Division has various sections, among them the general litigation section, the appellate section, and the refund trial section. As is the case with the other divisions at the Justice Department, the Tax Division's staff has no training in the area of computer litigation and related criminal matters. In an era when the computer is used daily to defraud the government of its taxes, such training is not only necessary, but imperative for the survival of tax laws.

Probably the most important division within the Justice Department is the Criminal Division. This section is charged with coordinating the enforcement of all federal criminal laws, with the exception of certain complex cases, such as tax and antitrust; these cases are handled by the more specialized units of the Department.[32] The Division consists of 11 sections, including organized crime and racketeering, which coordinates, with local federal prosecutors and other federal agencies, the strategy against organized crime. The use of computers by organized criminal elements would fall within its scope. At present, its staff has no training in the area of computer crime.

The narcotic and dangerous drug section directs prosecutorial efforts in the area of narcotics. The legislation and special projects section provides legal research and advice for the various local federal prosecutor offices. This unit would be of some value in the area of computer crime by assisting other federal prosecutors in developing a strategy and policy to contain such frauds. Probably the most important section within the Division, at least for the area of computer crime, would be the fraud unit. This branch coordinates efforts among the various units of the Justice Department in the area of white collar crime. The fraud unit has some expertise and specialization in this area and could use it effectively to deal with computer crimes.

The Justice Department's Washington, D.C. office acts as a clearinghouse for its many regional offices. The Department suffers from political and bureaucratic "indigestion." Policy, in many cases, is dictated by the political needs of a few groups rather than the needs of the nation as a whole. The Department has failed, historically, to develop a meaningful strategy against white collar crime and organized crime; heavily burdened with red tape and internal discord, it is unable to move swiftly and effectively. The Department's concern with inter-agency challenges to its jurisdiction has inadvertently closed the doors of federal courts to attorneys of other federal agencies and departments by requiring that all federal prosecutions be handled by Justice Department attorneys.

The local United States attorneys are, in many instances, students of the "old school" of legal theory who view the needs of modern criminology through the eyes of eighteenth century England. Judicial economy demands a modern standard of swift and effective prosecution. The Department must be stream-lined and professionalized. The offices of United States attorneys are too important to be left to amateurs. At present, the Department lacks the training, the knowhow, and the strategy to combat the criminal of the electronic age. The challenge of the computer age must be met by a rejuvenated Justice Department.

References

1. Hazel B. Kerper, *Introduction to the Criminal Justice System* (St. Paul, Minn.: West, 1972), pp. 430-431.
2. National District Attorneys Association Special Report, *Fighting the Forty Billion Dollar Rip-Off* (Chicago, Ill.: National District Attorneys Association, 1976), pp. 6, 7.
3. Ibid., p. 7.
4. Ibid.
5. Committee on the Office of Attorney General, *The Office of Attorney General: Organization, Budget, Salaries and Staff* (Raleigh, N.C.: National Association of Attorneys General, 1974), p. IV.
6. Ibid.
7. Ibid.
8. Special Committee to Study Federal Law Enforcement Agencies of the American Bar Association, *Removing Political Influence from Federal Law Enforcement Agencies* (Chicago, Ill.: American Bar Association, 1975), pp. 20, 21.
9. Ibid., p. 20.
10. Ibid.
11. Ibid.
12. Ibid., p. 21.
13. Ibid.
14. Ibid., pp. 21, 25, 30.
15. Ibid.
16. U.S. Department of Justice, *Annual Report of the Attorney General of the United States for 1975* (Washington, D.C.: U.S. Government Printing Office, 1976), p. 3.
17. Ibid.
18. Ibid.
19. Ibid.
20. Ibid.
21. Ibid.
22. Ibid.
23. Rabin, "Agency Criminal Referrals in the Federal System: An Empirical Study of Prosecutorial Discretion," 24 *Stanford L. Rev.* 1041 (1972).

24. Ibid.
25. Ibid., p. 1043.
26. Ibid.
27. U.S. Department of Justice, *Annual Report of the Attorney General of the United States for 1975*, p. 111.
28. Ibid.
29. Ibid.
30. Ibid.
31. Ibid., p. 138.
32. Ibid., p. 91.

7

The Investigators:
Part I

One of the most bizarre stories ever to come from police annals began to take shape in early 1977. It involved the large multinational firm of Imperial Chemical Industries (ICI) and Rodney Cox, a 25-year-old manager at one of that company's computer centers. Cox worked out of the center in Rozenburg, the Netherlands.[1] He had been passed over for promotion, and finally he was informed that he was fired.[2]

Soon afterwards, Cox drove to the computer center. The security guards allowed him in. They even helped him load about 1000 pounds of computer tape discs on his car.[3] The tapes contained all the future planning programs of the company. The tapes would be worth millions of dollars to any competitor of ICI.[4] Cox also stopped off at the ICI offices in Rotterdam to pick up the copies of the tapes. These were the "backup" tapes, in case the others were destroyed or stolen. Cox knew this. To restructure the data would take ICI many weeks.

Cox then sent a ransom note to ICI. He wanted $400,000 for the return of the tapes. Unlike the more sophisticated criminals, Cox had no contacts in the underworld or the world of industrial espionage. He was an amateur. It was lucky for ICI that he was not a sophisticated felon. ICI finally informed Scotland Yard. The police knew Cox was an amateur. They instructed ICI to inform Cox that before they paid the ransom they wanted to see copies of the tapes—to make sure that Cox in fact had them. He took the "hook." ICI received written instructions, and a meeting was set. The police followed, and Cox and an accomplice were arrested. The tapes were soon located. Cox had been no match; traditional police techniques paid off. But what if Cox had been a sophisticated felon? The outcome might have been different.

Thousands of computers receive, store, and update information on more than 50 million Americans. These computer banks have proven a tempting prize for criminals.[5] Fraud rings have devised ways to feed false credit histories into computers.[6] In 1971 such a group, the "Turner-Curtis gang," recruited computer personnel at several large data bank centers and fed false reports and credit ratings into the computers. In addition, the ring placed some of its members in key positions in more than a dozen banks and retail firms.[7] The job of the latter group was to feed false information into the data banks to which their employers subscribed.

The members of the gang not only used the false references themselves, but also sold them to others.[8] The Newport National Bank of Newport Beach, California, lost $200,000 in loans made on cars that didn't exist to bogus borrowers.[9] One of the ringleaders was eventually arrested, but the key figure behind the fraud remains at large.[10] Another gang, the "Spillane group," from 1970 through 1974 took various firms for more than $500,000 in goods and services. Many other rings are known to be operating, but the likelihood that they will be uncovered is small. As one prosecutor recently admitted, "Who will uncover them?" That is certainly the question. Even the best of laws and security measures are powerless if there is no one to investigate these crimes.

The decision to arrest is a police function. The role of the police includes the booking, taking of the accused before a judge, conferring with the prosecutor, and testifying in the trial. The investigatory apparatus of every society plays a key role in the enforcement of its laws. Without an adequate investigatory apparatus, there is no prosecution, no trial, no imprisonment. The police apparatus plays a key role in the enforcement of the laws of any society. It can be said that without such an apparatus, laws become meaningless.

Many countries, such as France and England, have a unitary police apparatus. The law enforcement agencies are usually highly centralized and, at times, specialized. In this country, law enforcement can be divided into two general areas: (1) local police, and (2) the federal police. The latter, however, take a series of complicated forms and shades. Our investigatory apparatus can be defined as a compilation of hundreds of various agencies and thousands of different departments. Many are poorly trained and ill-equipped in the electronic war that faces us.

The Local Police

Historically, Americans have resisted a national police apparatus. Our past has made us distrustful of a strong, centralized police agency. At the turn of the eighteenth century, police functions in this country were part of a *constable system.*[11] A constable was not a professional policeman, he was not trained in investigative techniques. Rather, the system was composed of private citizens. The citizens themselves performed the investigating and arresting functions.[12] In a small, agricultural society, such a system functioned well. All citizens of a community were expected to serve as constables. Those who did not were fined.[13]

The constables served only during the day. At night, the community was served by a system of night watchmen. However, their role was also neither investigative nor prosecutorial. Rather, the night watch kept a watch on fires, reported the weather, and called out the time. By the 1840s, with the growth of urbanization, the night watch was eventually incorporated into the smaller but more professional municipal police force.

The professional police forces themselves were often composed of criminals.[14] A system called the *compromise* had come into being. Under this system, the felon negotiated a return of part of the goods he had taken in exchange for a promise by the owner not to prosecute. The police force played the role of middlemen in these negotiations, and themselves received a fee in return.

It was only after the Civil War that police began wearing uniforms and sidearms. The development of our present local police agencies was slow, and it still continues. In fact, as a result of that evolutionary process, we have, at present, a highly decentralized and splintered police force. The police agencies consist of various forces, such as state police, county police, sheriff's departments, and city police. There are in this country, at present, more than 17,000 local police forces.[15] This number does not include the more than one hundred federal agencies, nor the large private police forces.

At the local level, more than 50 percent of these agencies employ fewer than 5 full-time employees.[16] Almost 70 percent of these employ fewer than 10 full-time employees.[17] One Presidential Commission has described present local law enforcement as being made up of small, separate groups, each acting independently of the other and, many times, in ignorance of what an adjoining jurisdiction is doing.[18]

One recent study found that only 6 percent of our urban centers employ more than 100 full-time police officers.[19] Only 61 percent of all police agencies surveyed had the ability to provide even the minimum police services.[20] Of those surveyed, 39 percent even failed to meet these minimum requirements.[21] The study concluded that:

... [W]ith the function of police becoming more technical and with the high mobility of the modern criminal, these small [police] departments find it increasingly difficult to meet generally accepted police standards.[22]

This study reflects the present dilemma of local law enforcement—a motley array of county, city, and state agencies. These are the units that must bear the brunt of investigating computer crimes where federal agents have no jurisdiction.

Presently, however, our local law enforcement agencies are not receiving any training in the area of computer crime. Many top local law enforcement officials do not view computer crime as a problem. One told me, "It's not our concern." A small number of local police forces have established fraud units; however, these are as yet too small and ill-trained to deal effectively with computer crime cases. Sufficient funds are not being allocated in this area. In fact, many local police forces rely on the federal apparatus to assist them. However, as I will note later, the federal agents are themselves ill-trained for this new crime wave. Training at the local level is, at present, not in sight.

Although local law enforcement lags behind in the area of computer crime, felons have, for many years, wreaked havoc in this area. What has spared us is our ignorance of what goes on, rather than our ability to deal with it effectively.

For example, one night in September 1967 several young men met in a New York City apartment and formed what later came to be known as the "Durham gang" (four of the gang's leaders came from Durham, North Carolina). Their objective was to loot the Youth Corps. One of the gang members became payroll director of the Corps. Plans were made to manipulate the Corps' computers, which issued more than 6000 checks weekly, more than 40,000 just during the 10 weeks of the summer.

During the period of January through June 1968, the gang siphoned off more than $700,000, another $1 million during the summer months. They created an army of fictitious Youth Corps members, assigned them individual Social Security numbers, fed the data into the computer, and many make-believe Youth Corps members received checks for work at nonexistent job sites. One of the gang members picked up the checks; the rest of the gang members then endorsed the checks and deposited them in a bank account they controlled. When the local authorities were later asked about the Durham gang, their reply was, "I never heard of them." A friend of theirs, when the matter finally surfaced, described them as "great people."

There have been other cases; the Durham gang is not the exception. For example, there is the case of the Dime Savings Bank clerk who took his employer for more than $1 million. Many of these crimes have surfaced by accident. Local police forces lack the training to uncover them; further, even once uncovered, unless the case is a simple one, prosecutors complain that local police do not know how to prepare these cases for prosecution. In the Dime Savings Bank case, the felon confessed his wrong. Further, his crime was a simple one, involving the juggling of customer accounts with the aid of the bank's computer. However, what if the case had been a complex one? Further, what if the felons were well organized and sophisticated? The police might have failed. Local police face a problem in this area; funds and training are badly needed to develop local capability. At present, such training is lacking.

The Federal "Cops"—The Regulatory Agencies

The federal investigatory apparatus, when compared to that of the localities, is a Goliath. It employs more than 2 million individuals; its budget exceeds $30 billion a year (excluding the military expenditures); and its structure consists of more than 50 different agencies and bureaus.[23] Its record in the area of computer crime, like that of the localities, also lags behind. It has fared no better. Computer crime detection techniques have been slow in the forming, and at present, save for small groups being trained at the Justice Department, there are no training programs in the many federal investigatory structures that police the vast economic sector, a sector that makes use of more than 90,000 computers and employs more than 1 million computer personnel. In fact, most of the major computer frauds have involved violations of federal law.

The federal investigatory structure rests on two key pillars: (1) the regulatory agencies, and (2) the nonagencies. The former constitute about 12 federal organs, headed by commissions. The regulatory agencies have their roots in the 1898 Interstate Commerce Commission (ICC) model. The regulatory agencies (henceforth, in this and the other chapters, will be referred to as simply *agencies*) police vast and important areas of the economy. The Securities and Exchange Commission (SEC), for example, polices the securities industry, which exceeds the $500 billion mark in value.[24] That industry makes large use of computers and is extremely susceptible to massive computer frauds, as was the case with the Equity Funding Corporation fraud. The Federal Trade Commission (FTC) is another important agency, assigned the task of policing the consumer area. Computer frauds have also involved this area. What makes these agencies unique is the manner in which they investigate and finally bring to prosecution cases involving violations of the federal law assigned to them to police.

The second key pillar of the federal investigatory apparatus consists of the nonregulatory agencies (henceforth, for purposes of this study, referred to as the *nonagencies*). These consist of the more than 30 different bureaus, departments, and divisions found within the vast investigatory apparatus. For example, the Internal Revenue Service (IRS) is a division of the U.S. Treasury Department; the Federal Bureau of Investigation (FBI) is a bureau of the Justice Department; the Customs Service (CS) and the Bureau of Alcohol, Tobacco and Firearms (BATF) are sections of the U.S. Treasury Department; the Postal Inspector's Office (PIO) is a bureau of the U.S. Postal Service; the Office of Special Investigations (OSI) is a division of the U.S. Air Force. There are many other units, for example, the Office of Investigations found within the U.S. Department of Health, Education and Welfare (HEW). All these units have one thing in common: unlike the regulatory agencies or agency model, they have no commissions. Their investigations, like those of the agencies, tend to deal with specialized areas of law. However, decisionmaking is not with the commission.

The commission is a decisionmaking entity with investigative, prosecutorial, as well as rulemaking roles. It alone can authorize its staff to initiate, investigate, and prosecute frauds they uncover. Thus, if a staff uncovers a computer fraud, it must first obtain the authorization of its commission to proceed to court with the case. If the commission fails to authorize action, then the matter dies within the agency. In addition, since most agencies hold their investigations up as being confidential, when a commission fails to authorize public action, then the public itself never knows what really happened.

Commission Investigations

All regulatory agencies have an enforcement section. This unit may go by different names within different agencies, but its role is to investigate violations of laws that its agency is authorized to police and enforce. Once the staff of this unit concludes an investigation, it will then recommend to the commission, which is the decisionmaking body, one of three actions: (1) referral to the United States Justice Department for criminal prosecution, (2) civil action by the agency itself, and (3) administrative action, also by the agency. The staff may recommend any of the above three, or even all three.

Investigations, however, take one of two roles: informal or formal. Once the staff receives information either from another law enforcement unit, or from an informer, or from a private police unit, that a violation of laws under its jurisdiction has occurred, the staff will then conduct an informal inquiry to determine the extent of the violation. If it is determined that the agency has no jurisdiction over the matter but that another agency or law enforcement unit (even a local one) has jurisdiction, the staff will then inform the commission and recommend that the matter be referred to the appropriate agency for further investigation. Since the commission is usually busy with numerous other matters, by the time a decision is made the culprits have erased their tracks. It may also mean that the commission may recommend no action, in which case the matter dies.[25] The staff is prohibited by law from going over the head of the commission. However, there are informal channels between different investigatory units. But, if the staff violates its own rules, the defendant can later attempt to quash the entire case against him on the grounds that it is the product of an illegal investigation; and members of the staff can be fired if discovered by the commission to have engaged in such activity.

If the agency determines that it has jurisdiction over the matter at issue and that a further inquiry is needed to determine its actual perimeters, it may seek from the commission authorization to conduct such an inquiry. The investigation, once approved by the commission, becomes formal. Some agencies, like the FTC and SEC, have the power to issue administrative subpoenas. The nonagencies, like the Federal Bureau of Investigation (FBI), which will be discussed later, do not have such powers.

An administrative subpoena, unlike a court-ordered subpoena, has no judicial support. If an individual fails to observe it, the staff must then go to the commission. The staff must request that it be given authority to go to court and seek subpoena enforcement. The commission must first approve the action before the staff can actually go to court and enforce its own subpoenas. Once in court, the adversary can oppose the enforcement of the subpoena by filing with the court a motion to quash the agency's subpoena. A court will then decide. If it decides to enforce the staff's subpoena, and the witness still refuses to abide by it, he will be held in civil contempt.

The problem with the agency model is that the staff must obtain the approval of the commission at every key stage of its investigation. Thus, in a sophisticated computer crime, the culprits have more than adequate time to destroy the evidence. Even if the agency can show that evidence has been destroyed, it must first obtain the commission's approval before referring the matter to the Justice Department for criminal prosecution. The individuals involved in the destruction of the evidence would probably be charged with obstruction of justice.

Once the agency obtains authorization to conduct a formal investigation, it will then begin questioning witnesses, many of whom will be deposed under oath; and it may issue subpoenas for the production of documents or for the appearance of uncooperative witnesses. The staff may also make onsight inspections of certain industries. For example, the SEC has jurisdiction over the brokerage industry. SEC staffers can make onsite inspections of the various brokerage firms. Whether an onsite inspection of a computer system will be of any assistance varies according to the expertise of the staff in areas of computer technology and crime as well as according to the sophistication of the felons involved in the fraud. It should be pointed out that, in some agencies, the commission must also approve every subpoena that goes out. This may add delays of weeks, or even months, to an investigation already overburdened with red tape.

Once the agency concludes its investigation, it makes its recommendations to the commission. If it finds criminal violations, it will recommend that the matter be referred to the Justice Department for prosecution. The staff will then prepare a *criminal reference memorandum.* This memo will outline the different violations of the law, the facts of the case, and will also list those individuals the agency recommends be named as defendants. The commission must then approve the recommendations. Once approved, the recommendations go to the Justice Department, where its staff will review them. On the average, it takes six months to a year before such a memo finally reaches the Justice Department.[26] In a computer fraud scheme—where time is of the essence, and where magnetic tapes, programs, and printouts are easily destroyed—the great wastes in time may play a key role.

Once at the Justice Department, the memo is assigned to one of its branches for scrutiny. The review process here may also take as long as six months. It should be added that the memo, both at the Justice Department level and at the agency level, usually goes through several tiers of review. The many tiers can occasionally have disastrous consequences, even in a traditional-type crime investigation. For example, a bizarre tale surfaced last year. Federal investigators had been informed that an underworld figure had been involved in a murder.[27] The event had occurred in 1973 in Fort Lauderdale, Florida. Two years later New York City police arrested the individual involved and returned him to Florida. He was then charged with murder in that state.[28]

Meanwhile, a federal agent was contacted by an informant who told him that the individual arrested had in fact confided during a private meeting with the informant that the suspect had been the "hit man" in the murder. The agent attempted to turn this information over to the local authorities in Florida.

However, the agency regulations required that he first obtain approval from his superiors in Washington, D.C. It took three months before he obtained the approval.[29] The memo requesting approval to inform the Florida authorities of the informant's "tip" left the agent's branch office on August 12. It arrived in Washington, D.C. at the home office on September 2. No action was taken until 20 days later.[30] A branch chief finally approved it in mid-October. Two more chiefs approved it afterwards. The three-paragraph request was then rewritten by the home office to conform with their "style," finally being approved by mid-November. The "murderer" was acquitted in late October. The information came too late to aid the local authorities.[31] Had this been a computer crime case, a delay of three months, just to inform the local agencies of a matter that would have taken a simple telephone call, could have proven just as disastrous. The culprits could have erased their "tracks."

Once a memo is at the Justice Department, various officials decide whether to act or not act. If the decision is to take no action, then the matter dies—no criminal action is forthcoming unless the staff finds a local prosecutor who will take the case. Even to do this, the staff must first obtain the approval of its superiors and finally that of the commission. If the Justice Department decides to take criminal action, it may then refer the case to the local federal prosecutor—a United States attorney. The majority of criminal referrals are usually declined, and die within the Department.[32]

"Shopping" for a federal prosecutor can be a tiring experience. If the prosecutor, after he reviews the case with his staff, concludes that there is "no case," the matter ends there. There is also the added problem that most federal prosecutors are ill-equipped in terms of both staff and training to handle sophisticated cases. A computer fraud case could easily tie up many members of the staff for lengthy periods of time and cost the office a substantial amount of money. These are certainly negative factors. A federal prosecutor makes his reputation by the number of cases he brings. If for the same effort he can bring six cases, as opposed to one, to a successful conclusion, then he will be inclined to reject the one that is "difficult." He can do it by simply saying, "We don't have a case here."

Once a local federal prosecutor is found, then the agency will usually assign one of its members to work with that office. Since federal prosecutors are not specialists, it is necessary that an agency investigator be assigned to the prosecutor's office. The investigator then outlines the entire case to the staff member assigned to take it to trial. Local federal prosecutors lack the expertise and the training in specialized areas of the law. They tend to be litigators. Further, no funds are provided for them to retain their own investigators. They rely entirely on the federal investigatory apparatus. Without it, they tend to be, as one prosecutor remarked, "prima donnas without a script."

The agencies generally hesitate to refer matters for criminal prosecution. There are various reasons for this. Some are political. For example, in one recent case, the governor of a Southern state openly intervened in a state investigation.[33] The state insurance department deferred regulatory action as a result. Although the federal agency was aware of the governor's obstructive tactics, and although those tactics may have hindered the federal investigation itself, no action was taken against the governor.

The agency is also concerned with its own image and budget. Typically, agencies attempt to show activity when in fact that activity is meaningless. Unfortunately, civil action in the form of an injunction will deter few, if any, criminals. The agency is also concerned with its annual budget. It must justify its requests. To do so, it must show activity by its staff. If staff members are assigned to the offices of federal prosecutors, some of them may have to work out of those offices for extended periods of time, sometimes as much as one or two years. The agency "foots" the bill and also gets little, if any, of the credit. If the criminal case succeeds, the credit is usually given to the prosecutor. If it fails, the agency (at least it feels so) will usually bear the blame.

Agencies, as well as staff personnel, are thus reluctant to work with the federal prosecutors. For example, the SEC was requested by the United States attorney for Newark, New Jersey, to assign an accountant to his office to work on a complicated securities fraud. The branch chief at the SEC, from whose branch the accountant was to be taken, declined on the grounds that he could not spare the manpower. The case was never prosecuted. The branch chief himself was concerned that if he did send his accountant to Newark, he might lose him for as long as one year. He certainly had little if anything to gain from the outcome. The accountant never left.

The Agency Games: Bureaucratic Politics

Under the present structure, even if agency investigators were given extensive training in computer fraud investigations, the federal prosecutors would have little access to them if they needed them. Further, it might only mean an intensification in the civil area to get publicity for the agency.

Agencies have direct civil jurisdiction. They can go, with their own lawyers, to any local United States district court and file a complaint against one or more individuals asking for injunctive relief. Agencies tend to favor this approach because in such instances the "glory" is shared with no one. It may thus mean that we will see more civil rather than criminal action in the area of computer crime, unless the forces that impel this kind of agency activity are curtailed or eliminated.

Once the staff uncovers violations, it may recommend to the commission that civil action be taken against various named individuals and/or corporations. The commission may decide to act against all of them, or some of them. The staff is then authorized to go to the federal district court to file action asking for injunctive relief. An injunction is a court order barring someone from doing or performing certain acts. It deals with anticipated behavior. In essence, the staff asks the court to stop Mr. X from stealing again, rather than punishing him for having stolen millions. It should be noted that the great Equity Funding fraud was, in large part, dealt with civilly in this fashion.

Thus, if a number of individuals were involved in a massive computer fraud, the agency would probably first proceed civilly and, once it had gotten the publicity, then refer the matter to the Justice Department. This may take several years, during which memories dim and witnesses disappear. By then, it may be too late. Further, the limelight now gone, the federal prosecutor himself may decline the case.

For example, the biggest fraud in American history, the Equity Funding scandal, cost the public more than $2 billion and resulted in the criminal prosecution of only a handful of individuals. Of the hundreds involved in this massive conspiracy, only about two dozen were prosecuted and convicted criminally. The rest were sued civilly or administratively. What also makes the Equity case interesting is the reaction of the federal agencies toward those who "blew the whistle."

The scandal first erupted in 1973. It became apparent that the president of the company, the chairman of the board, and other high officials were heavily involved. Management had used the firm's computers to create false insurance policies and to inflate its assets. A false picture of the company was presented to the public and the stockholders of the firm. The largest stockholders, it should be borne in mind, were the great financial institutions of this country—the First National City Bank of New York, Bankers Trust and Morgan Guaranty, and the Ford Foundation, to name just a few. The company filed numerous false financial statements with both federal and state agencies. None detected the fraud until it was finally brought to their attention by an outsider.

The fraud may have had its beginnings in the special class insurance policies the firm made available to its employees. These were offered to both employees and their family members with a free premium for the first year. The policyholder could eventually, so theory ran, cash in his "chips" and have a profit left over. This program, however, left the firm constantly in search of funds. The firm then embarked on a massive falsification scheme.

Of the more than 90,000 insurance policies recorded in the firm's computer, more than 60,000 were fictitious—they were created and recorded by company personnel in the computer files. The fictitious policies carried the designation code 99.[34] This enabled the computer billing programs to skip the bogus policies when bills were mailed out to the real policyholders. The bogus policies were sold to coinsurers.

Life insurance firms frequently sell large blocks of any insurance they underwrite to another firm. The latter is the coinsurer. The activity is known as *reinsurance*. The risk is thus sold to another firm. The firm will then receive most of the premiums paid by the insured. The original insurer will also receive part of these premiums so as to handle the bookkeeping and other paperwork expenses.

When Equity was asked for a listing of its policies, it produced the printouts. When further proof was asked, as for example, a random selection of policies, the firm's management would note that it was not immediately available. They stalled to buy time. During this time they forged the hard-copy files. The fraud had been going on probably since the 1960s. The fraud was first brought to the attention of one Ray Dirks, a securities analyst, by a former vice president of the company. Dirks conducted his own private investigation—he did not go to the authorities right away. Subsequently, the matter broke publicly. Dirks noted that he had no confidence in the authorities. If he had gone to them, he feared it would have taken months, even years, to get it exposed.[35] Presently Dirks is himself a defendant in a federal action,[36] because he did not go immediately to the federal authorities with his story.[37]

However, the slowness with which federal agencies act has been corroborated by a recent confidential document that appeared in the Dirks administrative trial.[38] It appears that as early as 1971 the SEC had indications of the Equity Funding fraud. A confidential government memo, now made public, reads as follows:

... it was common gossip on the [Wall] Street that for a number of years Equity Funding has been running fraudulent entries through the books of its various companies in order to show continued earnings, particularly for its end-of-the-year audits.[39]

The memo also makes note of a conversation between federal agents and a company source:

He admitted ... that he left the company [Equity] because he did not "understand" some of their accounting practices and did not want to put his signature to certain documents of which he did not approve. ... the company [Equity] seemed to be interested in having its books reflect an adequate cash flow and that he did not approve of some of the accounting methods used.[40]

There can be little doubt that there were strong indications that a fraud did in fact exist. However, the matter lay buried for several years. The real story on the great Equity Funding scandal will probably never be known. However, the slow and tiring process of the federal agencies appears to be ill-suited for the investigation of sophisticated computer crimes. The startling question about Equity Funding is why the officers of the firm, who had sufficient time to do so, never destroyed the magnetic tapes and computer programs. This would have certainly erased their tracks.

More than 90 percent of the agency civil actions culminate in consent decrees—a form of plea bargaining that the federal agencies have developed and nurtured to a new plateau. Critics charge that consent decrees are worthless, that they encourage rather than deter crimes. Nonetheless, if computer felons are to be deterred, it is imperative to understand the consent decree.

The Consent Decree Route

More than 90 percent of all agency investigations are confidential.[41] Agencies have statutory authority to conduct either open or closed investigations.[42] Agencies may, if they choose, announce that they are conducting an investigation into a specific conduct or industry.[43] However, this is rarely done. In fact, the trend is to conduct closed investigations. The entire decisionmaking process of investigation and prosecution is thus closed to the public. This makes it possible for agencies, for various political and internal reasons, to reach an accommodation known as a *consent settlement* with the targets of its investigation. In the case of a massive computer fraud, it may thus mean that a felon never even reaches the courtroom, but it resolves his problems with the agency through an internal and little-known avenue. It is important then that this route be understood.

The *consent decree* is not unique to the agency experience. The federal apparatus, however, has carried it to exaggerated proportions. Felons, who should have been prosecuted criminally, escape punishment through the consent route. For example, in one case, a well-known Chicago gambler, with possible underworld ties, entered into a consent agreement with the federal government.[44] In another case, the president of a publicly held firm admitted to federal sources that he had forged several contracts the firm allegedly had with national corporations. He was never prosecuted criminally, but instead entered into a consent agreement.[45]

As another example, in October 1974 a San Diego-based firm entered into a consent agreement with a federal agency. Under that agreement, the firm was to cease making false and misleading statements to the public.[46] The company was involved in the sale of real estate. It employed many young military officers. The land, sold mostly in parcels of 2 to 5 acres, allegedly was falsely promoted as having large growth potential.[47] Further, buyers were also told that local law would be amended to allow for gambling casinos in the area and that a large international airport would also be built in the area to service it.[48] In May 1977 a federal grand jury began to reinvestigate the entire case on grounds that the fraud had continued long after the consent agreement had been reached.[49]

The consent agreement itself is a contract between the government and the defendant or defendants—they may be individuals or corporations. The latter neither admit nor deny any wrongdoing. However, it is agreed by both sides that the defendant or defendants will not engage in certain illegal activities. Those acts and the statutes involved are usually spelled out. An agreement cannot be overbroad, because it will open itself to attack if the government ever seeks to enforce it. It should be pointed out, though, that these agreements are rarely enforced.[50]

If the defendant violates the provisions of the agreement—in theory at least—the government can go to court and enforce it. The defendant will then be held in contempt of court. The process is a civil one. Even if held in contempt, the defendant cannot be sentenced to more than 6 months imprisonment. Fewer than half a dozen such agreements have ever been enforced by the federal government in the last several years.

The agreement itself is not an admission of guilt. Thus those members of the public who have lost their funds as a result of the fraud cannot go to court armed with a certified copy of the agreement as proof of wrongdoing by the defendant. Further, the public itself has no input in the agreement. Unlike criminal plea bargaining, where the government prosecutors may consult with the victim and advise him or her of developments, in negotiations involving the consent agreement, the victim is never brought into the process. In addition, because the investigations are confidential, the victim may not even be aware of what is transpiring until the events are made public.

Further, the agreement itself is usually an extremely watered-down version of what really occurred. The agreement is negotiated. Attorneys for both the government and the various possible defendants will have numerous meetings to discuss the possible settlement. Usually, the negotiations begin in an informal setting. For example, when the government attorneys are ready to prepare their recommendations to the commission, the attorneys for the defense may meet with them.[51] First, they will ask the government lawyers if the latter contemplate recommending action against their clients. If the answer is yes, then the negotiations become more formal.

In some agencies, such as the SEC, once the defendant is informed that he or she may be the focus of a civil injunction or other agency action, the defendant, through counsel, may submit a brief arguing against such action.[52] The government attorneys must then prepare an opposition brief. Both briefs will then go to the commission and will accompany the staff's action recommendation. The commission will then review the matter and make a decision.

The staff, anxious to avoid prolonged internal delays—there is no limit as to the number of briefs a defendant can submit—may indicate to the commission that consent negotiations have begun with the defendants, or may even indicate that such agreements have already been informally reached. The commission usually rubber stamps those agreements. A good defense attorney will use the brief process to wear down the government's side into accepting a watered-down agreement.

If an agreement is finally reached, both sides review the papers before they are ever filed in court. When there is agreement that the papers are acceptable to both sides, the defendant and the government both sign these documents and they are then filed with the court. The defendant makes no appearance. The entire process usually involves a brief "run" to the court by one of the government's lawyers. The judge signs the agreements. The matter is then made public. However, at this stage, the victims have little to say in a process that is for all purposes a fait accompli.

The consent decree will usually also mean that few, if any, cases are prosecuted criminally. The incentive for an agency, once it enters a consent agreement, no longer exists to refer the matter to the Justice Department for criminal prosecution. Further, the Justice Department itself, unless there is a huge outcry from the public and various pressure groups, may not be interested in the case either. The publicity is too old, and the case itself may also be too old. Witnesses may no longer be available; victims may be reluctant to testify several years later since the pain of the loss has passed.

Cases, even when they are referred criminally after consent agreements, may have been so compromised along the way that the final conviction may be a watered-down prison sentence. For example, in one of the nation's biggest fraud cases, involving more than $200 million in land, only four top-ranking officers of Amrep Corporation received prison sentences, and these only 6 months each.[53] The many other individuals involved in the investigation entered into consent decrees. The judge noted that had the government not compromised its case with consent agreements, he would have meted out longer sentences.[54] The lawyer for the defendants pointed out to the court:

There is no reason to make an example of these men, . . . when the United States Government has been satisfied with civil remedies [consent agreements] in worse situations. A number of well-known public corporations, including I.T.T., Boise Cascade and Great Western United, have in the past engaged in land-sale activities as a substantial business. Only Amrep and its officers have thus far been the subject of criminal indictment and conviction, much less a jail term.[55]

Consent agreements are also common in the local juvenile courts of this country. Here individuals who have not attained majority status are prosecuted for various crimes they have committed. In the District of Columbia, the local prosecutor will occasionally enter into a consent agreement with a juvenile.[56] However, there are certain criteria. An offense must usually be the first for that individual; and the juvenile must not have been involved in other crimes. Second, the offense must not be a serious one. Third, the defendant, once he or she enters into this agreement, although he or she neither admits nor denies guilt, must agree not to violate the law and consent to meet with a probation officer, who in turn will monitor progress.

If a juvenile defendant who has entered into such an agreement with the government fails to live up to his or her commitment, the government may reinstitute the original charges and bring the matter to trial. If found guilty, the defendant can be commited until he or she reaches the age of adulthood. It may mean that if the defendant is 16 years of age, he or she can be sentenced to imprisonment until the age of 21. It is important to note that although the juvenile's consent agreement is processed and monitored by the criminal system, the consent agreement process in the regulatory model is neither monitored nor within the criminal system.

The agencies assign no one to monitor the defendants who have reached a consent agreement with them. Further, there is no demand that the defendant keep the agency abreast of his developments. There is no "probationary role" played by the agency. The entire process is civil. However, the violations may have been criminal. The decision to go civil is one dictated by the political needs of the agency and not the interest of the public. As such, the juvenile finds that his treatment can be harsher than that of his elders, even though they may have stolen large sums of money. The confidential nature of the agency proceedings ensures that the investigatory process is secret. The public never knows fully what has transpired.

In a massive fraud, for example, where the computer is used to create nonexistent assets or clients, the conspirators could easily evade criminal prosecution simply by using the consent decree route. With the rise of the Electronic Funds Transfer System (EFTS), the opportunities for computer felons are many and increasing. Thus by simply ensuring that their activity will fall within the regulatory agency model they can be assured of immunity from criminal prosecution. When and if prosecution does finally come, the case will be too old and the government will have compromised itself so many times that conviction may mean little more than a slap on the wrist.

The Administrative Route

The regulatory agencies also have administrative remedies available to them. For example, the agency may choose to take the administrative route instead of the civil or criminal. The administrative route, however, never culminates in a criminal conviction or imprisonment. The process may culminate in a fine, a censure, a suspension, or even the barring of the defendant from the industry the agency regulates. The SEC may bring charges in an administrative tribunal against a broker-dealer. If found guilty of the alleged violations, the defendant may be suspended from the securities industry for a period of time or be barred permanently. This latter punishment is rare and usually meted out against insignificant defendants, the small and powerless ones.

Thus, if a brokerage firm were found to be manipulating the stock of a public company, the firm and some of the officers of that firm could be brought within the administrative route and be charged with certain violations. The defendants could then either litigate the matter or enter into a negotiated settlement with the agency. They might voluntarily agree to be suspended from practicing in the industry for a period of time. If they decide to litigate, and if found guilty, they can appeal the matter to the United States Court of Appeals should the agency's commission uphold the administrative finding.

The administrative trial, usually called an administrative hearing, may be closed to the public. Further, the deciding officer is not a member of the federal judicial apparatus, but rather a member of the judicial division of the agency. All agencies have a judicial section—the administrative hearing examiners section. It means that the administrative trial judge, if his subpoenas are disregarded—and they may be—must ask the staff to go to the local federal courts for enforcement. In essence, a defendant can unilaterally delay the hearing. Further, the process itself is extremely slow. Thus it may take more than a year before the administrative judge comes down with a decision. All decisions must then be enforced in a federal court should the defendant refuse to comply.

Consequently, felons who make use of computers to manipulate corporate assets or the stock of a public corporation, if they are found to be members of the securities industry and within the gambit of the SEC's jurisdiction, may find that they can evade criminal prosecution through the administrative process.

In one instance, a government informer, in papers filed in a federal law suit, revealed a story that indicates the problems that lay in store with the area of computer crime. It bears grave forebodings. Mr. X, the informer, met in August 1976 with a member of one of the New York organized crime families.[57] He was introduced to a relative of the racketeer. The relative (referred to as Joey) had no criminal record and worked for one of Wall Street's more prestigious brokerage firms.[58]

Joey prepared computer programs for the firm's computer. The programs, in turn, controlled the record keeping of customers' accounts.[59] X was told by the racketeer that because Joey occupied a key position at the firm's margin desk, he could easily generate accounts for nonexistent customers and negotiate fictitious securities transactions for those customers.[60] Since Joey had no criminal record, no one would suspect him.

The scheme would work as follows. Joey would create a fictitious account on the firm's computer.[61] He would then have the account sell nonexistent securities. With more than $5 billion—Senate sources put the figure as high as $50 billion—of missing, stolen, or counterfeit securities, this would go unnoticed. Joey would then instruct the computer to pay for this nonexistent transaction. Joey could then cash the check and reprogram the computer to erase the entire fictitious transaction.[62] Joey, in his attempt to illustrate how easily this could be accomplished, showed X a check for over $500,000 made out to a fictitious account that he controlled.[63]

Had the regulatory agency (federal) uncovered this fraud, they would have probably settled it either through an administrative process or through a consent decree. More than 90 percent of their cases are settled in this fashion. For example, one alleged felon who had been involved in more than a dozen investigations and who was known by the investigators as having organized crime links was only temporarily suspended (through the administrative process) for his role in a number of frauds.[64] There is little to indicate that Joey would have met with different treatment.

The computer enables sophisticated criminal elements to perpetrate vast and complex frauds that touch all facets of our economy. To date, many of these frauds have come to the public's attention only by sheer accident. The majority of those which have been uncovered have involved minor figures. There is a growing view that perhaps the regulatory agencies have outlived their purpose, at least in the policing area. There can be little doubt that the commission model, with its mountains of red tape and bureaucratic trappings, hardly meets the needs of the computer age. It has proven ill-suited in the past, and may prove a disaster in the future when confronted with mass computer crimes.

References

1. Bernard D. Nossiter, "Scotland Yard Deprograms Great Computer Tape Heist," *Washington Post*, January 1, 1977, p. A-15.

2. Ibid.

3. Ibid.

4. Ibid.

5. G. Christian Hill, "Large Loan Swindles Spread with Reliance on Central Data Banks," *Wall Street Journal*, March 12, 1976, p. 1.

6. Ibid.

7. Ibid.

8. Ibid.

9. Ibid.

10. Ibid.

11. Evelyn L. Parks, "From Constabulary to Police Society: Implications for Social Control," in *Whose Law, What Order,* ed. William J. Chamblis (New York: Wiley, 1976), pp. 129-131.

12. Ibid.

13. Ibid.

14. Ibid.

15. National Association of Counties Research Foundation, *County-Wide Law Enforcement: A Report on a Survey of Central Police Service in 97 Urban Counties* (Washington, D.C.: National Association of Counties, 1975), p. 1.

16. Ibid.

17. Ibid.

18. Ibid.

19. Ibid., pp. 1, 5.

20. Ibid.

21. Ibid.

22. Ibid.

23. "The Bureaucracy Explosion," *U.S. News & World Report*, August 16, 1976, pp. 22-25.

24. U.S. Securities and Exchange Commission, *Annual Report 1976* (Washington, D.C.: U.S. Securities and Exchange Commission, 1977), p. 199.

25. August Bequai, "White Collar Plea Bargaining," *Trial Magazine*, July 1977, pp. 38-41.

26. Ibid.

27. Jack Anderson and Les Whiten, "IRS Red Tape Killed Testimony," *Washington Post*, October 19, 1976, p. B-13.

28. Ibid.

29. Ibid.

30. Ibid.

31. Ibid.

32. Based on my experience as a trial attorney with the Division of Enforcement, U.S. Securities and Exchange Commission, and also numerous interviews with both federal investigators and prosecutors.

33. "Louisiana Unit Delayed Insurance Case after Governor Intervened, SEC Says," *Wall Street Journal*, May 13, 1977, p. 21.

34. W.T. Porter, Jr., "Computer Raped by Telephone," *New York Times Magazine*, September 8, 1974, p. 35.

35. "The High Cost of Whistling," *Newsweek*, February 14, 1977, p. 75.

36. Ibid.

37. Ibid.

38. Priscilla S. Meyer, "SEC Data Indicate Equity Funding Probe by an Aide Long before Scandal Erupted," *Wall Street Journal*, February 10, 1977, p. 4.

39. Ibid.

40. Ibid.

41. Arthur F. Mathews, "Witnesses in SEC Investigations," *Review of Securities Regulation*, May 5, 1970, p. 923.

42. Ibid.

43. Ibid.

44. U.S. Justice Department, *Annual Report of the Attorney General of the United States for 1975* (Washington, D.C.: U.S. Justice Department, 1976), p. 91.

45. Based on a case I personally worked on while a trial attorney with the Division of Enforcement, U.S. Securities and Exchange Commission, 1973-1975.

46. Everett R. Holles, "Navy Men are Tried for Land Sale Fraud," *New York Times*, May 14, 1977, p. 23.

47. Ibid.

48. Ibid.

49. Ibid.

50. Ibid.

51. Attorneys for "targets" of a federal regulatory agency investigation usually meet with the federal attorneys and attempt to dissuade them from recommending that their clients become defendants in a government prosecution. At the U.S. Securities and Exchange Commission, these attorneys can also put their arguments in writing; the document or memo is known as a *Wells submission.* Through such tactics, defense attorneys can delay and tire the government attorneys down.

52. The brief can vary in length from 6 to several hundred pages.

53. "Four Get 6-Month Sentences in N.M. Property Scheme," *Washington Post*, March 11, 1977, p. C-26.

54. Arnold Lubasch, "Four Amprep Officials Get 6-Month Terms in Rio Rancho Case," *New York Times*, March 11, 1977, pp. D-1, D-11.

55. Ibid., p. D-11.

56. The Superior Court of the District of Columbia, among other jurisdictions, will place a first-time juvenile offender on a consent decree. The decree, however, is solely discretionary with the prosecutor and is usually given in cases involving nonserious offenses.

57. "John Doe Sues Dean Witter in Anonymity Necessitated by Mafia Tie, Fraud Effort," *Wall Street Journal*, January 28, 1977, p. 14.

58. Ibid.

59. Ibid.

60. Ibid.

61. Ibid.

62. Ibid.

63. Ibid.

64. Based on a case I worked on during the period of 1973-1975, while employed as a trial attorney with the Division of Enforcement, U.S. Securities and Exchange Commission.

The Investigators: Part II

The federal apparatus consists, in addition to the various regulatory agencies, of a myriad of other units. These, for purposes of this book, will be referred to as the *nonagencies*. Unlike the regulatory agencies, these other federal units have no commission structures to guide their investigations. Further, with the exception of the Internal Revenue Service (IRS), they lack subpoena power. They rely, in great part, on voluntary compliance, and also on the Justice Department.

There are, however, some similarities between these units and the regulatory agencies. For example, both groups have been delegated jurisdiction over well-defined areas of our economy. In addition, both groups have been given a legal arsenal with which to police their areas of responsibility. The nonagencies, as is the case with the commission structure, refer their criminal cases to the Justice Department for prosecution. If the latter refuses to act, the matter ends there. Like the regulatory agencies, they have administrative and civil jurisdiction over various violations of their statutes. However, some of the nonagencies rely on the Justice Department even for their civil prosecutions, adding further red tape to an already overbureaucratized structure.

Like the regulatory agencies, their investigations are usually confidential. Further, like the former, they too are noted for lengthy and overdrawn investigations, some averaging 5 years each. The nonagencies are extremely vulnerable to political pressure, and some have been even infiltrated by elements of organized crime. With the exception of the Federal Bureau of Investigation (FBI), the nonagencies have no programs to combat computer crime. There are some minor exceptions, for example, the U.S. Air Force Office of Special Investigations (OSI); but these are rare and too minor to play any key role. Their track record in this area of computer crime is no better than that of the commissions. I will now review some of these nonagencies.

Postal Inspector's Office

Several years ago, more than 400 investors lost millions of dollars in a scheme they thought would give them returns of 30 to 100 percent on their investments. In Florida alone, thousands of investors lost millions of dollars in land frauds.[1] In New York, a company falsified its records to cover the high count of bacteria in its ice cream.[2]

These cases reveal one common trait—all made use of the mails to perpetrate or conceal their frauds. The policing unit charged with regulating and ensuring that the mails are free of crime is the Postal Inspector's Office, which consists of more than 1700 postal inspectors throughout the country. These are the investigative agents of the U.S. Postal Service. The agents work with both federal and local law enforcement agencies.

Crimes committed within the postal system include mail fraud, illegal transmission of illegal goods, thefts of mail, and the mailing of dangerous and unauthorized objects. If use of the mails is made in a computer crime, even if only to further that scheme, the Postal Inspector's Office will have jurisdiction and the mail fraud statutes will control. Of all federal legislation, the mail fraud statutes are the least complicated and the least difficult to prove. All that is necessary is a showing that there was a mailing within the United States. If the mailing occurs outside the United States, however, the mail fraud statutes do not come into play.

For example, if a group of felons hatches a scheme based in Mexico and, from that country, manipulates the computer of an American firm also based in Mexico, and if checks are then forwarded for nonexistent services to "shell" companies in the United States, the mail fraud statutes would be of little value because the mailing took place outside the United States.

However, bankruptcy frauds, securities frauds, and thefts involving use of the mails, use of the mails to extort money, and trafficking in dangerous drugs through use of the mails, all fall under the jurisdiction of postal inspectors. For example, if explosives are mailed (with the objective of destroying a computer system) through the United States mail system, postal inspectors have jurisdiction to investigate.

If programs are taken and held for ransom, the postal inspectors also have jurisdiction if the mails have been used to forward the demands. However, postal inspectors have no jurisdiction outside the postal system or over a private courier system.

Postal inspectors have historically concentrated their efforts, as have other law enforcement units, on traditional criminals. Computer crimes have usually gone unhindered and unpunished. The postal authorities have no training in the investigation of computer-related crimes. However, the postal system itself has come to rely on computers for administrative purposes, and there are also plans to replace the written message by the electronic transference of data over a series of computer networks. A "mail-o-gram" may soon be replaced by electronic impulses, which carry the same message, but within a very short span of time and electronically. The Postal Service of the future may be a giant computer network, transferring information and funds over computer terminals. The present investigatory techniques and tools will be ill-adapted to meet those needs.

Secret Service

The Secret Service is not only charged with protecting the President of the United States and members of his immediate family, but also with protecting the integrity of the currency of the United States. In addition, it has the responsibility of detecting and arresting those who forge federal checks, bonds, and securities. Finally, the Secret Service is also charged with investigations relating to the Gold Reserve Act of 1934, the Federal Deposit Insurance Act, the Federal Land Bank Act, the Home Owner's Loan Act, and the Government Losses in Shipment Act.

The Service has several dozen branch offices in the major cities of this country. These offices have responsibility for enforcing the counterfeiting and forgery statutes of the Federal Code. For example, Title 18, U.S. Code, Section 8 defines the jurisdiction of the Service as including all bonds, certificates of indebtedness, national bank currency, Federal Reserve notes, Federal Reserve Bank notes, coupons, United States notes, Treasury notes, gold and silver certificates, checks, certificates of deposit, and other forms of currency. Section 8 makes no reference to computers or computer-related forms of currency. It makes no reference to electronic impulses, which may be a new form of currency, especially under a highly computerized banking system, such as an EFTS.

Section 481 makes it a crime to print, photograph, make, or sell any engraving, without authority, in the likeness of any genuine bond, note, obligation, or other security, or any part thereof, of any government, bank, or corporation.[3] This statute provides penalties of up to 5 years imprisonment, or up to $5000 in fines, or both. However, in an era when brokerage records have been largely computerized, the forging of corporate securities increasingly makes little sense. A felon needs only to create nonexistent securities by simply manipulating a firm's computer.

Section 504 prohibits the printing, publishing, or importation of plates necessary for the printing of postage stamps, revenue stamps, and other United States obligations.[4] The statute directs itself to the use of plates for counterfeiting purposes. However, it has no provision for situations where computers are used as instruments of forgery. One recent federal case, however, held that checks issued by a computer for nonexistent services at the direction of criminals are forgeries.[5]

Section 489 makes it illegal to make or bring into the United States any token, disk, or device in the likeness of any United States coins, or foreign currency, with intent to sell, give, or use in any manner. However, a duplicate, stolen, or forged computer program can be used to issue funds for nonexistent or inflated services; this statute would not cover the fraud.

The Service has, for many years, proven to be an invaluable arm of the federal investigatory apparatus. However, in an era of computerized transactions, where paper and coin currency will give way to electronic transfers, the Service is ill-prepared for this new role and needs to train special units to address the problem.

Federal Bureau of Investigation

The FBI is one of the largest investigatory police forces in the world. It employs more than 19,000 persons,[6] with 59 field offices; 494 suboffices, and 15 foreign liaison offices.[7] The FBI is charged with enforcing the federal criminal code, and it also trains local police forces at its academy in Quantico, Virginia. Unlike the regulatory agencies, this organization is a component of the Justice Department and reports directly to the U.S. Attorney General. It is one of the most important investigatory units of the federal law enforcement machinery.

The FBI has traditionally enforced dozens of statutes that are essential to this country's well-being. For example, it investigates crimes on the high seas involving American vessels, as well as crimes on Indian and federal reservations, including military bases. Tampering with military computers, or computers on any federal or Indian reservation, as well as on American vessels in high seas, could bring the FBI into the case. Computers destroyed while moving in interstate or foreign commerce would also bring the FBI into the case. Industrial or any other form of sabotage of computers moving in interstate or foreign commerce would also bring in the FBI.

The FBI also investigates use of the mails to convey a threat or a demand for ransom or reward. A threat to injure a computer, however, must also be coupled with an intent to extort in order for the FBI to intervene in the case. The use of wire, radio, or television to communicate threats in interstate commerce is also within the FBI's jurisdiction. Any such threats conveyed against a computer would bring the FBI into the case. Frauds against the federal government, as well as the presentation of false claims against the federal government, fall within the jurisdiction of the FBI; the fact that computers might be employed makes no difference.

The unauthorized wearing of an official uniform of the Armed Forces of the United States is also within the FBI's investigatory jurisdiction. Felons who impersonate military personnel at a military computer center would be investigated by the FBI, as would any felon representing a member of the military at any military installation. This also applies to the impersonation of employees of the federal government or foreign officials duly accredited to the United States.

The malicious interference with the federal government's telephone, radio, television, or other communication means—including those used for military or civil defense purposes—falls within the FBI's investigative ambit. Matters relating to internal security—espionage, sabotage, subversive activities, and related matters—are also within the FBI's realm. The sabotage of computers related to internal security work would compel FBI involvement.

Another area over which the FBI has jurisdiction is interstate transportation of gambling devices. Computers that, in any way, are used either directly or indirectly as gambling apparatus would come under FBI jurisdiction. The sending of communications in interstate or foreign commerce by radio, wire, or television with intent to defraud is also within the FBI's jurisdiction. However, use of wire to defraud within interstate commerce is not.

Interstate transportation of stolen property also falls within its ambit. It appears that the next important issue to be determined by the courts is whether electronic impulses are "property" as it is commonly understood. At least one court has held that they are not.[8] If property is taken and transported in intrastate commerce, it is not within the FBI's realm; but the theft of computers or computer-related equipment in interstate commerce may easily fall within the Bureau's jurisdiction.

The unauthorized interception of a radio, telephone, or telegraph message (except where authorized by the person transmitting it) is a federal violation of law and within the FBI's charge. However, if the interception involves coded data, it may not be a Bureau matter, since the intent was to give the FBI jurisdiction over oral or intelligible intercepted data. The rule, as it now stands, is that one cannot use for one's benefit data that one cannot intelligently discern.

The FBI investigates any and all matters arising out of the Veterans Administration, as well as any acts aimed at the overthrow or destruction of the United States government. Sabotage of computers connected with the Veterans Administration, or with the overthrow of the United States, would bring in the FBI to investigate. Use of computers by organized criminal syndicates in the furtherance of interstate transmission of wagering information would also bring in the FBI. The FBI also has jurisdiction over the Atomic Energy Act, and thus the disclosure of confidential data relating to atomic energy, or the attempt to do so, with the intent to injure the United States or secure an advantage to any foreign nation, or with reason to believe that either might result, is sufficient for FBI intervention.

The FBI can also investigate alleged antitrust violations. The Bureau is charged with investigating monopolies and combinations or agreements in restraint of interstate commerce. However, it has an extremely poor record in combating these problems. Historically, the FBI's past leadership has neglected this extremely difficult, but important, area. If computers were to be employed in furthering the antitrust schemes of large firms, the FBI would be of little assistance until it developed the sophisticated training and techniques needed in this area.

The FBI has concentrated most of its efforts in the area of bank robbery and embezzlement. It also investigates burglaries, larcenies, false entries in books or records, and the misapplication of funds of member banks of the Federal Reserve System, banks insured by the Federal Deposit Insurance Corporation (FDIC), banks organized or operated under the laws of the United States (for example, the banks in the District of Columbia), Federal Savings and Loan Associations, institutions insured by the Federal Savings and Loan Insurance Corporation (FSLIC), and the Federal Credit Union. The Bureau does not investigate crimes involving state banks; thus computer crimes involving state banks may not fall within the FBI's jurisdiction unless some violation of interstate commerce occurs.

The FBI has been slow to enter the area of white collar crime. Less than 30 percent of its manpower has been devoted to this area, despite the fact that these frauds have increased by as much as 300 percent in the last several years. To meet mounting criticism in this area, the Bureau has begun to train small cadres in the area of computer fraud. For example, a 44-hour course entitled Introduction to Electronic Data Processing for Law Enforcement has been added to the FBI academy's curriculum. The course is also available to local law enforcement agents. The objective of the course is to introduce the agent to the basic features of the computer.

Since January 1974 the FBI has also trained several hundred of its agents in the fundamentals of computer technology, in courses which vary from 2 to 4 weeks. Some of these agents also have an extensive background in accounting. Various professionals have observed that within the FBI there now appears to be a shift of priorities into this area; but to date, only 500 such agents have been trained. Whether such a small force can police the more than 90,000 computers in this country remains to be seen. In addition, it should be pointed out that training agents in computer techniques in and of itself is not enough. They must also be trained in the other variations that white collar crimes take. Only by understanding the fundamentals of white collar crime can an agent grasp the use of the computer in these areas.

The training has had some payoffs. For example, several years ago equipment disappeared from a military base; in fact, more than $100,000 in government equipment had been siphoned. A special agent with extensive computer training was assigned to assist other agents in the investigation. The thefts, it was later discovered, had been concealed through the creation of false requisition forms by the base computer. The property was then diverted to innocent civilian contractors. The felons then contacted the contractors and informed them that the shipments had been diverted by mistake. They then picked up the material and sold it to their sources. To insure that the periodic computer audit reports did not reveal their activities, the felons erased the identification records of the property from the computer system. Through this simple process, they stole more than $2 million in government property. When the scheme was finally uncovered, one of the key defendants received only a 3-year probationary sentence.

Another serious problem the FBI frequently encounters is the "phone freak." The latter, through the use of a remote terminal and a touch-phone, will attempt to enter a computer system, but theft is not his objective. The real motivation is the challenge of the computer. Phone freaks have been able to penetrate numerous systems and wreak havoc upon them. For example, in New Jersey, a computer firm donated several computer terminals to a local high school. It was later discovered that one of the students, with the aid of a terminal, had broken the system's security code and had instructed the computer to print out the message: "F___ you, the Phantom." This case was exceeded only by the case of a Midwestern bookmaker who used a local university's computer to calculate his handicaps.

The FBI's jurisdiction is far-reaching. However, it has had a history of antiquated practices; and although it is attempting to develop units capable of handling sophisticated technological crimes, it needs time. Whether it will have that requisite time depends on the ability of its leadership to prove flexible and dynamic. This remains to be seen.

The Military Investigators

The Department of Defense (DOD) employs more than 3000 computers. These are divided into two categories: (1) general purpose, and (2) special purpose.[9] The general purpose computers number more than 2000 and are generally employed in general management and administrative tasks.[10] The special purpose computers number more than 1400 and are usually employed in command, control, and intelligence functions.[11]

The importance of the computer within the military should not be underestimated. For example, DOD disburses, with the aid of computers, more than $25 billion yearly. Over $6.5 billion, or about 20 percent of this, is not subject to human hands;[12] it is all done by computers. In the area of logistics, the military disburses nearly $17.5 billion yearly. Of this, nearly 4 percent, or $0.7 billion, is handled by computers—again, free of human hands.[13] However, the military, like the civilian sector, suffers from the problem of computer fraud. The different branches of the military have already begun training their investigators in this area.

Of the three military branches, the U.S. Air Force Office of Special Investigations (OSI) is probably the best trained for the era of computer crime. OSI functions as a fact-finding agency. It investigates not only matters related to our intelligence community, but also frauds against the military. OSI operates both domestically and abroad. Outside the United States, its concern differs little from that of the British MI-5, the French Directorate of Military Security, or the West German Federal Agency for the Protection of the Constitution. OSI enjoys an excellent reputation and prides itself on professionalism. Domestically, it investigates crimes on U.S. Air Force bases involving personnel subject to the Uniform Code of Military Justice.

Perhaps one of the great limitations of OSI is its jurisdiction. Although well-trained and highly motivated, OSI has no jurisdiction over civilian criminals who prey on the military. OSI concerns itself with areas involving military procurement, nonappropriated fund activities, and other administrative irregularities. OSI investigators receive a mandatory 10-week course at the OSI school in Washington, D.C., as well as additional specialized courses.

In 1976 OSI revised its curriculum to include instructions on computer technology and fraud.[14] Past training programs contained 16 hours of instructions and 3 hours of practical problems.[15] A total of more than 60 investigators have gone through this program, some from other branches of the military. The objective of the training is to develop a cadre of specialized investigators capable of identifying computer crimes.

It should be reiterated that OSI investigators have no jurisdiction over civilians. In cases involving the latter, even when frauds are committed on military reservations, the FBI must be called in, and OSI investigators then assist the FBI in the investigation. All OSI criminal investigations are referred, with approval from the base commander, to the Justice Department for prosecution. OSI investigators have no subpoena power and, in many instances, work in isolation from the civilian agencies. Further, politically sensitive cases are always in danger of being quashed before they are referred to the Justice Department for prosecution. It may also occur that the Justice Department may not be interested in such cases. Conversely, military tribunals have no jurisdiction over civilians, and the latter can evade prosecution. They can only hear cases involving military personnel.

In 1974 OSI agents worked with the FBI in a case involving the fraudulent shipment of government property valued at over $800,000.[16] It was found that valuable military communication material had been diverted through the manipulation of a computer. More than 140 items had been diverted and sold to civilian sources. An additional 45 items had also been diverted, but eventually were recovered by the FBI.

OSI has identified more than a dozen other computer fraud cases.[17] These cases involved the manipulation or alteration of input data. Three of these investigations involved the entry of false requisitions in order to manipulate accounts; three other cases involved the manipulation of military leave time; and four additional cases involved the alteration of efficiency reports.[18] At least one case involved the entry of false data into the computer to allow an ineligible individual to reenlist.[19]

To test the security of its computers, the military has developed "Tiger Teams," or the "Penetration Approach."[20] A team consists of several computer scientists who conduct an ad hoc attack on the hardware and software security measures of a computer system.[21] Through these mock attacks the military has been able to test the weaknesses of its systems. The teams have been able to penetrate commercial computer systems with great ease. This should indicate that for a long time, industry has paid scant attention to security. We can no longer afford this luxury. OSI investigators are, on the average, better trained for the computer era than their civilian counterparts. However, OSI investigators have no jurisdiction over civilians. The civilian sector must develop its own expertise.

The Internal Revenue Service

The role of the IRS, in the overall federal enforcement program, cannot be underestimated. The IRS is feared by sophisticated and simple street criminals alike. The vast manpower of the IRS, its ability to issue administrative subpoenas, and its vast arsenal of important statutes enable it to be effective where the FBI and the other law enforcement units have failed. However, the computer also poses a problem for the IRS. The increasing use of the computer may mean that within a matter of years the IRS, which bases much of its investigative and enforcement capability on paper "trails," may have to revamp its apparatus to meet the challenge of the new technology.

The Investigative Apparatus

The IRS is part of the Treasury Department and is made up of various specialized divisions and branches. The key branch concerned with fraud is the intelligence division (ID). The ID is the criminal unit of the IRS; it investigates and refers all criminal violations of the IRS Code to the Justice Department. The ID is headed by a director, who has his offices in Washington, D.C., the location of the national office. The director is in charge of all ID activities and criminal referrals; he reports to the assistant commissioner for compliance and to the deputy commissioner of the IRS.

The IRS has regional offices in all large urban centers, such as New York, Dallas, San Francisco, and Chicago. The assistant regional commissioner within each region directs the ID personnel. The regions are divided into district offices—more than 50 in all. At the district level, ID personnel are directed by group managers. The ID investigator is known as a special agent (SA). The IRS has more than 2000 ID agents. They are assigned to the district offices and investigate all IRS-related frauds, conduct surveillance of organized crime figures, and also, with the Justice Department Organized Crime Strike Forces, participate in large-scale criminal investigations that involve the jurisdiction of many other federal agencies.

A distinction must be drawn between the SA and other IRS agents. Most IRS agents are simply involved in the collection of revenues. They also conduct field investigations to determine civil tax liabilities; if criminal violations are uncovered, they are referred to the ID. The SA is primarily a criminal investigator; his main concern is with criminal cases, though he may employ the assistance of non-SA IRS agents. Joint investigations between ID and the other IRS units are common. However, the presence of an ID investigator indicates that the IRS is conducting a criminal investigation. Unfortunately, ID agents, like their counterparts in the other federal agencies, have no training in the investigation of computer crime.

Key IRS Statutes

The burden of proving that a taxpayer has been guilty of a crime is with the IRS;[22] proof must be furnished "beyond a reasonable doubt."[23] Acquittal under the criminal statutes is not a guarantee of immunity from the IRS civil statutes. The IRS Code provides for numerous civil penalties. Conviction under the criminal statutes, however, may result in the application of the *collateral estoppel doctrine*, which would prevent the defendant from denying his fraud in a civil prosecution. Consequently, a convicted felon is also open to civil penalties. To date, however, prosecutors involved in the litigation of computer frauds have made infrequent use of the criminal and civil penalties under the IRS Code. As with some of the other federal laws, the criminal provisions of the IRS Code can constitute a powerful arsenal in the prosecution of computer crime. Although the computer has replaced the pen, the IRS statutes could find easy application.

Section 286 provides that whoever enters into an "agreement, conspiracy or combination" to defraud the federal government, can be fined up to $10,000 and/or imprisoned up to 10 years. All conspiracies or combinations that employ a computer to defraud the federal government can be prosecuted under this statute. The statute also applies to those individuals who only "aid" rather than directly participate in the conspiracy. Thus cases involving a conspiracy to file false and fraudulent claims with any branch of the federal government can be prosecuted under this statute. The fact that a computer was employed will make little difference. Also, a computer operator who only aids rather than directly partakes in the conspiracy can also be prosecuted under the statute.

Section 287 makes it a federal felony "to present" any federal officer with a false or fraudulent claim. The military branches are also covered under this statute. Thus employing a computer to file false or fraudulent claims (for example, for nonexistent services) will bring prosecution under this statute. Whereas Section 286 is aimed at conspiracies, Section 287 is aimed at "completed acts." The latter provides for fines of up to $10,000 and/or imprisonment for up to 5 years. These two sections could easily be employed to cover computer crimes involving the filing of false and fraudulent claims with the federal government.

Section 1084 provides for fines of up to $10,000 and/or imprisonment for up to 2 years for anyone engaged in the business of wagering or betting. However, the felon must make use of wire communications to receive information, money, or credit as a result of bets or wagers. The transmission must be in interstate or foreign commerce for the statute to apply. Use of a computer, to further such an operation, could fall under this statute. A Midwestern bookmaker was found to employ a computer in his wagering operations.

Section 1952 provides for up to $10,000 in fines and/or up to 5 years imprisonment for anyone who makes use of foreign or interstate commerce to:

(a) distribute the proceeds of an unlawful activity; or
(b) commit any crime of violence to further any unlawful activity; or
(c) otherwise promote, manage, establish, carry on or facilitate the promotion, management, establishment or carrying on, of any unlawful activity, and thereafter performs or attempts to perform any of the acts specified in subparagraphs (a) and (b).

This statute, although never employed in a computer crime case, might have applicability and could give the IRS jurisdiction where organized crime figures employ computers to perpetrate frauds.

Section 1621 is the "perjury statute." If a witness is questioned under oath by an IRS agent who has been authorized to administer such oath and should the witness "willfully provide" the agent with false information, orally or written, he can be found guilty of perjury. An individual convicted under this section can be fined up to $2,000 and/or sentenced for up to 5 years imprisonment. A suspect in a computer crime who perjures himself could be prosecuted under this statute. All that is required is for the prosecutors to show that: (1) the witness was under oath when questioned by the IRS investigators, (2) the investigators had been authorized to administer oaths, and (3) that the witness "willfully provided" false information, either in oral or written form. For example, if a computer programmer is questioned about the theft of some stolen programs and he tells the investigators that he has no knowledge, when in fact he was instrumental in their theft, and he makes the statements under oath and to agents who have been authorized to administer oaths, the perjury statute can be brought into play. There is, however, a requirement that the perjury be material. Federal prosecutors are hesitant to bring perjury charges unless they have at least two witnesses to the alleged act.

One of the more common statutes, under which tax evasion prosecutions are brought, is Section 7201, which specifies that anyone who "willfully attempts to evade or defeat" any tax or its payment, in any manner, shall be guilty of a felony. The statute provides for fines of up to $10,000 and/or up to 5 years imprisonment. Three elements are needed for prosecution under this statute: (1) an additional tax due, (2) an act or attempt on the part of the suspect to evade it, and (3) it must have been done willfully.

For example, an employee in the computer center of a city welfare department entered fraudulent data into the payroll system and stole more than $2.5 million.[24] He and several of his associates created a fictitious workforce and gave them fake Social Security numbers. These were processed weekly through the payroll routine. The computer automatically printed a check for each fake employee. The checks were then intercepted by the felons, endorsed and cashed. The case came to light when a city policeman discovered more than 100 of these checks in an overdue rental car he found illegally parked.

Had these felons failed to disclose the extra income in their filings with the IRS, they could have been prosecuted under this statute. Further, if federal funds were involved, Section 286 might also have been employed. If under questioning by federal officers the felons perjured themselves, Section 1621 might also be employed. A computer felon, like a narcotics dealer, is not apt to disclose his earnings from his criminal activity.

For the statute to come into play, the IRS must show the court that there was a tax loss by the government. The prosecutors must prove that additional income was due by establishing that there was unreported income, or that false deductions were claimed by the defendant. If an incorrect return is filed, willfully or not, this in itself is insufficient to require application of the statute. A tax must also be due,[25] but the IRS need not prove the exact amount of unreported income.[26] Thus, in the above example, it is sufficient to show that additional income (in this case more than $2.5 million) had not been reported by the defendants. It makes no difference that the illegal income in this case was the fruit of a computer crime.

Another example where the tax evasion statute might apply is the case of two felons who diverted more than $60,000 in bill payments sent by a number of insurance companies to a university medical center.[27] The two defendants deposited these funds in dummy accounts they had established. To cover their fraud, they deleted, for almost one year, accounts from the medical center's computer records by making them uncollectible or by purging them from the files. The crime was uncovered, as is the case with the overwhelming majority of such crimes, by accident. The felons mistakenly left one account in the system. A second bill was sent to the company. An investigation was initiated, and the crime was exposed. Had the felons divulged this additional income in their filings with the IRS, the statute would have been of no value. Few criminals, though, are so honest as to tell the IRS how much they steal.

However, it is not enough to show only that there was additional income, the IRS must also prove that the defendant made an affirmative act to evade his tax obligation. The affirmative action must constitute an attempt. There must be a willful commission of an act—a simple omission is not enough.[28] Failure to file a return is also not enough. It may be prosecuted as a misdemeanor under Section 7203 (discussed later) but not as a felony under Section 7201.

There are a number of acts that have been held sufficient to meet the test under this statute. For example, a firm that keeps fraudulent records through the use of a computer may be prosecuted under the statute. To date, though, no computer felon has been prosecuted under it. Destroying computer records would also fall under the statute, where the objective was to evade a tax. Concealing one's assets, covering up sources of income, or any conduct that attempts to mislead or conceal funds for tax evasion purposes would fall under the statute. The fact that a computer is employed makes no difference; the computer being only a giant "calculator." Admittedly, although the IRS Code was designed for traditional record-keeping procedures, it should prove sufficiently flexible to bring the computerized record-keeping process within its realm.

A defendant who personally files a false or misleading tax return meets the affirmative act test. The same could apply for a corporation. The fact that the IRS brings few criminal prosecutions should not be blamed on its statutes, but rather on the internal bureaucratic process and politics of the IRS. One who simply files no return, however, cannot be charged with being in violation of Section 7201. There is no misrepresentation made. But one who files a false return has attempted to defraud and mislead the IRS and can be charged with violating the statute, since by willfully filing a false tax return he meets the test set by the statute.

The willfulness requirement does, at times, pose a problem in criminal prosecutions under the statute. A specific intent must be shown, which is evidence of an evil intent to evade one's tax obligations.[29] The attempt must be voluntary and intentional, and it must be shown that the accused knew he had a legal duty to pay his taxes. In addition, from a practical prosecutorial standpoint, a substantial amount of money must be involved.

However, the fact that a computer is employed to defraud the public at large, or the government, does not excuse a felon from reporting that income. Using a computer to maintain a double set of books, to make false entries or alterations, or even to destroy data in computer banks does not affect application of the statute. Regardless of the criminal method of computer utilization, the statute applies to all such violations.

A less important, but nevertheless key, statute in the IRS arsenal is Section 7203. This section makes it a misdemeanor, punishable by fines of up to $10,000 and/or up to one year imprisonment, for willful failure to file a tax return, to keep such records, or to supply such information as required by the IRS Code. In order to establish a prima facie case, the prosecutors need only show the following: (1) the defendant was required by law to file a return; (2) he filed no return; and (3) his action was willful. Thus a computer felon who willingly fails to file a return, when so required by law, may be prosecuted under the statute. The defendant can also be charged with other violations of the tax code and can be ordered by the court to pay the costs of prosecution as well.

Section 7206 makes it a felony, punishable by fines of up to $5,000 and/or up to 3 years imprisonment, for an individual to file a return that is false. However, the falsity must be of a material matter. Under this statute, the IRS need only prove: (1) that there was a material falsity on the defendant's return, and (2) that it was willful. The crux of this offense, unlike Section 7201, is the willful furnishing of false information. The IRS need not show a tax deficiency, as in Section 7201.

Section 7206 also makes no requirement that there be an affirmative act. It will not be a defense if the defendant can show that he has made an adjustment for the deficiency. Paragraph (s) of this statute applies the same penalties to anyone who assists, advises, or counsels the defendant in the preparation of his false return. It is common, as a matter of strategy, for the IRS to charge an individual under both Sections 7201 and 7206.[30]

Section 7207 makes it a misdemeanor, punishable by fines of up to $1,000 and/or up to one year imprisonment, to file a false return or other false document with the IRS. The requirement of proof is very similar to that for Section 7206. Prosecutors, however, usually charge a defendant with a violation of Section 7206, since it carries a longer sentence.

The Computer Felon and the IRS

Although the IRS has the requisite manpower and legal arsenal, like the other units that constitute the federal investigatory apparatus, it too suffers from red tape and is in need of streamlining. Recently, a number of computer crimes have surfaced that not only involve the IRS itself but that, in fact, had it as their targets. What makes matters even worse is that the felons involved in these cases were simple street criminals who learned how to manipulate the IRS computer system.

The Gholston case illustrates the need by the IRS to train in this area. The case surfaced as a result of the investigative efforts of Phil Manuel and Fred Asselin, two Senate staffers assigned to the U.S. Senate Committee on Government Operations. The case involved two defendants, Marie Gholston and her daughter, Venita Huffman. In December 1976 both parties pleaded guilty to charges of fraudulently negotiating tax refund checks before a federal judge in Detroit, Michigan.

The two defendants were involved in a conspiracy that defrauded the federal government of more than $200,000.[31] The fraud involved the IRS computer. Marie Gholston, a receptionist by training with no background in computers, led a small group that filed hundreds of false tax returns with the IRS. The computer ordered that refund checks be mailed them. The scheme began in 1972 and continued undetected for several years. The conspirators first applied to the Social Security Administration (SSA) for Social Security cards, which were promptly issued by the SSA computer. The conspirators would then fill out blank W-2 tax forms, using false names, false Social Security numbers (provided by the SSA computer), and false employer identification codes. The W-2 forms were then filed with the IRS. The conspirators also filed a Form 1040-A for every fictitious W-2, claiming a refund ranging from $300 to $500.[32] Upon receipt, the IRS computer would process the forms and order that a check be issued. The checks were then deposited by the felons in the bank accounts of nonexistent companies.

The Secret Service was the first to become aware of this scheme. Apparently, the conspirators had unwisely and unknowingly invited scrutiny by employing the IRS computer for more than 300 refund checks. The IRS soon after uncovered a similar conspiracy operating out of East Detroit, which used the names and Social Security numbers of a group of welfare recipients to file for refund checks.[33] Before the second scheme was uncovered, however, more than a dozen refund checks, worth over $30,000, had been mailed by the IRS computer. Both rings had managed to defraud the IRS by simply mailing it computer refund returns.

Not to be outdone by the Gholston ring, Frank E. Ready, a convict at the federal penitentiary in Leavenworth, Kansas, defrauded the IRS of about $20,000 by filing false returns while incarcerated. Ready's former wife was also involved in this scheme. At his trial Ready told the court that many other inmates were also involved, and that numerous checks had been received.[34] One of the inmates implicated by Ready had been enrolled in a pilot Federal Bureau of Prisons program that trained inmates in the uses of computer technology.[35]

An even more bizarre case concerning the manipulation of IRS' computers involved David G. Robinson, a former IRS official. Robinson is quoted as saying,

I cheated Uncle Sam's tax computers out of more than half-a-million dollars in hard cash—and I could do it again any time I want. . . . It was easy. I knew exactly how the IRS computers work. I found major loopholes in the system. . . .[36]

Robinson had filed several separate income tax returns claiming refunds totaling more than $500,000; each time, he had used another name and a newly issued Social Security number. The mailing address he gave was the business address of a telephone answering service.

The Robinson case is one of more than a dozen cases the IRS has uncovered, involving over 900 returns with false claims in excess of $2 million.[37] The cases that have been uncovered all have one thing in common: they were detected only after the IRS computer sent out the checks. Through the simple process of filing false refund returns, unsophisticated felons (save for Robinson who had been with the IRS and knew its operations) have bilked the IRS's own computer system for large sums of money. These cases highlight the seriousness of computer crime—even the "cops" can be defrauded.

To respond to this technological challenge, the IRS has proposed a new tool—project TAS (Tax Administration System).[38] Under TAS, 10 IRS regional computer centers would be fed all the tax returns for the past three to five years of all the taxpayers in their respective regions. All the returns of that region would thus be available, instantaneously, to IRS agents at offices throughout the region on screens resembling a television set. Returns from other regions would be available through an IRS national computer center within a week or two.

The system would consist of more than 5000 terminals; more than 40,000 IRS personnel would run it; and the system would also link all data relating to a specific individual, such as forms filed by his employer, bank, and other business sources. An investigator would have immense data about a suspect at his disposal within a brief span of time. Project TAS, despite IRS pronouncements that it would be an excellent investigative tool, has met wide opposition.

More than anything else, TAS symbolizes the awe and suspicion with which government is held by the public. There is legitimate concern that TAS may open the individual citizen to Orwellian invasions of privacy. The possibility for abuse will be great. The project itself is also very expensive—$1 billion. There is also fear that TAS will be linked to the computer systems of other agencies, such as the Central Intelligence Agency, thus enabling the IRS to keep watch on Americans overseas. TAS may be a partial answer to the rise in technological crimes. However, given the vivid memories of governmental abuse in this post-Watergate era, TAS may not have an opportunity to be tested for many years to come.

However, the IRS has a formidable arsenal of statutes, as well as well-trained agents, to deal with computer frauds. Like many other federal police agencies, however, it suffers from bureaucratic red tape and poor leadership. The computer poses a new challenge, perhaps more far-reaching than the invention of the gun. Only through imaginative leadership, and a new strategy can the IRS adapt to the new challenge.

The Department of Health, Education and Welfare

This Department is the largest bureaucracy in the federal apparatus. It is a maze of divisions, units, and branches, employing a network of more than 160 computers. Its computer-related budget exceeds $300 million annually.[39] Each fiscal year its computers generate checks in the sum of more than $80 billion.[40] Although the Department of Health, Education and Welfare (HEW) makes extensive use of computers, it has few investigators trained to investigate, and prepare for prosecution, computer crime cases.

Aware of the growing problem of computer fraud, and under pressure from the U.S. Congress to take some action, HEW has assigned the task of solving this problem to the Deputy Assistant Secretary for Management, Planning and

Technology. HEW has a newly created unit charged with investigating frauds. This newly formed unit is known as the Office of Investigations (OI). Its director reports directly to the Under Secretary of HEW and is charged with the investigation of malfeasance, fraud, and misuse of funds, equipment, or facilities, as well as violations of terms or conditions of funding and conflict of interest by employees, grantees, contractors, and others working for HEW. In September 1976 the Director sent 20 to 25 key agents of OI to the FBI academy for a one-week course in computer training.

OI, like the other federal investigatory bodies, has no direct criminal jurisdiction. All frauds must be investigated, and, with the approval of the Secretary of HEW, must be referred to the Justice Department for criminal prosecution. HEW attorneys have no prosecutorial jurisdiction in criminal cases. In essence, HEW's investigatory unit suffers from the same malaise endured by other units: investigations must be referred to Justice Department for action. The latter need not take action at all if it concludes that the case has no merit. It should be noted that many of the HEW investigations are open to the same political manipulations and pressures found in other federal investigatory units, and may be killed within the HEW.

Further, HEW investigators are assigned to U.S. attorney offices to brief the federal prosecutors on the facts of cases. By the time an indictment is finally handed down, many of the participants to the crime may be difficult to locate, and documents may have been destroyed. Unfortunately, federal prosecutors are prone to the prima donna syndrome: many U.S. attorneys will not take a case if they consider it as being "non-newsworthy." Prosecutors also look for easy cases that will bring them unqualified victories and many headlines. HEW investigators often complain that after lengthy investigations many of their cases die within HEW simply because they cannot find U.S. attorneys who will prosecute them. Officials at HEW have disclosed that fewer than 10 percent of their cases are ever considered by the Justice Department for prosecution, and fewer than 5 percent go to trial. Deterrence is obviously lacking.

OI also suffers from its own internal difficulties. For example, all investigations must first be approved by either the Secretary or Under Secretary of HEW. If frauds are not brought to the attention of these two officials, OI cannot investigate them. Since HEW personnel are sometimes themselves directly involved in these frauds, there is little incentive by other divisions within HEW to bring these to the attention of either the Secretary or Under Secretary for referral to OI.

The resources HEW devotes to OI are characterized by one official as absurd. For example, HEW employs more than 120,000 full-time individuals.[41] However, OI is staffed by only 10 full-time individuals.[42] Consequently, many investigations average 5 years, and HEW has a 10-year case backlog. Although HEW has several other quasi-investigative units, these have been badly staffed and employed, and their investigators are rarely allowed to assist OI agents.

Understandably, none of these other units has even the minimal training in the area of computer crime.

A Congressional study has concluded that HEW poses a prime target for computer criminals. The HEW's centralized data system and payroll system are vulnerable to such attack.[43] The possibility of introducing false data into these computers is real, and could go undetected for long periods of time.[44] The study made several recommendations:

(a) pay and personnel records should be periodically audited to detect discrepancies between the authorized and actual data records;
(b) HEW should develop better audit trails and controls in present and planned systems;
(c) controls should be introduced over the master file data to ensure their integrity;
(d) master file data should be periodically reviewed to spot any discrepancies;
(e) programs should be reviewed periodically to ensure that changes have not been introduced;
(f) programming should be secured with lockout devices; and
(g) terminals should be located only in secure rooms.[45]

To date, few if any of the recommendations have been adopted. One knowledgeable source has described HEW progress in this area as a colossal mess.[46]

The majority of HEW's subdivisions have been found to be vulnerable to computer fraud attack.[47] For example, the Departmental Federal Assistance Financing System (DFAFS) is the branch through which letters of credit and U.S. Treasury checks are issued to local governments and grant recipients for the financing of grants awarded by HEW. DFAFS is a new system and has already developed a history of startup problems.[48] The original design did not provide the output data needed to establish controls over disbursements made by the system.[49] It is entirely possible that felons could use the DFAFS computers for their criminal ends with no difficulty.

There are additional areas that have been identified as potential problems for HEW. They are too numerous for this book to cover in any great length. However, among them must be counted the Office of Guaranteed Student Loans (OGSL). It processes claims payments and is a matter of serious concern to HEW investigators. Data are entered into its computers through remote terminals located in HEW regional offices. Supposedly, only authorized HEW personnel are to have access to these terminals, but security measures are so poor at HEW that "anyone" within OGSL actually has access.[50]

The finance section at the Office of Education (OE) is another possible target for computer felons. Although its computers do not create checks, they engage in transactions where payments are finally made. It handles student loan programs, basic education grants, and Indian program grants. Fictitious data could be generated with ease. Since the OE branch office that authorized the grants is usually the one that administers the payments, collusion within this branch office could lead easily to manipulation of the computers.

The Social Security Administration (SSA), in particular, has proven to be a problem for HEW. A survey of its data security led investigators to conclude that there is a definite need for security improvement.[51] About one-third of its backup data and input forms are not stored in secured places. The following areas were listed in a recent U.S. Senate study as being open to computer attack:

1. The physical security of the telecommunication system was found to be extremely poor.
2. Control over access to files by employees is poor.
3. Internal operations and audits have been few and infrequent.
4. There is no policy of periodic internal checks and audits.[52]

To date, HEW is aware of more than a dozen cases involving computer fraud. In one instance, an SSA employee found that a Social Security beneficiary had been overpaid. The SSA employee had the beneficiary write him a personal check for the overpayment. The employee then deposited it in his own account and entered a waiver of this overpayment into the SSA computer. In another case, an employee for a company under contract with HEW gave an employee of the latter false information regarding medicaid. The false data were fed into the HEW computer, and medicaid checks were then issued.

However, HEW's troubles, although numerous, have only recently begun to surface. In 1976 social welfare programs cost the American public more than $300 billion.[53] Such large sums of money present a tempting target for computer criminals. For example, a government study has revealed that some doctors have been overcharging Medicaid and Medicare patients by as much as 400 percent on tests done for them by commercial laboratories. In New York City alone, doctors are thought to be overcharging HEW by as much as $300 million annually.[54] In California, Mexican-American gangsters have gained control of a number of HEW social programs and have also made inroads into the student loan program.[55]

The FBI, IRS, HEW, and the other nonagencies like the regulatory agencies, suffer from excessive bureaucratic red tape. Investigations take many years; once completed, they must be referred to the Justice Department for prosecution. The latter may take as long as one year before it decides whether to prosecute or not. A U.S. attorney is then assigned to the case if a decision to prosecute has been made. Several years may pass before the case is finally brought before a court for trial. Some cases take as long as 5 years from the time the investigation is begun to the day they reach court for trial. Many cases, however, never see the inside of a court room. They are quashed, either within the investigatory body or within the Justice Department, by formidable political groups. More than 90 percent of all cases culminate in a consent decree. Thus both the nonagencies and the regulatory agencies have shown themselves to be too slow to act with the requisite speed. Computer crime, with its demands for speedy action and sophisticated investigatory tools, may yet spell the end of our present investigatory apparatus.

References

1. National District Attorney's Association, "Land Fraud," *Economic Crime Digest*, Volume III, No. 1 (November-December, 1975), p. 19.

2. Ibid., "Brooklyn D.A. Secures Guilty Plea from Good Humor Corporation," *Economic Crime Digest*, Volume III, No. 3 (March-April 1976), p. 106.

3. 18 U.S.C., sec. 481.

4. Ibid., sec. 504.

5. *United States* v. *Jones*, 414 F.Supp. 964 (1976).

6. U.S. Justice Department, *Annual Report of the Attorney General of the United States for 1975* (Washington, D.C.: U.S. Justice Department, 1976), p. 187.

7. Ibid.

8. U.S. Senate Committee on Government Operations, *Staff Study of Computer Security in Federal Programs* (Washington, D.C.: U.S. Government Printing Office, 1977), p. 235.

9. Ibid., p. 144.

10. Ibid.

11. Ibid.

12. Ibid., p. 146.

13. *United States* v. *Jones*, p. 964.

14. U.S. Senate Committee on Government Operations, *Staff Study of Computer Security in Federal Programs*, p. 147.

15. Ibid.

16. Ibid., p. 150.

17. Ibid., p. 144.

18. Ibid., p. 150.

19. Ibid.

20. Ibid., p. 158.

21. Ibid.

22. *Helvering* v. *Mitchell*, 303 U.S. 391 (1938).

23. Ibid.

24. U.S. Senate Committee on Government Operations, *Problems Associated with Computer Technology in Federal Programs and Private Industry* (Washington, D.C.: U.S. Government Printing Office, 1976), p. 358.

25. *Kooritz* v. *United States*, 277 F.2d 53 (5th Cir. 1960).

26. *Guzik* v. *United States*, 191 F.2d 993 (9th Cir. 1951), cert. denied, 342 U.S. 909 (1952).

27. U.S. Senate Committee on Government Operations, *Problems Associated with Computer Technology in Federal Programs and Private Industry*, p. 359.

28. *Spies* v. *United States*, 317 U.S. 492 (1943).

29. Ibid., p. 499; also see, *United States* v. *Cruessant*, 178 F.2d 96 (3rd Cir. 1949); and *Dillon* v. *United States*, 218 F.2d 97 (8th Cir. 1955).

30. *United States* v. *Lodwick*, 410 F.2d 1202 (8th Cir. 1969), cert. denied, 396 U.S. 841 (1969).

31. U.S. Senate Committee on Government Operations, *Staff Study of Computer Security in Federal Programs*, p. 129.

32. Ibid., p. 130.

33. Ibid., p. 131.

34. Ibid., p. 108.

35. Ibid., p. 109.

36. Ibid., p. 128.

37. Ibid., p. 127.

38. Evans Witt, "Lack of Privacy Feared with IRS Computer Plan," *Washington Post*, March 4, 1977, p. D-11.

39. U.S. Senate Committee on Government Operations, *Staff Study of Computer Security in Federal Programs*, p. 246.

40. Ibid.

41. Ibid., p. 252.

42. Ibid.

43. Ibid., p. 254.

44. Ibid., p. 255.

45. Ibid., p. 255.

46. Based on interviews I had with a number of prosecutors as regards HEW.

47. U.S. Senate Committee on Government Operations, *Staff Study of Computer Security in Federal Programs*, pp. 255-260.

48. Ibid., p. 256.

49. Ibid.

50. Based on interviews with HEW investigators.

51. U.S. Senate Committee on Government Operations, *Staff Study of Computer Security in Federal Programs*, p. 263.

52. Ibid.

53. "Welfare Tab Sets Record for 1976 at $331 B," *Washington Star*, December 15, 1976, p. A-26.

54. "Medicaid Mills Grind Out High-Price Care," *Washington Star*, August 30, 1976, p. A-1.

55. "California Probing Chicano Mafia," *Washington Post*, May 6, 1977, p. A-1.

9 Hearsay and Computer Litigation

The computer age has created some very serious problems for the attorney-litigant, whether he represents the interests of the government or the private sector. It affects both the civil and criminal areas of law and may eventually require changes in current evidentiary procedures as computer litigation becomes more complex. At present, the use, and abuse, of computerized data is rather primitive compared with what awaits us with future advancements in computer technology. However, those advancements are producing an immediate effect in the courts.

The computer substantially replaced the human hand in the areas of collection, collation, and calculation of data. Although the efficiency of record keeping has increased significantly, the contacts between the individual and the record-keeping process have proportionately diminished. Further, the record-keeping process has become more mechanized, and an ever-diminishing number of individuals possess an accurate understanding of the total picture. The computer complex is run by many who neither understand the entire process nor their role within that process. This situation results in a mechanized and tedious task. The programmer finds himself preparing material for a process he barely comprehends. The computer center itself may receive data from another computer system, many miles away, which in turn received data from another system, also a great distance away. Storage and reproduction are, in many instances, totally automated. In this arena, wire, radio and telecommunications come to play a strategic role.

The form in which data are found also differs from the traditional record-keeping process. The ledger sheet, popular for many centuries, has given way to the punch card, the magnetic tape, and other increasingly sophisticated modes of automation. The objective of the process is, and has been from the beginning, the eradication of waste, paperwork, and human involvement. It is not farfetched to anticipate a day when human involvement may become totally insignificant, and computers may in fact run the entire operation from the input through the output. Paper may become extinct in the record-keeping process of our business world.

Computerized data are not intelligible unless first translated into some sort of printout. The stored data itself are not generally cumulative. Entries, unlike the ledger system, are not added to the prior ones to create a permanent record. Rather, in a computerized system, data are usually updated by combining the old with the new. The old data are thus rendered unascertainable.

97

In such a system there is the real danger that serious errors may in fact be computerized.[1] For example, a federal government computer recently mailed more than 100,000 Social Security payments to the wrong individuals. The payments should have gone instead to the banks of the legal recipients.[2] U.S. Treasury Department officials later explained that the error occurred when the agency attempted to consolidate its records for all disabled recipients over 65 years of age.

The computer system also lends itself to penetration and manipulation. One United States Senator has already remarked that federal payments to Social Security recipients may have been tampered with.[3] Government officials have also confirmed that the Supplemental Security Income Program, begun in 1974, may have made more than $400 million in overpayments. Whether these were due to fraud or to error still remains a mystery. However, federal investigators have found more than $14,000 worth of checks on the desk of an absent employee of the Social Security Administration.[4] A Los Angeles grand jury in 1976 indicted a ring of six persons for allegedly manipulating the records of one of the nation's largest consumer-credit data banks.[5] The bank stores data on the borrowing habits of more than 50 million Americans.

Consequently, there is serious concern in the legal community, and rightly so, that the output data may not always be accurate and reliable. Courts, traditionally conservative, have shown a hesitancy to easily admit computer-related data in evidence. Thus, either in a criminal prosecution or civil litigation, the attorneys for both sides face serious evidentiary problems when attempting to introduce such data. However, although a growing minority of courts have begun to reassess computer-generated evidence, historical factors and a traditional approach to law still hamper serious litigation involving such data. As computerized data increasingly inundate our modern society, the courts will have to come to grips with this issue. The dilemma is neither illusory nor insignificant, and it demands immediate attention.

The Hearsay Rule Problem

An out-of-court statement, whether oral or written, when offered for its truth, is hearsay. Also certain conduct that amounts to an assertion of a fact may be hearsay even though no words have been spoken or written. The form the writing takes is immaterial. It may be a book, a magazine, a newspaper, a letter, or even a legal document. Thus, out-of-court statements, when offered for their truth, will be held inadmissible. The rule is binding in every type of judicial proceeding, whether it be on the federal or local level. Exceptions are sometimes made in an informal administrative proceeding. However, in all courts of law, the rule reigns supreme. The reason for the rule (its historical background will be dealt with shortly) is simple: the opposing party was not present when the statement was made and has not been able to test its accuracy and authenticity.

However, the hearsay rule is not inflexible. The courts, aware of the needs of a developing society, have allowed a number of exceptions to come into being. Some of these exceptions, such as the old "shop-book rule," have been codified both at the local and federal level. A litigant must thus attempt to bring computer-generated evidence into a trial under one of these hearsay exceptions. Several of these exceptions will be explored later.

Further, a litigant should keep in mind that the rule only applies when one of the parties to the case raises it—there must be a hearsay objection, the rule does not come into play automatically. In our adversary system, the court acts as a neutral arbitrator of events that transpire within its forum, but the court will not raise the hearsay objection. One of the litigants must object, preferably at the earliest possible moment. The objection should be made before a question is answered or a document introduced in evidence, when it is apparent that the answer or document is hearsay. It should be followed by a motion to strike the answer. If the hearsay answer is sufficiently prejudicial, the litigant should follow this with a motion for mistrial.

Hearsay objections should be made promptly, or as soon as it becomes apparent to the cross-examiner that the witness's testimony on direct examination was based on hearsay evidence. The opponent can move that the court strike all such testimony. It should be noted, however, that inadmissible hearsay evidence, unless objected to, may be admitted and considered by the court.[6] Such evidence, once admitted, will also be considered in posttrial motions and upon appeal. However, in the few reported cases involving computer-generated evidence, the parties involved, in most cases, have raised this objection in a timely fashion.

Why the Need for Hearsay Rules

During the reign of Edward I of England, special quasi-judicial bodies called Commissions evolved to investigate and report on issues in dispute. King Edward I, also known as the Law Giver, had learned well from the rebellions against his father, Henry III, that when one treads on the traditions of local communities, one does so at his peril. His father faced numerous serious rebellions. Under Edward I the common law developed, and the legal system began to assume an independence that it would maintain throughout most of England's history.

During this period, the practice evolved for small groups of citizens, or Commissions, to investigate the facts for themselves and then report to the court. Eventually, these Commissions began to assume the function of the present-day jury system. The practice of calling witnesses to court and having them testify in public began to take form under the House of Tudor.[7] However, a witness could speak only of what he himself saw and heard.[8]

King Henry VII, a member of the House of Tudor, in an attempt to quash his opponents, introduced the feared Star Chamber Court. Serious abuses took place, and witnesses were allowed to present hearsay evidence against defendants. The practice continued, although much abated, under the Stuarts in the seventeenth century. The latter, however, eventually faced a serious revolt as a result of their abuses, and King Charles I (Stuart) finally was executed by the forces of Parliament. King Charles II learned from the errors of his predecessor and displayed, at least publicly, a commitment to law and constitutional rights.

Critics charged that hearsay evidence was unreliable and that the defendant did not have an opportunity to test it through cross-examination; in addition, the witness who made the original statement was not under oath. By the end of the seventeenth century, the rule against hearsay evidence began to formalize. It must be viewed, in great part, as a reaction by the growing business class against the oppression of a tyrannical state, for both the Tudors and the Stuarts were in fact dictators.

The objections against hearsay took several forms, and many of these still survive, if not in substance, at least in form. The earliest critics charged that the declarant—the individual who made the original statement—was not under oath.[9] The oath, at least in an era of religion, played a key role in the minds of witnesses. In a church-dominated society, the "fires of hell" were very real. Many sincerely believed that those under oath would in fact give serious thought before perjuring themselves before the "higher" authority.

Further, there was concern that the witness reporting the hearsay evidence in court might do so inaccurately, either through error or through design. It should be noted that computer-generated evidence itself suffers, and is under attack by critics, because of this very same defect—there is serious, and real, fear that it may be either the outgrowth of error or manipulation, or both. In addition, while ledger sheets can be introduced into court and tested, both visually and experimentally, for alterations and omissions, this may not always be the case with computer data. The latter can be altered, manipulated, or destroyed; and if the culprit is sophisticated, he can easily erase his trail.

Another area of concern for both the early and present critics was the absence of cross-examination. Under the common law, it evolved that only through putting a witness through rigorous examination could one test the validity of his statements. The common-law lawyers attached little value to a witness who merely repeated what he had overheard. "Cross-examination," it has been said, "is the most efficacious test which the law has devised for the discovery of truth."[10] Critics, however, counter by saying that cross-examination rarely ensures that witnesses will tell the truth. Sophisticated witnesses can prove difficult and, at times, almost impossible to break down. Witnesses may confess in television fantasies, but rarely in the real court environment. Nevertheless, cross-examination may bring out inconsistencies in the testimony of a witness; it may put his memory to test; and it may also shed further light on the real facts.

Hearsay and the Confrontation Clause

The federal Constitution requires that in criminal cases, the defendant shall enjoy the right of confrontation. Under the Sixth Amendment of the Constitution, an accused is entitled to have the witnesses against him testify under oath, in the presence of himself and a judge, and subject to cross-examination. Nearly all the states have similar provisions in their own constitutions.[11] Typically, there are exceptions to this rule. For example, considerations of public policy and necessity require the recognition of such exceptions as dying declarations and the testimony of former witnesses who are no longer available.

In the 1930s, beginning with the case of *Snyder* v. *Massachusetts,* the United States Supreme Court began to speak of the confrontation doctrine as an aspect of procedural due process.[12] The Court began extending it to both state and federal noncriminal cases. For example, in the case of *In re Oliver* the Court went on to rule that cross-examination was essential to due process in a state contempt proceeding.[13] In 1965 the Court finally made the confrontation clause also directly applicable to the states. In *Pointer* v. *Texas* the Court ruled that a prosecutor's use of former testimony given at a preliminary hearing where petitioner was not represented by an attorney was a violation of the confrontation clause of the Constitution.[14] In a companion case, *Douglas* v. *Alabama*, a confession implicating the petitioner was put before the jury by reading it to the witness and asking if he had made that statement.[15] The witness refused to answer on grounds of self-incrimination. The outcome, the court noted, was to deny a citizen his right to confrontation and cross-examination. The confrontation clause ensures that an accused will have the opportunity to: (1) cross-examine his accuser, (2) test the accuser's testimony, and (3) enable the trier to better assess the credibility of the witness.

The confrontation clause may pose problems for computer-generated evidence. To date, no case has dealt with the issue of whether the admission of computer-generated evidence would violate the confrontation doctrine and due process clause of the United States Constitution. However, the doctrine has proven flexible. There are exceptions, and the courts now will allow former testimony if: (1) the witness is unavailable for trial, and (2) the accused has had the opportunity to cross-examine his accuser.

The unavailability of a witness may be explained on several grounds. The individual may be dead or physically unable to attend the trial or testify. If the disability is only temporary, then the adversary can ask for a continuation of the case until the witness recovers. The court, obviously, can use its discretion in this matter. However, the majority of the courts—especially in criminal, as opposed to civil, litigation—require that the disability be of a permanent nature.

Absence from a jurisdiction may also meet the unavailability test. If the absence is only temporary, and the witness is an important one, then the court could be asked to continue the matter pending the witness' return. The burden is on the opponent and not the proponent. If the proponent can show that he or she made a vigorous attempt to locate the witness, but to no avail, the test will be met, provided that the court is convinced and the opponent does not show otherwise.[16]

Exercise of a privilege can also meet the unavailability test. For example, an attorney cannot be ordered to testify against his client (this is covered by the attorney-client privilege). A doctor cannot be asked to discuss matters that have transpired between him and his patient in the official course of treatment; and a wife cannot be forced to testify against her spouse. Further, an accused can exercise his Fifth Amendment right in a criminal trial, and this too would meet the unavailability test.

Mental incapacity can also affect a witness's availability. If the individual, after a serious accident or illness, loses his capacity to observe, remember, and recount, this might meet the test. Retrograde amnesia may also meet the test. In *Wilson* v. *United States* the United States Court of Appeals for the District of Columbia noted that the test is not whether an individual suffers from a mental disorder, but whether he has sufficient present ability and a rational understanding of the proceedings.[17]

The issue of reliability also must be addressed. Former testimony will be allowed, provided it is reliable. The character of the tribunal and the form of the proceedings must also be reviewed. Testimony given before a legislative committee, or in the course of a coroner's inquest, has generally been excluded as being unreliable,[18] unless made competent by statute.[19]

The former testimony, once admitted, must then be proven. The testimony of a witness at a trial or hearing that was stenographically reported may be proved by having it duly certified by the person who reported the testimony. Where the stenographic transcript is offered as evidence, a proper foundation must be set down to support its admission. The foundation includes proof as to its truth and accuracy and identification of the contents as the evidence given at the former trial. There have been cases where a stenographer has testified from recollection.[20]

Generally, in both civil and criminal cases, if a proper foundation is established, a former hearing may be proved by the oral testimony of an individual who attended that proceeding and heard the witness testify. This individual can be a judge, an attorney, juror, reporter, or any layperson. There must, however, be a showing that the witness in fact heard the testimony and remembers the substance of the entire testimony for which it is sought to be introduced. The witness need not give the exact same words used at the former hearing; it is sufficient that he can state the substance of the testimony. The adverse party has the option of cross-examining him to test his ability to recollect, as well as his veracity.

Many courts will allow oral testimony as to former testimony, even though there might be a written transcript of it. However, the individual must satisfy the court that he is able to give the substance of all that the witness testified about relevant to the present litigation.[21] Also, unofficial notes of one who was present for the former testimony, generally are considered competent evidence to establish that former testimony.[22]

Computer-generated evidence admitted in a former trial (and the testimony surrounding that evidence) will usually be held admissible in a later trial, provided the former testimony exception is met. Through the latter, it is possible to evade the hearsay rule and also the confrontation doctrine. To date, there have been a few cases involving computer-generated evidence and testimony. As litigation in this area progresses, the exceptions to both the hearsay rule and the confrontation clause should be kept in mind. It should be noted that there are many exceptions available to the sophisticated litigator that can be employed to evade some of the procedural and evidentiary obstacles to computer-related testimony.

References

1. "Computer Sends 150,000 Checks to Wrong Addresses," *Washington Post*, May 9, 1977, p. A-4.

2. Ibid.

3. John Fialka, "SSI System Lacks Controls on Fraud," *Washington Star*, May 4, 1976, p. A-1.

4. Ibid.

5. Robert Lindsey, "Six Accused of Manipulating Credit Data Bank on Coast," *New York Times*, September 3, 1976, p. 1.

6. *Hayden* v. *Chalfant Press, Inc.*, 281 F.2d 543 (1960).

7. 5 Wigmore, *Evidence*, p. 12 (3rd ed. 1940).

8. 9 Holdsworth, *History of English Law*, p. 211 (1926).

9. 5 Wigmore, *Evidence*, p. 4.

10. *McCleskey* v. *Leadbetter*, 1 Ga. 555 (1846).

11. 5 Wigmore, *Evidence*, sec. 1397.

12. 291 U.S. 97 (1934).

13. 333 U.S. 257 (1948).

14. 380 U.S. 400 (1965).

15. Ibid., p. 415.

16. *State* v. *Ortego*, 157 P.2d 320 (1945).

17. 391 F.2d 460 (1968).

18. *Newman* v. *United States ex rel. Frizzel*, 43 App.D.C. 53 (1914).

19. *Los Angeles County* v. *Industrial Accident Commission*, 11 P.2d 434 (1932).

20. *Terry* v. *State*, 103 S.W.2d 766.

21. 29 Am. Jur. 2d, *Evidence*, sec. 763.
22. Ibid., sec. 765.

10 Getting Around Hearsay

A number of courts have held that computer-generated evidence, if offered for the truth of the statement contained therein, is hearsay. Consequently, a litigant must bring it in either as nonhearsay or else under one of the hearsay exceptions. The exceptions are numerous, and some courts may not hold them as being applicable to computer-related litigation. There is, however, a trend toward making at least some of these applicable to computer-generated evidence. These exceptions have in the past shown themselves to be sufficiently flexible to accommodate the needs of modern society. An ingenious litigator may be able to sway a court to accommodate them to this new electronic technology. It behooves both the investigator and litigator to be familiar with at least some of these exceptions.

The Affidavit

An *affidavit* is a statement put into written form and sworn to before an officer authorized to take oaths. When offered in evidence for the truth of any allegations it contains, the affidavit is hearsay. However, many states have, through legislation, made affidavits an exception. Some courts have also, through their own decisions, provided them with a special status. Affidavits may also come under one of the hearsay exceptions. For example, they may come in as admissions of a party opponent. A printout, in the form of an affidavit, signed and sworn to, may possibly be introduced in court under this exception.

Learned Treatises

An expert witness, either under cross-examination or direct examination, may call attention to statements contained in a published treatise. The publication may deal with one of several subjects, such as history, science, the arts, and other related matters. The expert witness, however, must first establish the treatise as being reliable authority. The court may, in some instances, grant it judicial notice. If admitted, the statements within the treatise may be read in evidence, although the document itself may not be admitted as an exhibit.[1]

Market reports, annuity tables, and even city directories have come in under the treatise exception.[2] It has been argued that polls and surveys of public opinion should be admitted as trade reports.[3] It appears that in many jurisdictions that apply a broad and flexible definition of *treatise*, computerized data could possibly come in under this exception.

Public Records and Reports

Public records and reports can also come in under one of the hearsay exceptions. The rule makes no distinction between state and federal agencies; its basis is the belief that public officials, in the performance of their daily tasks, will note daily events in their work, and the likelihood that they will leave information out is remote; the assumption is that public officials will perform their duties properly. There is also an awareness that a public official who daily transcribes numerous data will probably not remember what has been done that day. The cases allowing such reports and documents in as evidence are numerous.[4]

Weather bureau reports, Pension Office records, and General Land Office records have come in under this exception. Evaluative reports, however, have run into problems; the courts are divided on whether or not to admit these reports. Police reports are usually excluded, unless they report firsthand observations. However, at least on the federal level, various federal statutes provide for the admission of these reports. Section 78 of Title 7 of the U.S. Code provides for the admission in evidence of findings by the Secretary of Agriculture as regards the true grade of grains; other statutes make similar provisions. Computerized data could probably come in under one of these statutory exceptions.

When public records or evaluative reports are involved in an administrative hearing, the rules of evidence are relaxed.[5] Computerized data could easily be introduced, especially if in the form of a public document.

Federal Records Statute

Title 28, U.S. Code, Section 1733, provides in part, as follows:

(a) Books or records of account or minutes of proceedings of any department or agency of the United States shall be admissible to prove the act, transaction or occurrence as a memorandum of which the same were made or kept.
(b) Properly authenticated copies of transcripts of any books, records papers or documents of any department or agency of the United States shall be admitted into evidence equally with the originals thereof.

The statute applies, however, only to records, documents, and books of the executive branch of the federal government. Nevertheless, it covers more than 50 federal agencies. To be admissible, the records must concern matters to which an executive official could have testified in person.[6]

The statute has been held to render admissible numerous records and their "copies." Even reports of the weather bureau have been admitted under its provisions. There are, however, some exceptions, such as accident reports.[7] In a recent case, *United States* v. *Wilson,* a map prepared by the Navy Department was admitted in evidence where a witness, sufficiently qualified on cross-examination as an expert draftsman, identified it as one prepared by the federal government.[8] On the other hand, in *Yung Jin Teung* v. *Dulles,* government reports that did not relate to matters within the personal knowledge of persons who made them and that were made specifically for litigation purposes were held inadmissible.[9] Although the statute is not absolute, computerized data, to which someone with personal knowledge can testify, might qualify for admission under this statute if the material was not specifically prepared for litigation.

There are, however, two major problems when dealing with computerized data: (1) the individual who has personal knowledge may no longer be with that agency, and (2) the printout may, in fact, have been prepared specifically for litigation. Some cases that deal with the business records exception (Title 28, U.S. Code, Section 1732) seem to vacillate in this area. There is, however, a trend to acknowledge that although printouts are prepared for litigation, they may still be reliable. The matter is still in dispute. There is a strong possibility that Section 1733 might provide another vehicle for the admission of computerized executive agency data.

Other Public Records

Many of the exceptions to the hearsay rule, usually involving various types of public records, are governed by statute. If there is no statute, the common law generally provides for their admission on the grounds that these records are: (1) prepared by someone whose duty is to prepare them, and (2) who has firsthand knowledge of the records involved.[10]

Such records include, for example, a judgment of a previous conviction or certificates of marriage, birth, or death. Depositions may also be brought in, with accompanying exhibits. Computerized data may find admittance under one of the above. As to the matter of depositions, printouts that have been identified and discussed during the taking of a deposition may also find their way into a trial in this fashion.

Medical Records

Increasingly, hospital and physician records are being computerized. With the rising cost of medical services, computerization has come into vogue as a major attempt to introduce savings. With the increase in litigation involving both hospitals and physicians, computer records will be increasingly found at the center of this litigation. Courts have, over a period of time, extended some of the hearsay exceptions to noncommercial establishments. Medical records, either through judicial fiat or through statutes, have been recognized as falling within these exceptions.[11]

The criteria for the admission of hospital records differ very little from those set for commercial entries. First, the party having knowledge of the facts must testify that the records were made in the regular course of business. The problem, however, is that the individual who has the requisite knowledge may no longer be employed by the hospital. Second, the hospital or party that seeks the record's admission has the burden of locating the missing witness. In a highly mobile society, this may prove extremely difficult. However, some courts have relaxed the requirements of this exception, but many jurisdictions still remain conservative and hesitate to modify the rule.

Third, the entries should be made in the routine of the hospital. Finally, they must have been made contemporaneously with the event they describe. The problem is, especially when dealing with computerized data, that the reports may not have been formulated in the regular course of business, nor need they have been made contemporaneously with the event described. Many courts are hesitant, as they are in the area of commercial records, to dispense with these admission requirements when dealing with hospital or physician records.

Medical records, once computerized, face additional problems. The physician-patient privilege may pose a problem. A majority of states recognize this privilege.[12] Under this privilege, if a patient has consulted a physician for treatment and the purpose of the treatment is not illegal, the physician is barred from testifying against the patient. The records themselves are privileged and cannot be introduced into court against the patient unless specifically prepared for trial. The fact that the doctor is not employed by the patient is immaterial.

However, although the information secured by the physician is privileged, information on the dates of the visits and the number of visits is not privileged. Computer printouts, which fit the medical records exception, despite the physician-patient privilege, may be admitted to show such matters as the number and frequency of visits to the physician.

Past Recollection Recorded

A memorandum or other writing regarding a matter about which the witness once had knowledge but no longer has may be introduced under the past recollection recorded exception.[13] Nearly all the jurisdictions recognize this exception. However, it must be shown that the writing was made while the matter was still fresh in the witness's mind, and that the knowledge recorded is correct.

Where the memorandum is made by someone other than the witness who testifies in court, the writing may still be introduced if the witness testifies that, at the time when his memory was fresh, he read the writing and knew it to be true. Thus, where the entrant and the reporter are produced, and the former testifies as to the correctness of the facts and the latter testifies as to the correctness of his reporting, the record will be allowed under this exception.

A plausible argument could be made that computer-generated writings, especially as computer technology becomes more advanced, should be able to be brought in under this exception. Large computer firms are presently working on machines that can write legal briefs. The Common Pleas Court in Philadelphia has begun an experimental program where a computer network, Computer-Aided-Transcription (CAT), will be employed to prepare court transcripts. The court reporter employs a stenotype machine that has been modified to record the information on a cassette tape. This can be read by a computer. When a request is put in for a court transcript, the computer then prepares a final transcript. The system costs about $100,000 and may be the answer to the large backlog in the preparation of court transcripts. Computers will soon be employed to produce similar transcriptions in non-court-related matters.

CAT-related writings could come in under this exception, by simply having the witness who has knowledge of the matter testify that it was transcribed by a reporter while still in his memory. Also the reporter should testify that he took down what was reported to him. Then both the witness and the reporter should testify to the correctness of the writing. The writing should then be able to come in evidence. If the reporter alone testifies, and the witness is not available, he should testify that at the time he prepared the writing his memory was fresh, and that he read the writing and knew it to be correct. Under the CAT system, the court reporter usually reviews the first draft of the transcript to ensure that it is correct and may make corrections. These will then be incorporated in the final draft of the document.

Computer technology is still in its infancy. This technology will in the future replace the pen and paper as a vehicle for writings. An individual with the assistance of a computer may soon be able to produce voluminous writings. It could easily be argued that computer-generated writings should fall under this hearsay exception.

Present Recollection Refreshed

Writings may also be employed to refresh a witness' memory. However, it is necessary to first demonstrate that: (1) the witness needs to have his memory stimulated, and (2) that the writing is used only for that purpose. The witness must then testify from an independent recollection of the facts. The writing is only employed to refresh his obscured memory.[14]

The writing itself may take any one of several forms. It may be a diary, letters, personal as well as commercial records, and even a computer printout.

For example, a witness can use the minutes of a board of directors meeting to refresh his recollection as to what transpired at that meeting. Grand jury testimony has been known to be used to refresh a witness's memory. Courts have used great latitude in determining what form the writing may take. The adverse party may inspect the writing and cross-examine the witness with regard to it. There is every reason to believe that a printout or other computer-generated "writing" may also be used to refresh a witness's memory.

The Jencks Exception

In any criminal prosecution brought by the federal government, if a government witness testifies, and the defense attorney makes a motion, the court will order the government to produce any and all statements the witness gave the government officers. However, the statements must relate to the subject matter of the testimoy in question.[15]

The term *statement*, under the Jencks Act (as this requirement is called) covers a variety of things:

(1) a written statement made by said witness and signed or otherwise adopted or approved by him; or
(2) a stenographic, mechanical, electrical, or other recording, or a transcription thereof, which is a substantially verbatim recital of an oral statement made by said witness to an agent of the Government and recorded contemporaneously with the making of such oral statement.[16]

Statements that have been computerized may in fact be covered by the Jencks Act provided that the "writing" is a "substantially verbatim recital"; and is recorded "contemporaneously" with the making of the oral statement. The first part would pose no problem. However, the second part of this requirement might pose a problem when dealing with computer data since they are not usually recorded contemporaneously with the act. Some courts might nevertheless relax this requirement, if it could be shown that the writing were in fact accurate and reliable.

The progress of computer technology and its impact on our laws is a recent and almost unnoticed development. The Philadelphia CAT system has cut court transcription time by almost one half. The new system makes use of this technology—computers are utilized to prepare court transcripts.[17] At present, in the majority of our courts this is done by hand. As computers come into greater use, much of the writings now being prepared by hand will eventually be prepared by a computerized system, perhaps similar to CAT, thus enabling greater storage and speed in the preparation both at the court and police levels, possibly resulting in the expansion of this exception to include computerized data.

Admissions of a Party-Opponent

A voluntary acknowledgment (either through words or acts) of the existence or truth of a fact that is contrary to an adverse party's defense is an *admission.* To be admissible, an admission must be relevant and of a material nature. For example, if Mr. Smith acknowledges a contract as having been signed by him and later denies ever having entered into that same contract, his former admission may be entered against him.

Admissions by an agent acting within the scope of his employment are also admissible. For example, admissions by an officer of a corporation are admissible against the firm. The only question in dispute would be whether the officer had the authority to act. An admission may also be contained in a deposition or a pleading, but it must be a statement of fact.

In litigation involving computers, an admission by an operator or a programmer, made either before or during the trial, that the system had developed many technical problems or was prone to fraud or errors could be used to show that the system was unreliable, or to attack the authenticity of the data. If the adverse party attempted to introduce a printout under one of the hearsay exceptions, the admission of a party-opponent could be used to undermine the evidence. For example, the test, when employing computer data, is to demonstrate the computer's reliability and accuracy; testimony that could shed an adverse light on that reliability and accuracy might be of use. The party against whom the admission is being used, however, can introduce rebuttal testimony to support his position.

An admission may take various forms. For example, a party's failure to answer a written statement may, at times, be taken as an admission. This rule, however, is limited to civil cases. In criminal cases, one's failure to reply to a written inquiry or statement will not be admissible as an admission. However, if the parties involved have conducted frequent exchanges and have discussed a specific subject, one party's reference to that specific subject and the other party's failure to reply might be taken as an admission. In the business world, for example, the rendering of a bill to Mr. Smith and his failure to reply (when the two parties have had frequent correspondence on that specific subject) might be taken as an admission of the transfer of that bill.[18] Computerized bills could possibly be entered as admissions where the other party, after frequent exchanges as to a specific bill, fails to reply. Thus the printout itself may not be necessary as proof of the existence of this obligation.

There are numerous instances involving a computer system when admissions may be admissible. One such admission takes the form of behavior. For example, if a company disposes of its computer because of frequent problems with errors and returns to traditional record-keeping systems, this might be allowed as an admission by that party that the system was faulty and that it was responsible for the financial injury suffered by the other party. The company has a right to attempt a rebuttal. The weight accorded the admission is a matter for the court. The plaintiff may employ the admission rather than introduce numerous printouts, and face the problem of hearsay. The admission of a party-opponent may also be used in conjunction with other exceptions.

Declarations against Interest

Where a declarant is unavailable and has made statements that are against his pecuniary or proprietary interest, these will be admitted. However, the declarant must have been a witness to the facts involved. The theory behind this exception is that an individual will not make statements damaging to himself unless they are true.[19] The statements themselves are viewed in the context and the environment within which they were made. For example, an agreement by Mr. Jones to testify against an associate in return for the prosecution's promise to drop its charges against him must be viewed within the proper context of the then-existing situation; the statements are not made in a vacuum.

The criteria for the admission of such statements varies from jurisdiction to jurisdiction. For example, some states limit these declarations to situations where their reliability has been proven;[20] other states, if they find a motive to falsify, will exclude the declarations.[21] However, in a computer litigation case, a declaration by one of the parties that he did in fact falsify the data is a declaration against interest and is admissible in evidence. It is against his pecuniary or proprietary interest, especially in matters involving civil litigation, and there is little reason to doubt its authenticity.

Confessions

An acknowledgment by an individual of his guilt is a *confession*. To be admissible, however, it must have been made voluntarily; inducements and threats must not have been used (except perhaps an agreement by the prosecution not to press the case against the defendant if he implicates his associates). There must be corroboration, and the individual's constitutional rights must be respected. A confession, in computer crime cases, could easily facilitate prosecution and save the government from the quagmire of litigating a complex computer fraud case.

Above all else, there must exist proof that an act did take place—a corpus delicti must be proved. For example, in a case affecting a computer crime, there must be proof that a crime did take place; that the computer was destroyed, manipulated, bugged; or that its software was stolen. Further, the confession must be voluntary.[22] No threats, force, or inducements can be used to influence its outcome; it must be the product of free will. In custodial situations, the defendant must be appraised of his constitutional rights and may have an attorney present if he requests one.[23] It is a violation of the Fifth Amendment to force an individual to be a witness against himself.

Many computer cases can easily be solved if one or more of the parties to the crime openly confess. For example, in December 1976 four individuals were indicted in Maryland in a computer fraud case that bilked a District of Columbia pension and health plan of more than $500,000 over an 8-year period.[24] Their scheme was simple. The defendants had fabricated a number of accounts in the memory banks of the computer. The computer then directed checks to be mailed to one of the defendants. More than 600 checks were mailed. The checks were then cashed at one of the local Maryland banks. Several spot audits indicated to trained investigators that something was wrong.

The prosecutors dropped charges against two of the defendants, but the remaining two agreed to plead guilty to a lesser charge. Had the prosecutors gone to trial, procedural objections could have been raised by the defense, and the hearsay rule could possibly have been used to bar the introduction of all or part of the computer data. A difficult and tiresome criminal trial was circumvented. Civil litigation in this matter is still pending and has been going on for about two years, with no end yet in sight.

In this case, no force or coercion was employed to obtain the open-court confessions. The defendants were accompanied by counsel; there was a corpus delicti; their constitutional rights were protected; and their confessions could easily have withstood the challenge of an appeal should the defense have attempted one. In dealing with serious white collar felonies, an investigator and prosecutor should guard against providing the target of their efforts with an array of procedural motions with which the defense can later delay and tire the prosecution. Confessions, when obtained within constitutional confines, can prove a blessing in computer crime cases. It should also be pointed out that defense attorneys are as yet unsophisticated in this area. Those who acquire the needed sophistication could easily impede the government until it either abandons its prosecution or works out a favorable plea arrangement with the defense.

Statements in Ancient Documents

In the great majority of jurisdictions, documents that are: (1) 30 or more years old, (2) in the proper custody, and (3) free of any indications of fraud or forgery are admissible as an exception to the hearsay rule.[25]

In the future, it is possible that printouts, if 30 or more years old, if they have been in proper custody, and if free of indications of fraud or forgery may be admitted under this exception. However, since computer technology is relatively young, and since few if any printouts could meet the criteria of this

114

exception, it is doubtful that the exception has any real present application. The problem with applying the exception to computer-stored data is that false and erroneous data could easily be introduced. Computer systems are vulnerable to attack and infiltration by felons and manipulators; such unauthorized introductions defeat the criteria set for the exception.

There are a number of other exceptions to the hearsay rule, but the key ones have necessarily been discussed. However, the exceptions most often raised (and most widely discussed) in computer-related litigation deal with the old shop-book rule and the business records exception. These will be discussed in the next chapter.

References

1. Robert S. Hunter, *Federal Trial Handbook* (San Francisco, Calif.: Lawyers Co-operative, 1974), p. 596.

2. See *Williams* v. *Campbell Soup Co.,* 80 F.Supp. 865; and 6 Wigmore, *Evidence,* sec. 1704.

3. Charles T. McCormick, *Handbook of the Law of Evidence* (St. Paul, Minn.: West, 1954), p. 620.

4. *Bailey* v. *C.V. Hunter, Inc.,* 148 S.E.2d 826 (1966); and *Matthews* v. *United States,* 217 F.2d 409 (1954).

5. Such hearings, whether at the state or federal level, are usually highly informal, and the rules of evidence are relaxed. Hearsay evidence is usually allowed to come in.

6. *Vanadium Corp.* v. *Fidelity & Deposit Co.,* 159 F.2d 105 (1947).

7. 49 U.S.C., sec. 1441.

8. 535 F.2d 521 (1976).

9. 229 F.2d 244 (1956).

10. 5 Wigmore, *Evidence,* sec. 1638(a).

11. 6 Wigmore, *Evidence,* sec. 1707.

12. 8 Wigmore, *Evidence,* sec. 2380-91.

13. *United States* v. *Kelly,* 349 F.2d 720 (1965).

14. Charles Kramer, *Evidence in Negligence Cases* (New York: Practising Law Institute, 1973), p. 8.

15. 18 U.S.C., sec. 3500.

16. Ibid.

17. "System Being Developed to Speed Court Transcripts," *Washington Post,* May 16, 1977, p. A-7.

18. *Megarry Bros., Inc.* v. *United States,* 404 F.2d 479 (1968).

19. *Donnelly* v. *United States,* 228 U.S. 243 (1913).

20. *Cameron* v. *State,* 217 S.W.2d 23 (1949).

21. Charles Kramer, *Evidence in Negligence Cases,* p. 31.

22. *Miranda* v. *Arizona,* 384 U.S. 436 (1966).

23. Ibid.

24. "Four Indicted in $500,000 Fraud by Computer from Union's Funds," *Washington Post,* December 16, 1976, p. C-1.

25. *Clark* v. *Owens,* 18 N.Y. 434 (1892).

11

Business Records Exception: State Level

In response to the needs of a growing mercantile society, English courts were increasingly faced with the need to deal with the problem of allowing business records into court as an exception to the hearsay rule. English jurists, however, have always been concerned with the accuracy and authenticity of the evidence, particularly in cases involving businessmen. The courts feared that merchants would prepare self-serving records in preparation for litigation. Clearly some business records had to be admissible, but how was the court to ensure that false and misleading evidence would not be allowed in court?

A single case, *Price* v. *Lord Torrington,* in 1703 lies at the heart of the common-law development regarding business records.[1] The case involved an entry made by a drayman shortly before his death concerning some beer he had delivered. The question before the court was whether the records should be admitted in evidence. The court set three conditions for its admission: (1) the declarant must be proven dead—clearly if he were alive, there would be no need for the document, since he himself could testify; (2) the entry should have been made contemporaneously with the act; and (3) it should have been made in the regular course of business.

The *Price* Doctrine

Many of the early American cases, including many of the statutes enacted by our states to address themselves to the problem of business records as an exception to the hearsay rule, were heavily influenced by the *Price* case. That holding goes far to explain the present dilemma regarding the admissibility of computer records. Many of its provisions still control in many of our states today. The case, as such, merits some further elaboration so that we may better understand our present problems.

One of the criteria set by *Price* was that the declarant be proven dead. It would mean that his identity and status must first be determined. Further, it means that there must be no doubt in the court's mind that the declarant is in fact deceased. If he were alive, he would be expected to testify. Early eighteenth century English society lacked the mobility of later times. People usually spent most, if not all, of their lives in one locality. There would be little, if any, problem in proving someone dead.

However, in a highly mobile society, *Price* could pose a problem. In a

117

computerized society, where employee turnover is extremely high and rapid communications enable individuals to travel from one continent to another in a matter of hours, it is no easy task to prove someone dead. Under the *Price* doctrine, unless one could prove that the declarant was dead, the record would be inadmissible or else the moving party would have to locate the declarant and have him testify personally in open court.

The *Price* doctrine poses an added problem for computer litigation. It requires that the declarant be identified. In today's business world, with its large offices and staffs that number in the thousands, identifying the declarant could pose a difficulty. Further, since a task is divided among many employees, no one individual would have knowledge of the total act. Security measures employed in large computer centers, through design, prevent any one individual from having total knowledge of the act required by the *Price* doctrine.

Price also requires that the entry have been made contemporaneously with the act. In eighteenth century England, business entries were usually entered contemporaneously with the act. However, in a world of corporate conglomerates and multinational firms, such is not the case. Computerized bookkeeping is not contemporaneous. Entries may be made weeks or even months afterward. Original source documents are usually destroyed. Even if at best the entry is made by an individual who has knowledge of all the facts, the recording of the data may take place weeks later, only after numerous records have been accumulated.

Price also required that the entries have been made in the regular course of business. It implies a specific duty by a specific individual. As already noted, this requirement would have little meaning in a modern business setting. In a computerized system, entries are not usually made contemporaneously with the act, but rather days or weeks later. Further, the security measures employed in a computer center ensure that no one individual learns too much about the system, and there is constant rotation of personnel. No one individual knows the full operation of the system. This could further add to the difficulties of bringing in a computer printout as an exception to the hearsay rule under the *Price* doctrine.

The American courts made some minor modifications in the *Price* doctrine. For example, the moving party was no longer required to prove that the defendant was dead. He could merely show that the declarant was unavailable because he was out of the court's jurisdiction or seriously ill.[2] However, the courts continued to require that the entries be made near or at the time of the act, and that they be made in the regular course of business. These latter two requirements were retained to ensure that the records be accurate and be kept in the regular course of everyday business, thus ensuring their authenticity.[3] Out of the original *Price* doctrine, many offshoots to handling the business records exception have evolved. Different jurisdictions have adopted variations of the doctrine.

At present, the business records exception to the hearsay rule takes on several forms: (1) the old shop-book rule of the common law, which is still recognized in many common law jurisdictions; (2) the Uniform Rules of Evidence Act, found in a minority of our jurisdictions; (3) the Uniform Business Records as Evidence Act, found in more than half of our states; (4) the Texas Act; and (5) the Federal Business Records Act, adopted by the federal government in 1936 and still used in federal courts. The federal rules have also been invigorated and modified by the New Rules of Evidence. This chapter will review the various state rules.

The Shop-Book Rule

The most immediate offshoot of the *Price* doctrine in America, was a common-law rule that came to be called the *shop-book rule*. About a dozen states still retain this common-law exception to the hearsay rule.[4] Some 20 states have changed this common-law rule through statutes;[5] and the state of Texas has evolved a model of its own.[6] The federal courts have adopted their own rules in this area. However, there are some basic similarities between the various statutes and the shop-book rule. The latter sets the following criteria for the admission of business records in a trial: (1) the records must have been made routinely during the regular course of business; (2) the entry must have been made contemporaneously or within a reasonable time of the transaction recorded; (3) the entry must have been made by a person who is unavailable as a witness; (4) who has personal knowledge of the event; and (5) who had no motive to misrepresent or misstate the facts.

The reasoning behind the rule was twofold: (1) reliability, and (2) necessity. The rule served the business needs of nineteenth century America well. However, a computerized society faces serious obstacles under the rule. A number of computer-related cases have already failed the test under this common-law exception. Computerized entries are not usually made contemporaneously or within a reasonable time of the facts recorded. Most entries are not computerized until days or even weeks have passed. Backlogs and priorities in the computer system make it difficult to do otherwise.

In addition, many computer entries are not made in the routine of one's regular course of business. A large business conglomorate with offices and subsidiaries in many states and countries may not computerize its data for long periods of time. The entries in the computer system are certainly not made in the regular course of doing business. In many instances, the ledger sheets on which the entries are routinely made are usually destroyed once the data are fed into the computer.

The requirement of unavailability poses no problem for computerized data. Many of the personnel who had access to and worked in the computer system are probably no longer with the firm, and thus unavailable. The rule, by relaxing the death requirement under the *Price* doctrine, has in fact facilitated the admission of computer records in a trial.

There is an added problem: the personal knowledge requirement. Few, if any, of those who are employed in the computer center have knowledge of a personal nature of the events they record or enter into the computer banks. The theory of computer security provides for just the opposite situation. This doctrine requires that no middle- or low-echelon personnel have knowledge of the entire process. The doctrine further requires that only those on a need-to-know basis should have access to the data. Many who work with the computer will neither have personal knowledge, nor will they be informed, of how their work fits into the overall scheme. In addition, personnel are also constantly revolved around the system, again with security in mind. Too few of them will have sufficient access to acquire the bare minimum requisites to meet the criteria of personal knowledge. The thrust of the doctrine of computer security is to keep them in the dark as much as possible.

In a large firm, with a system that spans several states and which employs hundreds of personnel, even in the absence of security measures the computer personnel are too far removed and isolated from the rest of the firm to have personal knowledge of the facts. Further, in some firms, top management itself may be engaged in a long-term practice of keeping false records. For example, the giants of the aerospace industry have engaged over a period of time, in payoffs to foreign agents. Some firms have also engaged in illegal domestic payments. The former chairman of one of the nation's largest airline companies recently told the federal government that his firm had engaged in systematic payoffs since 1934.[7] He stated that the practice was common and systematic in the industry for many years.

In a series of other revelations, one large conglomerate has admitted making illegal payments to foreign officials exceeding $2 million.[8] Other large firms have engaged in both illegal payments to foreign political leaders and "kickback" schemes that laundered corporate funds that eventually made their way back to the pockets of these corporate officers in various disguised forms. Some firms, in dealing with the American intelligence community, have purposely falsified their records to disguise these dealings. One federal prosecutor recently said that at least one large firm was suspected of keeping two sets of "books" within its computer banks. It showed "false ones" to the government for purposes of paying fewer taxes.

The intentional falsification of records by top level company officials raises serious questions about the commercial records exceptions to the hearsay rule. For example, do fraudulent entries qualify under the hearsay exception as regular business records? If the record is admitted to prove the truth of the matter asserted in it, can it still come in under the hearsay exception if that matter is in fact false? The low-level personnel in a computer center would not be privy to this fraud. This differs markedly from the case of a small firm, where the falsification of records would probably be known to its employees. In fact, if the records have been falsified, the matters asserted in them are not authentic and there is no hearsay problem. The hearsay records exceptions would not apply. The only purpose for admitting these records would be to support the charge that a fraud was being committed. The evidence would have to come in as nonhearsay. The personal knowledge requirement in a large and complex business setting has little meaning, nor can it ensure the authenticity of the records.

The rule also requires that a moving party show that the maker of the record had no motive to misstate or misrepresent the facts. This may be difficult, especially when an individual has a past criminal record or is known to associate with criminal types. Computer personnel, even those who have access to confidential material, usually undergo only a routine background screening. Fingerprinting and more stringent security measures are usually limited only to those few with access to intelligence and secret material. Felons and even impostors can easily find employment in most computer centers today.

As an example, the staff of the U.S. Senate Government Operations Committee, in a study conducted by Phillip Manuel and Fred Asselin, found that convicted felons at the federal prison in Leavenworth, Kansas, were employed as programmers for various federal agencies. These programming services included: accounting, budgeting, payroll projects, and even keeping track of the movement of prisoners in the Federal Bureau of Prisons system. In litigation, the adverse party can and should bring to light conduct that may affect the motives of those involved in operating the computer system.

The shop-book rule has served the courts well in the past. In *Vosburgh* v. *Thayer,* in 1815, a New York court allowed the proponent of the evidence to introduce his business records when he showed: (1) that he kept fair and honest books, (2) that no regular clerk was kept who could testify firsthand as to the entries, and (3) that the entries established regular business dealings between the parties.[9] In *Rathbone* v. *Hatch,* a century later, another New York court took a less broad position.[10] The business records of a stockbroker had been offered in evidence concerning the price of a stock. The manager of the firm testified that he had knowledge of the prices and reported them accurately to the messenger who then relayed the information to the firm's bookkeepers. The latter recorded the information in the firm's books. The messenger, however, had not been called to testify. The court, applying the rule, held that the records were inadmissible since the messenger had not testified that he had reported the information given to him accurately.

The shop-book rule, although consistently being replaced by legislation, still retains its force in many states. Some courts have broadened it and adapted it to the needs of a changing society. However, many courts are still reluctant to do so. Although American courts have proven more flexible than their English counterparts in developing a more liberal application of the rule, they still have to go a long way in meeting the needs of a computerized business society.

The Uniform Business Records as Evidence Act

A general dissatisfaction with the shop-book rule led some jurisdictions to find alternatives. The large urban states were the first to take this lead.[11] In 1927 the Commonwealth Fund of New York proposed a model statute to broaden the common-law rule. The suggested statute provided as follows:

> Any writing or record, whether in the form of an entry in a book or otherwise, made as a memorandum or record of any act, transaction, occurrence or event shall be admissible in evidence in proof of said act, transaction, occurrence or event if the trial judge shall find that it was made in the regular course of such business . . . at the time of such act, transaction, occurrence or event or within a reasonable time thereafter.[12]

The proposed legislation followed closely the common-law evolution in this area. It was not a radical departure from the shop-book rule.

The Commonwealth Fund, however, went a step further. It suggested that all other circumstances of the making of such writing or record, including lack of personal knowledge by the recording party, should not affect the admissibility of the record, but rather the evidentiary value or weight it was to be accorded.[13] The Fund also proposed that the model statute include within its definition of *business* not only the traditional world of business, but also the professions, and most other occupations.

The Fund's proposal met with favorable acceptance in many corners of the legal and business establishment. It would play a dominant role in the state and federal legislation that would follow in the next several years. However, the very next year, New York became the first state to enact the proposals of the Fund. The New York Civil Practice Act, section 374(a), superseded the state's old shop-book rule. The act was later modified in 1963, but in substance it has remained the same to this day.

The New York statute provides as follows:

> Any writing or record, whether in the form of an entry in a book or otherwise, made as a memorandum or record of any act, transaction, occurrence or event, shall be admissible in evidence as proof of that act, transaction, occurrence or event, if the judge finds that it was made in the regular course of any business.[14]

The requirement of personal knowledge was minimized. Henceforth, it would only affect the weight accorded rather than the admissibility of the writing itself.

The New York Act was later adopted in one form or another by more than

20 jurisdictions. It sets forth three key criteria that have to be met in order for the record to be admissible in evidence. First, it requires that a record be made in the regular course of business; second, that the regular course of business involve and include the keeping of records; and third, that the record be made at the time of the transaction, event, or occurrence, or within a short time thereafter.

In a computerized record-keeping environment, this first requirement presents certain problems. Printouts are rarely prepared unless needed. Thus, although the data may be fed to the computer in the regular course of business, they will be stored in the computer's banks until there is a need to retrieve them. An adversary could argue that a printout is not a record or writing kept in the regular course of business, but rather a copy of the real record, prepared for litigation.

The problem to resolve is an exact definition of the phrase the *regular course of business*. In 1965 a Nebraska court made an attempt to address itself to this problem. That state had adopted a statute patterned along the lines of the New York model. In the case of *Transport Indemnity Co.* v. *Seib*, the Nebraska court rejected the argument that a printout is a writing specifically prepared for trial.[15] The court noted that although the data had in fact been retrieved for trial purposes, the information and calculations thereon were made in the usual course of the business.

The *Seib* court appeared to be departing from a strict construction of the Nebraska statute, which provided that:

A record of an act . . . shall, insofar as relevant, be competent evidence if the custodian or other qualified witness testifies to its identity and the mode of its preparation, and if it was made in the regular course of business, at or near the time of the act, condition or event, and if, in the opinion of the court, the sources of information, method and time of preparation were such as to justify its admission.[16]

The proponents of the printouts in the *Seib* case went through great lengths to demonstrate how the computerized system worked, and also to demonstrate the accuracy and reliability of the computer record-keeping process. It would appear that the court was impressed and gave the statute a liberal interpretation.

It should also be borne in mind that the *Seib* court decided the matter in 1965, before the American public heard of the revelations involving Equity Funding Corporation, the domestic and international illegal corporate payment schemes, the numerous computer crimes that have since surfaced and have led many sources to question the accuracy and reliability of computerized data in a white-collar-crime-infested environment. More than a dozen years have passed since *Seib*, and the courts are still reluctant to relax the criteria for allowing computerized records in evidence.

The New York statute suffers from several additional problems. It requires that the regular course or conduct of business also include the keeping of records. Some corporations, especially subsidiaries of larger firms, usually maintain only the bare skeletal records. The more elaborate data are passed over to other divisions of the parent company for record-keeping purposes. Further, small independent firms usually share one computer system, and this may pose problems. Large multinational companies may keep records in several countries, and each record is kept in conformity with the laws and requirements of the area where they do business. For example, it is customary for large multinational firms doing business in Afro-Asia to maintain several books. The practice is known as *double books*. Company records are intentionally fabricated so as to evade local taxes. However, it cannot be said that these books were kept in the regular course of business, as defined by the statute. The intent of the statute is to ensure that accurate and reliable business records are maintained. It cannot be said that the above practice conforms with the intent of the statute.

There is also the added problem of the time factor. At common law, and later by statute, the requirement is that an entry or record be made within a reasonable time after the event or act has transpired. In a computerized process, information is rarely fed into a computer soon after an event or act has transpired. There is a time lag between the time of the event and the entry of that data into the computer. This time lag affords criminals an opportunity to manipulate the process. For example, the vice president of a large New York bank, with the assistance of several cohorts, stole more than $500,000 from his employer by simply running a float fraud between his bank and another local bank for a period of about four years. Since records of deposits were not computerized at or shortly within the period of the event, the felons were able to alter these records while stored at the computer center, so as to make them appear as deposits. The felons then simply withdrew the money from the bank.

A similar case involved the chief clerk of another New York bank. A police raid on a gambling operation came across his name; he was one of the large bettors. Gambling records showed that he had been betting as much as $30,000 a day. A further investigation disclosed that the teller had access to one of the bank's key computer terminals. For more than two years, he had been using it to bilk the bank out of more than $1 million. The operation was simple—he pocketed many of the customer deposits and then later, with the assistance of the terminal, entered false data in the computer. He also instructed the computer to transfer funds from one account to another. No one checked his work, nor would a visual examination have been of much assistance.

Cases of this sort lend credence to the argument that entries should be made contemporaneously or soon after the act. The time interval between the act and the entry of the data in the computer enables felons to take advantage of the situation and manipulate the information as it best suits their needs.

In 1936 more than 20 states, including New York, passed legislation adopting a more liberal approach to the record-keeping exception to the hearsay rule. The new legislation, later adopted by some additional states, including Texas in a hybrid statute, came to be known as the Uniform Business Records as Evidence Act. The act provides, in part, that a business record include the following:

A record of an act, condition or event, shall, in so far as relevant, be competent evidence if the custodian or other qualified witness testifies to its identity and to the mode of its preparation, and if it was made in the regular course of business, at or near the time of the act, condition or event, and if, in the opinion of the court, the sources of information, method and time preparation were such as to justify its admission.[17]

The act also defines the term *business* to include every kind of commercial business, profession, occupation, calling, or operation of institutions, whether carried on for profit or not.[18]

The 1936 act differs somewhat from the 1927 proposal of the Commonwealth Fund statute. It includes "conditions" within its scope, in addition to "act or event." The term *conditions* could be interpreted as applicable also to computerized record-keeping transactions. The 1936 act also relaxes the requirement that had hampered litigants under the shop-book rule—the need for the record keeper (entrant) to testify. It qualifies this by providing that any "qualified witness" may testify, not only the entrant.

The act further confers upon the court discretion and power to admit evidence it believes to be from reliable sources. When contrasted to the common-law rule, this is a further broadening of the record-keeping exception.

The ALI Model Code

In 1942 the American Law Institute (ALI) proposed a revision of the business records exception rule. The ALI model had as its objective the further broadening of the 1927 Commonwealth Fund proposed statute. The ALI model, rule 514 of its code of evidence, provides as follows:

A writing offered as a memorandum or record of an act . . . is admissible as tending to prove the occurrence of the act or event or the existence of the condition if the judge finds that it was made in the regular course of business. . . .[19]

Rule 514 retains the requirement of personal knowledge, also that an entry be contemporaneous, and that it be made in the regular course of business. The ALI proposal, hailed by some as progressive, was in fact only a modification of the New York statute of 1928 and never had as its objective the elimination of the hearsay rule. Rather, it sought to evade some of its obstacles by giving the court greater power over business records being submitted in evidence.

The ALI model also did not require that the person having knowledge make the memorandum himself. If he transmitted this knowledge to someone, who in turn made the memorandum, the record would still be admissible, provided the court was satisfied that it met the other requirements. Although the ALI proposal influenced other states in modifying their laws, it was never adopted by any state. It represented an added attempt to handle the litigation problems connected with a growing and complex business world. It did not address itself specifically to the computer. The latter, as yet, had not made its entrance in the business world. The ALI statute would not have met the needs of computer-related litigation even had it been adopted in its entirety.

The Uniform Rules of Evidence Act

In 1965, three local jurisdictions adopted the Uniform Rules of Evidence Act. This was one more modification of the 1927 Commonwealth Funds proposal. Rule 63(13) addressed itself to the business records problem. It provided, among other things, that if:

Writings offered as memoranda or records of acts, conditions or events to prove the facts stated therein, if the judge finds that they were made in the regular course of a business at or about the time of the act, condition or event recorded, and that the sources of information from which made and the method and circumstances of their preparation were such as to indicate their trustworthiness . . . [20]

then those writings would be admissible in evidence. Only Kansas, the Panama Canal Zone, and the Virgin Islands have adopted this rule.

The Uniform Rules of Evidence Act was not drafted with the computer in mind. It addresses itself only to the problems of traditional record keeping. The intent of its drafters was to facilitate the admission of business records in evidence, in light of the pressures of an ever-growing and complex business society. For example, the statute notes that if a court is satisfied that the sources of the data and their compilation are trustworthy, it may admit the writing, provided it also meets the other tests. Rule 63(13), although admittedly progressive, falls somewhat short when applied to computers. It continues to require that the records be made in the regular course of business. Further, that they be made at or near the time of the act or event recorded. These two elements pose a problem for computer-related litigation. The drafters did not have the computer in mind when drafting this statute. This is not surprising, since the first computer-related litigation did not occur until 1965.

The Texas Model

In 1929, in the case of *Watson Company* v. *Lone Star Service Station,* a Texas court held that entries made in a permanent record are admissible in evidence.[21]

Forty-two years later, in the well-known case of *Arnold D. Karmen & Company* v. *Young*, another Texas court faced a somewhat different problem.[22] A defendant sought to introduce computer records as evidence that the plaintiff was not entitled to commissions on various sales he was claiming. A senior partner from defendant's firm testified that data had been punched into computer cards and had been sent to the tabulating center. The court ruled that the computerized records were inadmissible on the ground that none of those who testified had personal knowledge of the information punched on the cards.

The Texas business records exception to the hearsay rule, like that of most states, is statutory. However, it is unique in that only Texas has adopted it. The Uniform Business Records as Evidence Act, passed in most other states, essentially provides wide discretion for the trial judge. If he is satisfied that the computerized records are trustworthy, he may then admit them. Further, the act does not require that the entrant have personal knowledge, nor is it required that the normal course of business include personal knowledge of who the entrant is. Personal knowledge only goes to the weight of the evidence and not to its admissibility.

However, the Texas statute is much more restrictive. It appears to resemble more the Commonwealth Fund model statute rather than the Uniform Business Records as Evidence Act. For example, the Texas statute differs in two key respects from the latter. It sets the following criteria for a memorandum or record to be admissible in evidence. Under the Texas statute it must be:

(a) made in the regular course of business;
(b) the regular course of that business for an employee or representative of such business with personal knowledge of such act, event or condition to make such memorandum or record or to transmit information thereof to be included in such memorandum or record;
(c) made at or near the time of the act, event or condition or reasonably thereafter.[23]

The statute also sets guidelines for the introduction of records in evidence. A proponent must first identify and explain to the court the mode of preparation of the record. This may be proven:

by the testimony of the entrant, custodian or other qualified witness even though he may not have personal knowledge of the various items or contents of such memorandum or record. Such lack of personal knowledge may be shown to affect the weight and credibility of the memorandum or record but shall not affect its admissibility.[24]

The Texas statute thus limits the discretion of the trial judge, whereas similar statutes in most states increased that power. No mention is made of a role of the court in this process. However, the admissibility requirements are well defined. The record must have been made in the regular course of business. Further, either the entrant or the one who transmits the data to him must have personal knowledge of the information. Other witnesses will not do.

The statute defines *business* to include every kind of regular organized activity whether conducted for profit or not. The statute, however, incorporates a novel approach—one left out by the other statutes. It allows for the admissibility of an omission of a record as evidence that the event did not occur. For example, it states that evidence to the,

effect that records of the business do not contain any memorandum or record of an alleged act, event or condition shall be competent to prove the non-occurrence of the act, event or the non-existence of the condition in that business if the judge finds that it was the regular course of that business to make such memoranda or records of all such acts, events or conditions. . . .[25]

In a more recent Texas case involving computerized records, *Railroad Commission* v. *Southern Pacific Railroad Company,* the court set out the following criteria for the admission of computer data in evidence: (1) they must have been made in the regular course of business; (2) the records must have been kept in the regular course of business; (3) the entrant must have had personal knowledge; and (4) that they were prepared by someone who understood the operation of the equipment and whose duty was to operate it.[26] This last requirement makes it difficult to admit computer data, since security guidelines in computer systems provide for keeping personnel in the dark. In complex computer systems, few would understand the operation of the process.

Texas courts, when applying their statute to computer data, have interpreted the statute to require not only personal knowledge of the information but also knowledge of the operations of the system. In addition, the statute also requires that the memorandum be made at or near the time of the event or act, or reasonably soon thereafter. If the Texas courts apply a rigid test as to the time requirement, this will also pose a problem. The Texas statute, however, unlike the common law, makes no requirement that the memorandum or record be an original. It can be a copy or even a transcript.[27]

The Texas statute addresses itself to traditional record keeping. Like the other state statutes that were drafted to address the problem of hearsay, it concentrates its thrust on that which its drafters knew best—the commercial world of the 1920s and 1930s, an era without computers. Critics have suggested that the statute be amended to include records that are produced by automated systems like the computer.[28] However, even if the statute is amended, the courts need not be bound by a liberal interpretation. Judges, if given free reign by badly drafted legislation, will continue interpreting the law as their whims dictate. In both Texas and the other jurisdictions we need statutes specifically addressing the problems related to computer litigation. The majority of our states do not have such legislation on the books. Two states, however, have taken a bold step in that direction.

The Computer Statutes

North Carolina and Delaware have adopted statutes that address the specific problems connected with computer litigation.[29] The statutes are nearly identical. Rhode Island has also enacted a law that addresses itself to the computer.[30] However, this statute addresses itself more to the problem of computer crime than the evidentiary problems related to litigation.

The Delaware statute authorized corporations to keep computer records. These records can be admitted in evidence, provided the following two conditions are met: (1) they are maintained in the "regular course of business"; and (2) they must be maintained in such a manner that they can be converted into a legible written form within a reasonable period of time. In addition, individuals entitled to inspect these records can do so. Thus stockholders and parties to a litigation have access to these computer records also. Delaware has also continued to retain its old business records statute. This exemplifies that state's awareness that computerized records have unique properties of their own and require a special statute that addresses itself to these unique features.[31]

The North Carolina statute differs somewhat from that of Delaware. The Delaware statute has recently been amended to require that when data are reproduced for inspection or trial, it be "clearly legible." The North Carolina statute makes no such requirement. The initial Delaware statute made no requirement either. It now does require that the record be "written." It appears that the Delaware legislators apparently felt that the ability to inspect printouts in the form of cards, tapes, or video displays would not prove sufficient. They felt that a written and legible output would prove more meaningful. In North Carolina, a party may be given computerized data in the form of tapes, cards, or video displays. There is no statutory requirement that the output data be in the form of a writing or clearly legible. In civil cases, parties without funds to convert the data into a writing may find the statute of little value. In fact, the statute may serve just the opposite purpose and make meaningful discovery of the data impossible unless a party can have them translated into a legible writing. Data that cannot be read are of little, if any, value at all.

The Delaware statute also suffers from similar drawbacks. It does not specify who is to bear the cost of inspecting a computer's records. Printouts can be extremely expensive to produce. Further, the regular course of business requirement has also been retained. This too can pose problems. Some commentators take the position that perhaps the best way out of this dilemma is through further development of the case law.[32] However, if a statute is to be meaningful, it should address this problem. Both the North Carolina and Delaware statutes are a step in the right direction, and we should learn from their drawbacks. The state of Florida has also amended its business records statute to provide for a "record kept by means of electronic data processing."[33] Other states may soon follow suit. Whether the change comes from the courts or the legislatures matters little. Presently, it has been slow in coming and too limited as yet to set any meaningful pattern for the future.

There is a need for legislation that specifically addresses the problem of computer litigation. Attempting to apply the old common-law rule and business records statutes to this new technology is ill-advised. It results in loss of time and also loss of confidence in our legal system.

References

1. 91 Eng. Rep. 252 (1703), discussed in 5 Wigmore, *Evidence,* sec. 1518, p. 349.
2. See 5 Wigmore, *Evidence,* sec. 1521; also see *In re Fennerstein's Champagne,* 70 U.S. (3 Wall) 145 (1865).
3. See 5 Wigmore, *Evidence,* sec. 1522.
4. Among these states are found Alaska, Colorado, Indiana, Kentucky, Louisiana, Maine, Mississippi, Massachusetts, North Carolina, South Carolina, Virginia, and West Virginia.
5. The majority of states have adopted the Uniform Business Records as Evidence Act; fewer than half the states have adopted the Uniform Rules of Evidence Act.
6. Comment, "The Texas Business Records Act and Computer Printouts," 24 Baylor L. Rev. 161 (1972).
7. William H. Jones, "Airline Says Payments Since 1934," *Washington Post,* May 18, 1977, p. E-1.
8. John F. Berry and William H. Jones, "Boxfuls of SEC Documents Reveal Firms Secret Deals," *Washington Post,* May 18, 1977, pp. A-1, A-6.
9. 12 Johns. 461 (N.Y. 1815).
10. 80 N.Y.S. 347 (1903).
11. Comment, "Admissibility of Computer Business Records as an Exception to the Hearsay Rule," 48 N.C.L. Rev. 689 (1970).
12. Colin Tapper, "Evidence from Computers," 8 Ga. L. Rev. 591 (1974).
13. Ibid.
14. N.Y. Crim. Proc. Law 4518 (McKinney 1963).
15. 132 N.W.2d 871 (1965).
16. Neb. Rev. Stat., sec. 25-12, 109 (1964).
17. 9 A.U.L.A. 504, 506 (1965).
18. Ibid.
19. Colin Tapper, "Evidence from Computers," 8 Ga. L. Rev. 591 (1974).
20. 9 A.U.L.A. 598 (1965).
21. 16 S.W.2d 151 (1929).
22. 466 S.W.2d 381 (Ct. Civ. App. Tex. 1971).
23. Tex. Rev. Civ. Stat., art. 3737e (Supp. 1973).
24. Ibid.
25. Ibid.
26. 468 S.W.2d 125 (Ct. Civ. App. Tex. 1971).
27. Comment, "The Texas Business Records Act and Computer Printouts," 24 Baylor L. Rev. 165 (1972).
28. John J. Robinson, "The Admissibility of Computer Printouts under the Business Records Exception in Texas," 12 South Tex. L. Rev. 302 (1970).
29. See N.C. Gen. Stat., secs. 55-37.1, 55A-27.1 (Supp. 1973); and Del. Code Ann., tits. 8-9, sec. 224 (Supp. 1973).

30. National Conference of State Legislators, *The States Combat White Collar Crime,* (Washington, D.C.: National Conference of State Legislators, 1976), p. 13.

31. Del. Code Ann., tits. 10, sec. 4310 (Supp. 1970).

32. Roy Freed, "Providing by Statute for Inspection of Corporate Computer and Other Records Not Legible Visually—A Study on Legislating for Computer Technology," 23 Bus. Law 457 (1968).

33. Fla. Stat. Ann., tit. 7, ch. 92.36(2) (Supp. 1972).

12 Business Records Exception: Federal Level

In 1936 the federal government followed the example of the states and enacted the Act of June 20, 1936.[1] The act provides that:

> In any court of the United States and in any court established by Act of Congress, any writing, or record, whether in the form of an entry in a book or otherwise, made as a memorandum or record of any act, transaction, occurrence, or event, shall be admissible as evidence of such act, transaction, occurrence, or even if made in the regular course of business. . . .[2]

The statute continues the requirement that the entry be made in the regular course of business. However, the statute notes that the entry can be made in a book or "otherwise." Whether the latter could be interpreted to include computerized records remains to be settled.

Under the statute, *lack of personal knowledge* by the entrant or maker of the record may be shown to affect its weight but not its admissibility. The definition of *business* has been expanded to include any business, occupation, or calling.

The statute also provides that if an original document has been destroyed but has been reproduced either by any photographic, photostatic, or another process in the regular course of business, such reproduction, when satisfactorily identified,

> . . . is as admissible in evidence as the original itself in any judicial or administrative proceeding whether the original is in existence or not and an enlargement or facsimile of such reproduction is likewise admissible in evidence if the original reproduction is in existence and available for inspection under direction of court. The introduction of a reproduced record, enlargement, or facsimile does not preclude admission of the original.[3]

One could argue that a computer printout, like any copy of an original, should be able to come in through the statute.

For a record to be admissible under the Federal Business Records Act, it must meet the following test: (1) it must have been made in the regular course of business; (2) it must have been in the regular course of business to make such record; and (3) it must have been made at or near the time of transaction or event. The federal act, as was the case with the statutes, never had the admission of computer printouts as its objective. However, in the last few years, some courts have given the act a broader interpretation, which has facilitated computer-related litigation.

In the case of *United States* v. *Ahrens,* a federal court held that the Federal Business Records Act does not require that the maker of the record have personal knowledge of the act or event as a condition precedent for the admission of that record.[4] In *United States* v. *Scallion,* another federal court held that the fact that the maker of a record did not testify did not make that record inadmissible.[5] However, in *Palmer* v. *Hoffman,* an accident report prepared by an employee of a firm was held to be inadmissible by the U.S. Supreme Court because it was not prepared in the regular course of business.[6]

The preceding cases, and others that have dealt with the business records exception, have usually dealt with traditional forms of record keeping. The computer poses a new challenge. To respond to the needs of this new record-keeping technology, and in awareness of the limitations of the Federal Business Records Act, the federal system has adopted the New Rules of Evidence Act. The new rules attempt to handle the problem of computer printouts in federal litigation.

Rule 801 defines *hearsay* as any statement, other than one made by the declarant while testifying at the trial or hearing, offered in evidence to prove the truth of the matter asserted. The drafters of the new rules, like the scholars of the common law, sought to preserve the integrity and accuracy of business records by continuing to require: (1) that a witness, not necessarily the maker of the record himself, personally testify; (2) that he do so under oath; and (3) that he be opened to cross-examination by the opposing party. Rule 802 specifically bars hearsay statements from admissibility in a court.

The new rules, although admittedly a step forward, must not be viewed as some radical departure from the *Pierce* doctrine. On the contrary, the new rules have merely expanded that doctrine to meet the needs of computerized record keeping. They have not swept the old hearsay rule or its exceptions under the rug. The rule still lives on.

The hearsay exceptions under the new rules are not too dissimilar from those found under the common law or the state statutes. For example, rule 803 lists more than a dozen of these. The key exceptions are the following:

"Excited utterances"—statements, relating to a startling event or condition, made while the declarant is under stress

"Recorded recollections"—memoranda or records concerning a matter about which a witness once had knowledge

"Records of regularly conducted activities"—records of acts, events, conditions, opinions, or diagnoses, made at or near the time by, or from information transmitted by, a person with knowledge, all in the course of regularly conducted activity, unless the sources of information or other circumstances indicate lack of trustworthiness

"Public records and reports"—these include any reports, statements, or data compilation, in any form, of public offices or agencies

"Records of vital statistics"—these include records of births, deaths, or marriages, in any form, if made to a public office; and also "judgements of previous convictions."

Rule 804 goes on to include the former testimony of a party, as well as statements of personal or family history. A computer printout could possibly come under one of these listed exceptions in rules 803 and 804 to the hearsay rule.

The new rules also provide for the identification and authentication of records as a condition precedent to their admission in evidence. Rule 901 provides that the requirement will be met if evidence is given that describes the process or system employed to produce the records, and there must also be a showing that the process or system produces an accurate result. Thus, if through the use of witnesses familiar with the process, the moving party can show that the computerized records were a product of this process, and can further demonstrate that the process was not open to error or fraud, the printouts could possibly come in. The opposing party should move to challenge the authenticity and reliability of the process.

The new rules also include electronic recording devices within their realm. Rule 1001(1) defines a *writing* as:

... letters, words, or numbers, or their equivalent, set down by handwriting, typewriting, printing, photostating, photographing, magnetic impulse, mechanical or electronic recording, or other data compilation.

Printouts could easily qualify under this broad definition of what constitutes *writing*. The new rules go even farther than any other statute or rule within this country. Rule 1001(3) specifically addresses itself to computer printouts, and notes that:

... data ... stored in a computer or similar device, any printout or other output readable by sight, shown to reflect the data accurately, is an "original."

The new rules, however, retain the common-law requirements that the writing be accurate and authentic. However, if a moving party can demonstrate that the process was not error prone or fraudulent, it will be allowed to introduce a printout in evidence just as if it were a written document.

Although much has been said about the new rules, they have not done away with the hearsay rule. Further, the new rules continue to require that the data be compiled in the regular course of business, and that they be entered on or about the time of the event. In computerized transactions this is not always possible.

The printout may, in fact, not be the product of a regular course of business. Entries are not always made contemporaneously to the event recorded.

The new rules also require that the record must be produced by individuals with knowledge of the information that is recorded. Although the drafters were certainly aware of the problems associated with computer-generated data, and had hoped to resolve some of these issues, they neglected to consider information that may have been transmitted from one or more computers by wire to another computer, totally eliminating the role of the individual. As computer systems and their employment grow, the role of the individual will increasingly diminish. The drafters of the new rules probably anticipated these problems. However, the new rules, as presently drawn, unless further broadened by court decisions, may in fact be unable to handle the many problems associated with litigation in an advanced computer system.

At present, there exist more than a dozen exceptions to the hearsay rule. Various state statutes, including the common-law shop-book rule, continue to define the business records exception in traditional terms. However, the rapid advances in technology, especially in the computer record-keeping area, have made it increasingly difficult for our legal system to adjust with sufficient speed. Some scholars have suggested relaxing the hearsay rule even further than the new rules, while others have noted that the hearsay rule should be abolished as an anachronism of an old era, that the only criteria in judging the admissibility of business records and other evidence should be reliability and accuracy. The majority of jurists, however, oppose any such radical change. Technology poses a challenge, and not a choice. The computer, either for good or bad, is here to stay. The vast economic powers and resources behind it make it an impossibility to dismiss as a passing matter. At stake is not only the hearsay rule, but the very ability of our rules of evidence to survive this new challenge. The new rules are a beginning.

References

1. 28 U.S.C., sec. 1732 (1970), initially enacted as the Act of June 20, 1936, ch. 640, sec. 1, 49 Stat. 1561.
2. 28 U.S.C., sec. 1732(a).
3. Ibid., sec. 1732(a).
4. 530 F.2d 781 (1976).
5. 533 F.2d 903 (1976).
6. 318 U.S. 109 (1943).

13 Best Evidence Rule Problems

In the interest of justice, courts, as a matter of policy, require that where a party has a choice of proving his case by several types of evidence he do so by presenting the strongest (best) evidence, and not secondary (a copy of the original) evidence. This rule, known as the *best evidence rule,* requires that the contents of an available document be proved by the introduction of the original document itself. Under the rule, to prove the content of a writing, recording, or photograph, the original writing, recording, or photograph is required. The problem in computer-related litigation is that the printout, which is considered a copy of the original, although admissible under one of the hearsay exceptions, may be barred by this rule. It should be pointed out, however, that this rule, as with the other rules of evidence, must be raised by a timely and specific objection in order for it to bar the admission of a copy in evidence. Otherwise, the adverse party waives its right to object, and the secondary evidence will be admissible.

The rule took roots during the evolution of the common law. There are differences as to when in fact it became part of English law. At least one early eighteenth century English case, *Ford* v. *Hopkins,* has held that the best evidence is required in a trial.[1] However, although there are differing views as to when the rule took hold, there is agreement that the rule is not rigid nor sacrosanct. There are exceptions to it.

The rule, in general, is applied where the contents of a document are in dispute. The document itself must be produced. However, the rule has no application in cases where the fact sought to be proven has an existence independent of any writing. The moving party, in such a case, may prove the fact in dispute by oral testimony, even though the fact may have been reduced to writing. Furthermore, the rule generally applies to private writings. Properly authenticated public documents may be used in lieu of the original. The rule will not bar their admission.

The rule will not apply where secondary evidence is not offered to prove the contents of an original writing.[2] For example, if X denies having entered into a written agreement with Y, the latter may introduce secondary evidence as to the contents of the agreement without producing the original writing. The issue is not the contents itself, but rather whether X and Y had entered into an agreement. Applying the analogy to a printout, if the latter is introduced as evidence of an event rather than as evidence of the contents itself, it could come in under this exception. The printout could also come in if it were an authenticated public document.

138

There are also several justifications for circumventing the rule. For example, where the original writing has been lost or destroyed without the fault of the moving party, it will not be barred by the rule. However, if the opposing party can demonstrate to the court that the original writing was destroyed in bad faith, the rule will apply. In addition, if the moving party claims that the original document is lost, it must usually demonstrate that a diligent search was made to locate it. In cases involving printouts, the moving party could easily argue that the original writing was either lost or destroyed. If he can demonstrate that it was not done in bad faith, the printout should be admissible.

If the moving party can demonstrate that the writing is in the possession of a third party who is presently outside the court's jurisdiction, the rule will not apply. However, the moving party must demonstrate to the court that it has attempted to obtain the original document but has failed to do so because the third party is outside the subpoena power of the court. A printout could thus come in this way if the original writing is beyond the court's jurisdiction and the moving party has made sincere attempts to obtain it.

Where the writing is in the possession or control of the adverse party to the litigation, and the latter fails to produce it upon reasonable and advance notice, the secondary evidence will be held admissible. However, the moving party must demonstrate that the adverse party was put on notice, by the pleadings or otherwise, that the contents of the original writing would be the subject of proof at the trial. The adverse party's failure to produce the original writing thus waives the rule. Where the original documents are in the possession of an adverse party to the litigation, and the latter fails to produce them even after having been put on notice, the printout might be admissible as secondary evidence.

Where the original writings, recordings, or photographs are so voluminous that it would be impractical to produce them in court, the Judge, on motion, may hold the rule as being inapplicable. It would be not only inconvenient but also impractical to introduce voluminous documents in a trial. In its place, the court might allow a summary of the material. However, it must be shown that the material was summarized by a competent individual, and that the originals are and have been made available to the adverse party to examine or copy at a reasonable time and location. For example, in a 1965 Nebraska case, *Transportation Company* v. *Seib,* the court allowed a summary, in the form of a printout, of a voluminous exhibit.[3] The director for accounting, under whose direction the material has been prepared, testified.[4] The defendant in this case had ample time to examine the documents and copy the material had he so chosen. The defense was not taken by surprise. Other cases have allowed accountants to testify as to summaries they have prepared for trial.[5]

However, more than 30 states have enacted special legislation to deal with the problem of the rule. The statute, called the Uniform Photographic Copies of Business and Public Records Act, provides as follows:

If any business, institution, member of a profession or calling, or any department or agency of government, in the regular course of business or activity has
kept or recorded any memorandum, writing, entry, print, representation or
combination thereof, of any act, transaction, occurence or event, and in the
regular course of business has caused any or all of the same to be recorded,
copied, or reproduced by any photographic, photostatic, microfilm, microcard, . . . or other process which accurately produces or forms a durable medium
for so reproducing the original, the original may be destroyed in the regular
course of business . . . unless its preservation is required by law. Such reproduction, when satisfactorily identified, is as admissible in evidence as proceedings. . . .

The act provides for the admissibility of a copy of an original writing made by
"any process," provided it was made during the regular course of business. The
act would probably allow a computer printout in evidence as an exception to the
rule. In 1969 a Mississippi court, in the case of *King* v. *State ex. rel. Murdoch
Acceptance Company,* allowed a printout in evidence in spite of the rule.[6] A
Nebraska court in the *Seib* case had done the same several years before.
However, Mississippi had not adopted the act at the time. Nebraska had, and its
move could be interpreted as applying the act to computer printouts. The
Mississippi court, in the *King* case did, however, note that:

Records stored in magnetic tape by data processing machines are unavailable and
useless except by means of the printout sheets such as those admitted into
evidence in this case. In admitting the printout sheets . . . we are not departing
from the shop-book-rule, but only extending its application to electronic
recordkeeping.[7]

The *King* and *Seib* cases represent a minority trend toward allowing
printouts in as exceptions to the rule. The act, however, specifies that the copy
of the original record must be made during the regular course of business. The
Seib court found no problem with this requirement in waiving the rule. Other
courts, however, may. Although the trend appears to be in the direction of
allowing printouts in as exceptions to the rule, the majority of state courts have
yet to decide in this area.

The act has its federal counterpart.[8] The federal statute allows copies made
in the regular course of business to be employed in place of the original in
evidence. However, the copy must be properly identified. It makes no difference
if the original is in existence or has been destroyed. The federal statute applies to
both the private and governmental sector. It includes copies made by any
photographic, photostatic, microfilm, microcard, or other process. It could
easily be argued that it also encompasses printouts. There are a small, but
growing, number of federal cases that have allowed printouts in evidence.

However, at the federal level, other developments have also taken hold and
will probably further facilitate the introduction of printouts in evidence in

140

federal cases. The new developments are the New Federal Rules of Evidence. The rules go further than any other existing statutes in liberalizing the admission of secondary evidence. Although rule 1002 still retains the requirement that an "original writing" must be produced, rule 1001, for example, defines a *writing* as consisting of:

... letters, words, or numbers or their equivalent, set down by handwriting, typewriting, printing, photostating, photographing, magnetic impulse, mechanical or electronic recording, or other form of data compilation.

Rule 1001 goes on to note that an original writing included data stored in a computer or similar device, and a *printout* is defined as being an "original document." It was the intent of the drafters to include a printout within the definition of an *original writing.*[9]

Rule 1001 makes it abundantly clear that if a proper foundation is laid to show that the printout was made within an accurate and reliable system, it will be admitted as an original writing. The adverse party bears the responsibility of showing that in fact the process is neither accurate nor reliable. If the proper foundation is laid by the proponent of the printout, then there should be no problem with admitting it in evidence. The rule, however, applies only to federal cases.

Rule 1004 provides that an original is not needed where it has been lost or destroyed, where it is not obtainable, or where it is in the possession of an opponent. Rule 1003 provides that a copy will be admissible unless it can be shown: (1) that there is a genuine question raised as to the authenticity of the original, and (2) that it would be unfair in certain circumstances to admit the duplicate in lieu of the original. Even if the admission of a printout under rule 1001 is defeated by the adverse party, there is a possibility of bringing it in under either rules 1003 or 1004.

The best evidence rule, in the past, has posed a problem for the admission of copies of an original writing in evidence. The courts and legislatures have relaxed their criteria. There is presently a trend toward admitting printouts at both the state and federal levels. With the growth of computer-related litigation, the best evidence rule may have to be relaxed even more to allow for expedient litigation. The present trend appears to be to bring the rule in harmony with the needs of the computer age. The rule, in the near future, should pose few difficulties for litigants who seek to have printouts admitted in evidence.

References

1. 1 Sald 283, 91 Eng. Rep. 250.
2. *Chicago C.R. Company* v. *Carroll,* 68 N.E. 1087 (1903).
3. 178 Neb, 253, 132 N.W.2d 871 (1965).

4. Ibid.

5. *Stephens* v. *United States*, 41 F.2d 440 (1930), cert. den. 282 U.S. 880.

6. 222 So.2d 393 (1969).

7. Ibid., p. 398.

8. 28 U.S.C., sec. 1732(b).

9. Paul F. Rothstein, *Understanding the New Federal Rules of Evidence,* (New York: Law Journal Press, 1973), pp. 149-150.

14

Computer Litigation: State Level

To date, computer litigation has involved only a few cases, and these have dealt solely with printouts. There have been no complex cases, no sophisticated litigation, and no trials involving the sophisticated frauds, such as in the Equity Funding case. However, trends have appeared: some courts have shown a willingness to accept this new technology; others still cling to a conservative position.

In 1965 the now landmark computer case of *Transportation Company* v. *Seib* was litigated in the state of Nebraska.[1] The *Seib* case involved an action for insurance premiums. The defendant was a company that operated a fleet of trucks in several states. The plaintiff was an insurance firm. The defendant had an insurance policy with the plaintiff, which covered bodily injury, property damage, and cargo liability. To establish the amount of premium due, the plaintiff offered a computerized record at the trial. The printout of this record was prepared at the plaintiff's Los Angeles office.

The printout had been prepared under the direction of the company's chief accountant. This individual had personal knowledge of the computations involved and was presented as a witness at the trial. On direct examination, he testified as follows:

[*Question:*] ... was Exhibit 14 [the printout] computed, say by an I.B.M. or other tabulating machine?

[*Answer:*] Those calculations are prepared by machine, yes. They are all electric computers. We have our formulas set out, first, as to the type of policy this is. There are different plans of insurance which you can pursue ... so you have to have a formula in order to feed this particular information into the machine, and each time you have a case, we feed that formula into the machine, and the machine does the calculating work.... It just does what used to be done by keeping books.[2]

The plaintiff's witness also explained how the record keeping was carried out. He informed the court that the information as to losses was fed into the computer, which in turn recorded them and stored them in a tape. Each accident was recorded by date, the name of the driver involved, the type of accident, the amount and type of loss, and other information from which the premium could be computed. The record was made in the regular course of business. A cumulative record was sent quarterly to the defendant.

The information, the witness added, was stored on a tape; the computer

143

could retrieve it at any time, and in a printout note a record of all losses, their dates, and the premiums paid and due. The chief accountant also gave a detailed explanation of each phase of the operation. He told the court that the record and computations were kept in the usual everyday business of the plaintiff and not specifically prepared for litigation, and that the record was also kept separate.

Plaintiff's witness also noted that the Nebraska statute, Section 25-12, 109. R.R.S. 1943, specifically provided that a record:

... of an act, condition or event, shall ... be competent evidence if the custodian or other qualified witness testifies to its identity and the mode of its preparation, and if it was made in the regular course of business or near the time of the act, condition or event, and if, in the opinion of the court, the sources of information, method and time of preparation were such as to justify its admission.[3]

The Nebraska statute provides three key elements: (1) the record is broadly defined to include not only an act, but also a condition; (2) the personal knowledge requirement is relaxed, and any qualified witness can testify as to its identity and mode of preparation; and (3) the court is given broad discretion to decide if the record meets the test of reliability and accuracy. However, the statute, as is the case with most state business record statutes, still retains two crucial requirements that make the admission of computer records difficult. The record must have been made: (1) in the regular course of business, and (2) at or near the time of the act, event, or condition.

In concluding that it was not error to allow the printout into evidence, the court stated that past Nebraska cases had held: "The purpose of the act [the statute] is to permit the admission of systematically entered records without the necessity of identifying, locating, and producing as witnesses the individuals who made entries in the record in the regular course of business. . . ."[4] The court noted that in this case, the plaintiff had established the requisite foundation required by the statute; as a result, it was not necessary for plaintiff to produce and identify the witnesses who originally supplied the information that was recorded on the computer's tapes. It should be noted that the court's holding was fortunate for the plaintiff, because it would have been physically impossible to produce all the employees who had personal knowledge.

The court was also satisfied with the detailed explanation and information supplied by the plaintiff's witness. Citing another court, it noted that the expert witness had: ". . . testified to a well-established business procedure not only in the trade, but specifically in the very company which had prepared the document. . . . The hallmarks of authenticity surround this document, since it was made pursuant to established company procedures. . . ."[5] The court wanted to interpret the statute broadly and in light of the new developments in the world of business. It recognized the advent of the computer as a tool for book-keeping purposes, and was satisfied with the "sources of information, method, and time of preparation" of the printout.

The court also noted that original sources for the preparation of the printout had come from the defendant himself. The defendant did not question the substance or the authenticity of the record. However, the defendant did raise the argument that the printout had been prepared for litigation. But the court, acknowledging that this was so, indicated that, nevertheless, the taped record itself was made in the usual course of business and for the purpose of the business alone. Thus the defendant's objection was without merit.

The Nebraska court gave the statute a broad interpretation. Further, the defendant's objection had not centered so much on the authenticity, accuracy, and reliability of the process as on the fact that the record was produced specifically for litigation. The testimony of the plaintiff's witness, the broad interpretation other state courts had given the statute, and the defendant's failure to raise doubts as to the accuracy of the printout all led the court to allow the record into evidence. The court also acknowledged that a strict interpretation would probably have meant also barring the original documents if an attempt had been made to introduce those into evidence.[6] Ultimately, a broader approach was adopted.

In 1968 two key cases came before the Arizona Court of Appeals. These would play a major role in establishing a small but growing trend among states regarding computer printouts. In *Merrick* v. *United States Rubber Company* the defendant appealed from a lower court decision that had been favorable to the plaintiff, United States Rubber Company.[7]

In 1961 defendant Merrick had formed a firm with another individual, under the name of City Tire Company. The plaintiff furnished the company with merchandise on consignment and with an open account; these two accounts were handled separately. Periodically, there was an inventory of consigned goods and City Tire was billed. In 1963 City Tire developed financial difficulties. The company then assigned, through one of its partners (not defendant Merrick), the accounts receivable to the plaintiff. The assignment instrument was on plaintiff's printed form.

Plaintiff soon afterward sued the two partners. The complaint prayed for a judgment of $20,978.18 and was accompanied by an itemized statement. The verification was by an employee of the plaintiff. A pretrial conference was later held, followed by a pretrial order. At the conference, all the exhibits that were to be used at the trial were marked in evidence.[8] Exhibit I of plaintiff's exhibits consisted of eight multipage documents in support of the itemized account attached to the complaint. These were computer printouts from plaintiff's IBM accounting equipment.

To support the admission of its computer printouts, the plaintiff called as a witness one of its employees who worked in the credit department. The witness testified that he himself had no personal knowledge of the physical operation of the plaintiff's IBM computer equipment. The latter was located in the firm's home office in Los Angeles. The witness did testify, however, that he was generally familiar with the plaintiff's accounting records. The defendant charged that a proper foundation had not been laid. The plaintiff answered that it had met the requirements of the Arizona business records rule.[9] The defendant, however, raised no objection to the use of copies of the original records, the best evidence rule objection.

The Arizona statute provides, in part, the following:

Any record of an act, condition or event, shall, insofar as relevant, be competent evidence if the custodian or other qualified witness testifies to its identity and the mode of its preparation. . . .[10]

However, the record must have been made: (1) in the regular course of business, and (2) at or near the time of the act, condition, or event. Further, if in the opinion of the court, the "sources of information, method and time of preparation were such as to justify its admission," the court could allow it into evidence.[11] The statute, however, retains the requirements of certainty, accuracy, and reliability.

The court cited an old Arizona case in support of the proposition that trial courts have "great discretion" concerning the admission of records kept in the course of business.[12] The court also cited the Nebraska decision in *Seib*. It compared that case with the case before it, and said:

. . . a more meticulous foundation was laid in the Nebraska case than was laid in the case now under consideration in the matter of the testimony of a person immediately in charge of the record-making equipment.[13]

Nevertheless, the court deemed the foundation laid in the case before it adequate. Further, the defendant had offered no evidence to challenge the substance of the records, nor evidence to challenge their accuracy.

The court further noted that, in fact, the defendant himself had acknowledged occurrence of the transactions, although he had no recollection as to their dates. Thus the case, when viewed in its entirety, addressed primarily the issues of the accuracy and reliability of the records themselves. The court refused to bar their admission into evidence solely upon a narrow construction of the business records rule. The court, in support of its conclusion, cited *Seib*, and outlined its reasoning as follows:

The Arizona statute was intended to bring the realities of business and professional practice into the courtroom and the statute should not be interpreted narrowly to destroy its obvious usefulness.[14]

The court was swayed by the needs of a modern business environment; and in weighing those needs against the possibility of computer error, it found that the substance of the records was never challenged and, like the *Seib* court, drew a broad interpretation of the statute. The *Seib* court was sufficiently honest to openly admit that printouts, under a more strict application of the hearsay rule, "would probably be inadmissible."[15]

That same year, in *State* v. *Veres,* the Arizona Court of Appeals addressed, for the second time, the problem of computer printouts in litigation.[16] This involved a criminal case. In December 1962 the defendant entered into a lease arrangement for a trailer and made his deposit by check. Several days later he entered into another leasing agreement with the same company. He made this second deposit by check also. The checks, when presented to the bank by the lessor, were not honored due to insufficient funds. The vehicles themselves were never returned. On January 30, 1963, the defendant was charged with one count of grand theft (embezzlement) of a trailer and one count of grand theft (embezzlement) of a truck-tractor.

Soon afterward, he was charged with two more counts, relating to the two checks. All counts were alleged to be felonies, and defendant entered pleas of not guilty. The two criminal cases were consolidated for purposes of trial. As regards both grand theft charges, the jury returned two verdicts of not guilty. However, on the two counts relating to the checks, he was found guilty and placed on probation.[17]

The facts showed that the defendant and his wife maintained a joint checking account at the bank on which the two checks were drawn. These checks were in the sum of $35.00 and $65.00, respectively. Over the objections of defendant, the bank records were introduced into evidence in court. The records consisted of four separate sheets that were received as a single exhibit. Various overdrafts were disclosed that extended over a period of months. An official of the bank, testifying during the introduction of the records, identified the more than 40 entries. These clearly indicated that there were insufficient funds in the checking account.[18]

The defendant had objected to the use of these computerized bank records in his prosecution. A bank official, who identified himself as an assistant cashier in charge of operations and procedures, had testified during the trial. The witness identified the records as being those of the defendant. He testified that he had not prepared the records, but that they had been prepared by an "automatic machine" (computer). He also noted that he was not familiar with the workings of the computer, but that another employee at the bank was in charge of that operation. Further, he stated that his own knowledge was based on "his access" to the records. The witness also indicated that the checks and deposits were "encoded by machine."

The prosecution, in introducing the records into evidence, relied on the Arizona business records rule,[19] which declares, in part, that any record of an act, condition, or event shall be competent evidence if the custodian or other qualified witness testifies.[20] The statute will admit a record: (1) if it was made in the regular course of business, (2) if it was made at or near the time of the act, condition, or event, and (3) if, in the opinion of the court, it justifies admission. A *business* is defined by the statute as any kind of business, profession, occupation, calling, or operation of institutions, whether or not carried on for profit.

The court also noted that not every entry in a business record is automatically admissible. It added, however, that courts have wide discretion, as provided in the statute. The defendant's testimony, the court held, indicated that he knew his bank account "was not in good condition." The trial judge was not impressed by the defendant's arguments.

Veres gave Arizona courts great latitude under the business records rule, regarding the admission into evidence of computerized business records. Although the defendant argued that his bank records were not in good condition, he did not challenge the accuracy of the computer record-keeping process. The defendant did not object to the reliability of the records, but rather to their admissibility under the states statute. The defense made no challenges to the lack of timely entry of these records, nor to the lack of personal knowledge of the witness. The defendant, in turn, did not offer his own expert testimony to challenge the accuracy and reliability of the computer process. Neither did the defense challenge the qualifications of the witness offered by the prosecution. The court's decision to allow the records in evidence was in large part due to the defense's lack of challenges to the reliability and accuracy of the computer records. The court also held that a liberal interpretation of the statute was necessary to meet the needs of the business community.

In 1969 a Mississippi court faced the problem of admitting computer printouts in evidence. What made this case, *King* v. *State ex rel. Murdoch Acceptance Corp.,* unique was that it involved a common-law jurisdiction that still adhered to the old shop-book rule.[21] The case involved an appeal from a decree of the Chancery Court of Alcorn County, and the question centered on whether the old rule could accommodate the new technology.

Appellee Murdoch was a finance company engaged in the financing of automobiles and mobile homes through the purchase of conditional sales contracts. One of the dealers financed by Murdoch was Serl Anderson, who operated a large distribution center and sold mobile homes. One of Anderson's agents was John H. Putt of Corinth, Mississippi. Murdoch purchased six conditional sales contracts from Anderson, two of which had been cosigned by Putt. Anderson later went bankrupt, and Murdoch summoned Putt as a witness at the creditors meeting. Murdoch also contended that Putt was liable to it for about $16,000. Putt, however, had made a settlement offer of $11,000 to Murdoch. Putt agreed to hand over to Murdoch a note signed by his wife and parents and secured by a deed of trust on the property of his parents. Murdoch agreed to the settlement. The note and deed of trust were delivered by Putt and had purportedly been signed by Putt's family.

Putt eventually defaulted on this obligation, and Murdoch filed suit. Putt's family also filed suit to enjoin the sale of the property because they had not signed the note and deed of trust. These last two bore the notarial certificate of one Hershel King. Thereafter, suit was also brought against King, the notary public. King lost, and judgment was entered against him. He then appealed this decision.

Among the many arguments raised by King in his appeal, was one touching on the admissibility of Murdoch's business records. These were computer records, and printouts of the records had been offered into evidence at the lower court. At the trial, in order for Murdoch to prove the amount of damages, it was also necessary to prove the amounts paid on the note. Murdoch introduced printouts to prove the balances due on some of the conditional contracts. The printouts contained a complete record of each account.

At the trial level, the assistant treasurer for Murdoch, who was also in charge of the data processing department, gave extensive testimony on the subject. He testified that the material had been prepared under his supervision and that the computer used was a Burroughs B-280. The witness testified that the machine was recognized as efficient and accurate. All the records were maintained on magnetic tape. He testified that the information was fed into the computer by an efficient and competent staff of operators. The essential information was keypunched on a card, which was then verified by another operator. If the card was not punched correctly, the verifying machine would not allow it to go through. Correct cards would then be fed into the computer, and the information would be stored on magnetic tape. This was how Murdoch kept a permanent record of its customer accounts.

In addition, the witness testified, records were kept of each payment, and the branch offices recorded all payments made. These records were then sent to the home office for verification and were afterward fed into the computer. The paper records were microfilmed, and the originals were destroyed. The information the home office received was fed daily, the witness further testified, into the computer in the regular course of business.

King, however, argued that the computer printouts did not meet the test set out by the shop-book rule. Mississippi, he argued, was a common-law jurisdiction, and the old rule still applied. The printouts, he argued, were not original documents and not within the rule. The Appeals Court acknowledged that if the records had not been computerized, there would have been no problem as to their admissibility. The question, however, to be resolved was whether Mississippi would grant computer printouts the same recognition. The Appeals Court also noted that many jurisdictions had adopted the Uniform Business Records as Evidence Act. Mississippi, though, had evolved its own common-law rule on a case-by-case development. However, the law must keep abreast of the needs of society.

The court cited some of its own past cases to illustrate its awareness of the needs of the new business era. The court also cited the *Seib* case, noting that a number of experts had declared that:

> [The] scientific reliability of such machines [electric computing equipment], in the light of their general use and the general reliance of the business world on them, can scarcely be questioned.[22]

Records stored on magnetic tapes are unavailable and useless except by means of a printout. In admitting these, the court noted, it was actually following rather than departing from the old common-law rule. It was only extending its application to electronic record keeping.

In sum, the Appeals Court held that printouts are admissible in evidence if they are: (1) relevant, and (2) material. There would be no need to identify, locate, and produce as a witness the employee who made the original entries if it could be shown that: (1) the electronic equipment is recognized as standard equipment; (2) the entries are made in the regular course of business, at or near the time of the happening of the event recorded; and (3) the foundation testimony satisfies the court that the sources of information, method, and time of preparation were such as to indicate its trustworthiness and justify its admission.[23]

The court had given the common-law rule a liberal interpretation. Murdoch produced a witness who in fact testified as to the reliability of the computer—that the Burroughs B-280 computer enjoyed a good reputation in the industry. The witness also testified that the entries were made in the regular course of business, at or near the time of the event. The court was satisfied with Murdoch's foundation testimony, and also with the sources and method of preparation of the printouts.

Further, King put forth no expert witness of his own to challenge the accuracy and reliability of Murdoch's computer system. King also did not raise questions regarding the computer entries themselves: whether they were made at or near the time of the event. If King had taken an aggressive posture and presented his own experts, he might have been able to raise serious questions about the operation of the system. That he did not further reinforced the court's determination that computers are reliable and, although admittedly different from other traditional modes of record keeping, play an essential part in the present-day business world. The Appeals Court attempted to bring the common law into modernity, aware of the role computers play. For this it cannot be faulted, but the defense failed to raise serious questions that could have easily been raised.

Two years later, the *Southern Pacific Transportation Co.* case was litigated in Texas.[24] The Southern Pacific Transportation Company (Company) had applied to the Texas Railroad Commission (Commission) for authority to discontinue its railroad agency in one of the small towns in Texas. The

Commission denied its request and the Company filed suit in a local court. The trial judge held for the Company. The Commission appealed his decision and raised several points of error. One of these errors dealt with "seven exhibits" the court allowed the Company to introduce in evidence. The Commission claimed that these exhibits were hearsay.

The evidence in question covered operations of the Company for a period of two years. They included summaries of revenues and expenses, summaries of train stops and shipments. The exhibits were introduced through a witness who had worked for the Company for more than 20 years, the last 12 years having been spent in the production of cost analyses.

The bulk of the evidence comprised volumes of computer printouts. The witness testified as to the manner of making the records. The Texas court noted that business records are admissible in evidence, if the proponent shows the following:

(a) that the record was made in the regular course of business;
(b) that it was the regular course of that business for an employee or representative of such business with personal knowledge of such act, event or condition to make such memorandum; and
(c) that it was made at or near the time of the act, event or condition or reasonably soon thereafter.[25]

In referring to the state's business records statute, the court noted that the witness called by the Company did not qualify as the custodian of the records, nor was he offered as an employee having sufficient knowledge of the records to prove their accuracy. The Company did not offer any testimony from any witness who had been in charge of its computer system or under whose direction the material had been prepared. The Company offered no testimony as to the type of computer it employed, the nature of the record storage, or the manner in which daily information was fed into the computer.

The court held that the Company had failed to meet the test of the Texas statute. Electronically maintained business records have become increasingly prevalent, noted the court, but the underlying criteria remain unchanged: they must be proven accurate. There should be proof that: (1) the computing equipment being used is recognized as standard equipment; (2) the records were made in the regular course of business; (3) the records were based on information within the personal knowledge of an individual whose duties included the collection of such information; and (4) the records were prepared by individuals who understood the operation of the system and whose regular duty it was to operate the equipment.

The Company's witness held a supervisory position and was a statistician by training. He had engaged in many reviews and had analyzed the firm's revenues for a number of years. However, the court noted, hearsay is not waived merely because a witness testifies on facts about which he has no personal knowledge.

He was not a custodian of records, nor did he understand the workings of the system. The Company had not met the statute's test, and the printouts were inadmissible.

That same year, Texas courts heard a second case concerning the computer—*Arnold D. Kamen & Co.* v. *Young.*[26] This case involved an action against Arnold D. Kamen, brought by Young, who sought to recover commissions allegedly due for his services as a broker with the company's commodity brokerage offices in Dallas. The company, however, maintained that Young had incurred deficits, that these were deducted from his commissions, and that he was thus not entitled to any payment. The trial court entered a judgment for Young, and the company (Arnold D. Kamen) appealed the case.

Among the 11 points of error cited by the company, point 8 dealt with the admission into evidence of the defendant's Exhibit 9, which was actually a computer printout of various financial statements. It consisted of 8 pages of data, and the company had contended that it should be admitted under the Texas business records statute. A witness for the company testified that the information contained in the records had been punched on keypunch cards by employees of the firm's Chicago office. The cards had then been taken to a tabulating service, which had run them through a computer and then had returned the data to the company in the form of a printout, (similar to Exhibit 9). Young objected to the admission of these records on the grounds that they did not comply with the state's statute. Young also argued that the company had not laid a proper foundation by simply offering evidence that the original data had been prepared by someone who had personal knowledge of the act or event to be recorded.

The Texas Court of Appeals concurred with the lower court's ruling that the individual who prepared the computer cards or other data should also have had personal knowledge of the information punched onto those cards. The company's witness, however, merely testified that the computer cards had been prepared by an employee of the firm's Chicago office. He did not testify as to whether he had personal knowledge. The company had failed to meet the statute's test, and thus the lower court had properly rejected the admission of Exhibit 9. If the company had produced a witness who did have personal knowledge and had met the other tests summarized in the Texas statute, a different result might have been reached.

In 1972 the courts of Illinois confronted their first criminal case involving computer printouts. The case of *People* v. *Gauer* presented the court with the question of whether a proper foundation had been laid for the admission of computerized telephone records.[27]

The defendant was an employee of the Illinois Bell Telephone Company. In 1970 the company was faced with a strike. The defendant and other company employees went on strike, although other employees refused to strike. The defendant made telephone calls to two of the nonstriking employees, but no words were spoken. After several calls, the complaining witnesses requested that a trace be put on their telephone lines. Eventually the calls were traced to the defendant, who, in turn, was charged with disorderly conduct.

The state relied on the company's records to substantiate the charges. A company employee was called as a witness, and he testified that his duties concerned the maintenance of the firm's records, and that in this capacity he had responsibility for supervision and control over these records. Among the records brought into court were two sets of punched IBM Trouble Recorder Cards. These company business records were made in the regular course of business, at or about the time and dates reflected thereon.

The witness testified that the company's records were reliable, and that the firm placed "a lot of faith" in them.[28] The trial court admitted the records into evidence. The defendant later appealed the admission. A State Court of Appeals noted that, in light of the large use of computers in the business world, the "scientific reliability of such machines can scarcely be questioned."[29] The court also referred to the *Seib* and *King* cases. In those cases, the method and preparation of the computer records was fully explained by experts in court. The *King* court also stated that a trial court must be satisfied from the foundation testimony that the sources of information, method, and time of preparation indicate trustworthiness before it could admit computer printouts. That state's Court of Appeals concurred with the lower court's decision.

However, in the *Gauer* case competent testimony was lacking, and consequently, an adequate foundation had not been laid. The State's Court of Appeals reversed and remanded the case for a new trial because the state had failed to produce the foundation testimony necessary to prove the accuracy and reliability of the material. The defense, however, made no attempts to demonstrate the ease with which computers have been victimized by criminals. In addition, the defense also erred by not making use of its own experts to attack the reliability of computer data and to demonstrate to the lower court that the prosecution had failed to meet the test of the state's statute.

The following year, the Supreme Court of Wyoming faced a somewhat different problem in the case of *Harned* v. *Credit Bureau of Gillette*.[30] The plaintiff sued the defendants for an alleged balance due, and recovered a judgment at the local district court; the defendants then appealed.

The defendants had been customers of the Petrolane-Wyoming Gas Service Company. The plaintiff alleged that the defendants had not paid for all the gas delivered and services rendered for the period of 1967 through 1970. Defendants maintained that, in fact, they had made the payments. In support of this claim they introduced 23 cancelled checks made out to the company.

When the company delivered gas to a customer, the truck driver completed an invoice that showed the number of gallons delivered and was made in quadruplicate. One copy of each went to the company's Wyoming office, to its California office, to the customer at delivery, and to the same customer during billing periods. Upon receiving the invoice, the California office fed it into the firm's computer, and it then appeared in a printout. The computer printout was mailed monthly to the firm's Wyoming office and at that point became a permanent record of that office.

The firm had the manager of its Wyoming office testify at the district court trial. She testified that she was in charge of all the firm's bookkeeping in Wyoming and that she had prepared the plaintiff's exhibit, which was a recapitulation of the printouts received from the California office. Defendants raised the defense of the best evidence rule, which requires that the original or primary evidence of an obligation be produced and no evidence that is secondary or substitutionary shall be received if the original evidence can be had.

The plaintiff's witness also testified that the original invoices were available. However, no attempt was made to produce them, nor was their nonproduction explained to the court. Further, the plaintiff's witness began to work for the firm one year after the controversy in this suit erupted and was therefore not familiar with the company's policy as to past billing procedures. Although the firm's exhibit showed the service charges, it did not show the basis for these charges. The plaintiff, of necessity, argued that the records were admissible under the state's business records statute.

The Wyoming Supreme Court, however, reversed and remanded the case for a new trial. It did not accept the company's argument that the records came under the state's business records statute. The records, it noted, were "not made in the 'regular course of business at or near the time of the . . . event.' "[31] The Wyoming statute itself provided that the:

. . . record of an act, condition or event, shall . . . be competent evidence if the custodian or other qualified witness testifies to its identity and the mode of its preparation . . . and if, in the opinion of the court, the sources of information, method and time of preparation were such as to justify its admission.[32]

It was apparent to the judges that the company did not provide a qualified witness to testify at the district court trial; the company's witness had no knowledge as to the identity or mode of preparation of the record. The court also added:

It is a frightening prospect to think that a person could be sued for services rendered and have the plaintiff base its claim solely upon a recapitulation of computer printout sheets.[33]

The court expressed the general concern of many other courts—computer records are not always correct and are vulnerable to error and manipulation.

In 1973 the Supreme Court of Missouri, in the case of the *Union Electric Company* v. *Mansion House Center North Redevelopment Co.,* addressed the legal issue of computer printouts.[34] The plaintiff, the Union Electric Company

(Union), was in the business of providing electric and heating services. The defendant, Mansion House Center Redevelopment Company (Mansion), was one of several limited partnerships engaged in the operation of apartment and commercial buildings.

Prior to the time that these buildings were constructed, both plaintiff and defendant held several meetings to discuss the merits of various energy systems, the objective being to develop an efficient and economic energy system for defendant's buildings. The parties finally signed a series of contracts. However, several years later the defendant complained to the plaintiff that its billings exceeded the estimates developed in the negotiations. After the protest failed to reduce the costs, the defendant withheld part of the costs due the plaintiff. The latter then brought suit to recover the unpaid sum.

At the trial, the plaintiff introduced its records into evidence regarding the amount owed by the defendant. The records were offered under the Missouri Uniform Business Records as Evidence Law, which provides that the:

... record of an act, condition or event, shall, insofar as relevant, be competent evidence if the custodian or other qualified witness testifies to its identity and the mode of its preparation, and if it was made in the regular course of business, at or near the time of the act ... and if, in the opinion of the court, the source of information, method and time of preparation were such as to justify its admission.[35]

The disputed records in this case were the plaintiff's computerized records. To establish their admissibility, the plaintiff offered the testimony of several of its officers.

The defendant objected on the grounds that the plaintiff had failed to "lay an adequate or proper foundation to qualify the exhibits [records]."[36] The Missouri Supreme Court, however, held the defendant's objection as being inadequate because it did not inform the court "in what respect there had been such a failure."[37] The defendant had failed to state "fully and correctly the grounds" for his objection.[38] To say only that the records are not accurate, the court held, only goes to the probative value of the evidence and not to its admissibility. Further, the defendant did not offer any expert witnesses of his own to challenge the records.

The defendant also objected on the ground that the plaintiff had not attempted to "interpret and prove the accuracy or the meaning of the computer punching on various cards."[39] The plaintiff argued that computer records were a new development, but that a number of cases had already addressed themselves to the problem, and that in instances where the question of their admissibility had been raised some courts had held them admissible.

The court concluded that the Missouri statute was drafted with the intent to bring the changing needs of the business world into the courtroom; the statute was never intended to be interpreted in such a narrow way as to destroy its function. The court gave the statute a broad interpretation, thus enabling the plaintiff to introduce into evidence his computer printouts. It should be pointed out that the defendant had not offered opposing evidence or witnesses to challenge the reliability and accuracy of the computer system. Further, there was no attempt made to challenge the witnesses' knowledge of the company's computerized operation. The defendant did not raise the question of whether the plaintiff's witnesses were qualified to testify on the identity and mode of preparation of the records. Absent from the trial was also the issue of whether the records were made in the "regular course of business, at or near the time of the act. . . ."[40] In future litigation, those opposing the admission of computer records should be prepared to recognize and challenge the frailties of the computer system.

That same year, North Carolina courts faced their first computer-related case. In *State* v. *Springer* that state's Supreme Court heard an appeal from the Catawba Superior Court.[41] The defendant had been charged by the police with "unlawfully, willfully and feloniously" witholding a credit card from one Mabel L. Long in violation of the state's credit card theft statute.[42] The indictment alleged that the credit card—a Bankamericard—had been issued to a Ms. Long on September 20, 1971, when in fact this was an error, and the correct date was September 15. Defendant had argued that this discrepancy, together with others, rendered the bill of indictment defective.

A special investigator with Bankamericard had testified for the state. He noted that the North Carolina National Bank's IBM computer printout is the official record pertaining to credit cards. Over objections by the defense, he was allowed to testify as to the "official computer printout regarding" the credit card in question.[43] He noted that the card had been used for purchases totaling more than $1000 since the time its owner reported it missing.

The Supreme Court of North Carolina acknowledged that the changing business environment had led states and courts to reassess the old rules of evidence. It would be impossible, the court noted, to produce in court all those who had knowledge and who had recorded each individual transaction. Admittedly, very few courts had addressed the problem of business records stored on computers. The court made reference to the state statute on business records, which noted that:

. . . records maintained by a corporation in the "regular course of business," including its stock ledger, books of account, and minute books, may be kept on, or be in the form of, punch cards, magnetic tape, photographs, microphotographs, or any other information storage device. . . .[44]

The numerous storage devices listed by the statute could easily also include those which hold computerized records. For example, the statute specifically includes "magnetic tape" with its definition of a storage device.

The statute also states that such records are admissible, provided: (1) that they can be converted into clearly legible form within a reasonable time; (2) that a corporation shall convert these records upon the request of any individual entitled to inspect them (although no provision determines who will pay the costs); and (3) that they can be authenticated. The statute, according to the court, is meant to give legislative approval to computerized records for use as evidence.

However, the statute does not address itself to the problem of reliability and accuracy, nor does it establish any standards for testing these. The court did, however, state that printouts should be admitted if they met the following tests: (1) they were made in the regular course of business; (2) they were made at or near the time of the transaction involved; and (3) a proper foundation has been laid by the testimony of a witness who is familiar with the records and methods under which they were made, so as to satisfy the court.[45] However, this evidence may be refuted to the same extent as may evidence of traditional records.

In the *Springer* case, the court noted that the testimony of the special investigator was inadmissible, nor had a requisite foundation been laid by the prosecution. In fact, the printout itself was never offered into evidence. Instead, the state's witness merely testified as to its contents. The evidence, the court held, was likewise inadmissible under the best evidence rule. The state had made no effort to circumvent this barrier. Admission of the printouts by the lower court had constituted prejudicial error requiring a new trial.

The prosecutors had not only failed to lay the adequate foundation necessary for the admission of the printouts, but they also had failed to provide the actual records, or explain their absence. The government opened itself to attack from both the hearsay rule and also the best evidence rule. The state's statute specifically required that the "records so kept can be converted into clearly legible form within a reasonable time," and that a "duly authenticated readout or translation shall be admissible in evidence, and shall be accepted. . . ."[46] Curiously, the government presented no record in evidence, and only the testimony of one witness, who had no personal knowledge of the matter involved and who testified that the printout was in fact the only record kept. The problem here lay not so much with the court's reluctance to allow printouts into evidence, but rather with the prosecution's poor presentation of its case. Even had the state's attorney attempted to introduce traditional records, they may have faced a similar outcome. The court specifically noted that modern business needs dictate a "revision of the [old] rule of evidence."[47]

On a rainy evening in October 1972, Robert B. Heath, while driving on a four-lane highway in Washington State, collided with a motor vehicle owned by a Ms. Marlene Owen.[48] The testimony of the parties differed as to who was responsible. At trial Heath testified that although he was aware of the collision, upon inspecting his vehicle he found no damages and continued on his way. Ms. Owen followed Heath and copied down his license plate but never identified herself to him. Four days later, Heath was approached by the Seattle Police and interviewed by a detective of that department. He was advised of his rights and gave a voluntary written statement about the accident. He also told the questioning detectives that "I haven't gotten around to going and getting a driver's license...."[49]

Soon afterward Heath was charged with several violations, including negligent driving, leaving the scene of an accident, and driving without a valid license. A trial was held in municipal court and defendant Heath was convicted. Heath then appealed his conviction and the Court of Appeals for the State of Washington heard it. In the case of *City of Seattle* v. *Heath,* the Court of Appeals faced, among other matters, the question of whether the admission of computer printouts had been an error.[50]

During the trial the prosecution had introduced Exhibits 1 and 2, which were abstracts of the defendant's driving record and the status of his driver's license. The defendant, however, charged that the admission of these exhibits was in violation of the state's business records statute. As grounds, he cited sections of that statute:

[A]n act, condition or event . . . shall . . . be competent evidence if the custodian or other qualified witness testifies to its identity and to the mode of its preparation. . . .[51]

In addition, the statute also required that a record be:

. . . made in the regular course of business, at or near the time of the act, condition or event, and if, in the opinion of the court, the sources of information, method and time of preparation were such as to justify its admission.[52]

The exhibits in question were computer printouts. The Washington statute differed little from that of other states, and like those, had never dealt with the problem of printouts.

The defendant charged, among other things, that the state's testimony was insufficient to show that the entries were made in the routine course of business. He questioned whether the recorder himself had personal knowledge of the events and whether the entries were made at or near the time of the transaction. The defendant also charged that the testimony of the prosecution's witnesses failed to show how the computer exhibits had been prepared, and the state had thus failed to lay a proper foundation. The Court of Appeals disagreed and held that the foundation was sufficient.

The prosecution had called the Assistant Director of the Traffic Violations Bureau of the Seattle Municipal Court to testify. The witness had informed the lower court that his office kept records relating to traffic violations by the name of each defendant. The witness stated that the municipal court had a teletype and printer with a direct terminal to a city computer at the Department of

Motor Vehicles. He identified Exhibit 1 as being an abstract of the defendant's driving record, as recorded on the city's computer at the Department of Motor Vehicles. The abstract, according to his testimony, showed violations by date, place, and type. He identified Exhibit 2 as an abstract of the status of defendant's driver's license, as contained in the computer banks.

The official further informed the court that records are retrieved by feeding into the computer the name and birth date of the individual involved; the computer then discloses the status of the driver's license. He added that the exhibits in question had been personally obtained for him by the clerk in the Traffic Violations Bureau under his personal direction and observation.

Under cross-examination by the defense, the state's witness testified that he was a custodian of the records once they came over the teletype from the computer, that these records were in printout form, but that he was not the custodian of the records at the Department of Motor Vehicles nor of its computer system, and finally, that the printouts also contained the dates on which requests were made for information on a driver's status.

The Washington Court of Appeals upheld the lower court's holding. It was influenced by several factors in its decision. First and foremost, it noted that the decision of a trial judge in admitting or excluding business records is "given much weight" and will not easily be reversed unless there is manifest injustice.[53] In the case at issue, the court pointed out that the defendant had made a written admission to the police that, in fact, he did not have a license to drive his car. Further, Ms. Owen, the other party involved in the auto accident, had personally followed the defendant and taken down his license plate number. There was little question that the preponderance of the evidence clearly indicated the defendant's guilt, irrespective of the exhibits at issue. The trial court's findings were supported by "substantial evidence."[54]

The court also addressed the issue of computerized business records. The witness could be "either . . . the custodian of the record or a qualified witness."[55] Although the prosecution's witness was not the custodian of the computerized records at the city's Department of Motor Vehicles, he was the custodian of the teletype printouts. The purpose of the statute, the high court stated, is to allow business records into evidence if made systematically and in the usual course of business. Its purpose would be defeated if one had to locate, identify, and produce as a witness each individual who made the original entries. The record need not appear in any specific form, since all forms that meet the criteria outlined by the statute are acceptable. The high court held ultimately that a record that has been computerized and stored in a computer's data bank is admissible, like any other form of record.[56] In addition, reference to the *Seib* and *King* cases was made. To summarize, a printout will be admitted, said the court, if testimony indicates: (1) that the computer system is recognized as standard equipment, (2) that the entries were made in the regular course of business at or reasonably near the time of the happening of the event recorded, and (3) that the foundation testimony satisfies the court.

In the *Heath* case, the testimony of the Assistant Director of the Traffic Violations Bureau apparently had impressed both the lower and higher courts. Also, there was testimony that the entries were made in the regular course of business, and their mode of preparation satisfied the test for accuracy and reliability. The courts in *Heath* also faced a serious dilemma: if the business records statute were interpreted narrowly, it might mean that many traffic violations would go unpunished, unless proven by other testimony, independent of computerized evidence. As a matter of policy and in recognition of the difficulties a narrow interpretation of the statute could have on law enforcement (where data have been computerized), the higher court supported the lower court's decision. The ruling was also influenced by the fact that the prosecution presented its testimony within the criteria set by the statute.

The majority of local cases dealing with computer-generated evidence have come from states with business records statutes, and from jurisdictions where sophisticated and complex business related litigations, or major frauds, have been infrequent. However, in 1974, in *Ed Guth Realty, Inc.* v. *Gingold,* the New York State Court of Appeals addressed the issue of printouts.[57] It appears inconsistent that a major urbanized and commercial state, where complex business dealings and frauds are an everyday affair, should follow rather than lead the smaller states in this area. Possibly, though, both government and private attorneys have hesitated to risk major cases merely on the admissibility of printouts. However, as computer use increases, it will be increasingly difficult for the large urbanized states to evade litigation that specifically addresses the issue of allowing into evidence computer printouts and other forms of related data.

The *Gingold* case involved several cross-appeals within a series of proceedings brought under article 7 of the New York Real Property Tax Law. This case also saw the introduction of computer printouts. In support of their admission, one of the parties had the Director of Research and Statistics for the New York State Board of Equalization and Assessment testify as a witness. He interpreted the printouts, explained how the data had been collected, and showed how they pertained to the matter at issue. The opposing party made no attempt to argue that the data were not relevant, nor was any attempt made to impeach them. However, the adverse party did argue that the printouts could not come in under the state's business entry statute, and also that they were not "best evidence."[58]

The New York Court of Appeals differed. It noted that the statute is essentially based on the concept of *routinism.* The routinism of an entry, in the usual course of business, tends to guarantee truthfulness because of the lack of motivation to falsify.[59] Compiling and feeding data into a computer is routine, as required by the statute. The court also noted that although there were no past New York cases dealing with printouts, the Federal Rules of Evidence Act provided guidance in this area—rule 803 provides for the admission of data compiled by computer.[60]

Additionally, the adverse parties did not challenge the "routinism" of the data stored in the computer. As for the best evidence rule, the court stated that the voluminous writings exception to that rule would apply.[61] The exception permits the admission of summaries of very extensive records or entries, provided that the party against whom it is offered can have access to the original data if it requests. The adverse party did not object on grounds that it had been denied access to the original documents but merely raised the rule. This would not suffice when standing alone.

As a result of these factors, the court relaxed the state's business records act to allow for the introduction into evidence of computerized business data. The opposing party never raised the issue of whether the data had been prepared in the regular course of business, nor whether the witness had any personal knowledge. Further, it did not attack the accuracy and reliability of the printouts. It did not offer testimony from its own experts in opposition to the admission of the evidence. Had these issues been raised, the court could have dealt more completely with the case as a whole and could have further clarified the state's statute regarding computerized business entries.

In 1975 the case of *John Edward McGee, Jr.* was heard by a Middlesex County judge, in New Jersey.[61] McGee had been stopped on the New Jersey Turnpike by a police officer, who, after searching McGee's car, found a .22-caliber gun. The police officer later testified at trial that a check with the FBI's National Crime Information Center (NCIC) computer terminal operator confirmed that the gun had been stolen. The county court allowed the NCIC printout into evidence, above the defendant's objections, as a business record.[62] The defendant then appealed.

A superior court judge heard the appeal and held that the NCIC printout, unless corroborated by other evidence, is not sufficiently trustworthy on its own.[63] The document was held as being hearsay. The prosecution then appealed, and the case was heard by the appellate division. It reaffirmed the superior court judge. It noted that such evidence, on its own, was not sufficient to overcome the hearsay rule objection. The proponent of the evidence should have had the operator of the NCIC computer testify as to the trustworthiness of the information contained in the printout.[64] The prosecution should also have introduced testimony to demonstrate how and when the information about the stolen gun had been reported to the FBI, how and when it had been computerized, and how and by whom it had been retrieved. The court was not willing to relax the hearsay rule, even for printouts prepared by the FBI's NCIC computer.

Serious problems arise when computer printouts are admitted into evidence. For example, if the records are intended to be prima facie evidence of a crime in a criminal case, they may deprive the defendant of his constitutional rights of confrontation and cross-examination. In addition, it should be noted that all the state cases to date dealing with computer-generated evidence have dealt with printouts. The cases themselves have not involved any complex commercial matters or sophisticated criminal frauds. Fewer than a dozen such cases have involved criminal proceedings. The majority of computer-related cases have dealt with such areas as records of thefts, missing and stolen property, and traffic violations. To date, no state case has ruled on the use of computers in highly complex financial transactions, nor on criminal cases where the computer itself is the tool used to perpetrate a massive fraud. On the state level, many questions still remain unanswered. Although some courts have shown a willingness to broaden their business records statutes to include computer printouts, many continue to refuse. The problem of computer crime is a complicated one and must be attacked on various levels. At the state level, legislators can do well by providing for statutes that specifically address themselves to the problem of computer-related litigation. Without such statutes, both civil and criminal litigation at the state level remain a problem.

References

1. 132 N.W.2d 871 (1965).
2. Ibid., p. 873.
3. Ibid., p. 874.
4. The court cited the Nebraska case of *Higgins* v. *Long River Public Power District,* 159 Neb. 549, (1955).
5. The court cited the 3rd Circuit's holding in *United States* v. *Olivo,* 278 F.2d 415.
6. *Transportation Company* v. *Seib,* 132 N.W.2d 874-75 (1965).
7. 440 P.2d 314 (1968).
8. Ibid., p. 316.
9. Arizona, like many other states, has replaced the old common-law rule with legislation.
10. *Merrick* v. *United States Rubber Company,* 440 P.2d 316 (1968).
11. Ibid.
12. *Builders Supply Corporation* v. *Shipley,* 341 P.2d 940 (1959).
13. *Merrick* v. *United States Rubber Company,* p. 317.
14. Ibid.
15. *Transportation Company* v. *Seib,* p. 874.
16. 436 P.2d 629 (1968).
17. Ibid., pp. 631, 632.
18. Ibid., p. 635.
19. Ibid.
20. Ibid.
21. 222 So.2d 393 (1969).
22. Ibid., p. 398.

23. Ibid.

24. *Railroad Commission* v. *Southern Pacific Company,* 468 S.W.2d 125 (Tex. Civ. App. 1971).

25. Ibid., p. 128.

26. 466 S.W.2d 381 (Tex. Civ. App. 1971).

27. 288 N.E.2d 24 (1974).

28. Ibid., p. 25.

29. Ibid.

30. 513 P.2d 650 (1973).

31. Ibid., p. 653.

32. Ibid.

33. Ibid., p. 652.

34. 494 S.W.2d 309 (1973).

35. Ibid., p. 313.

36. Ibid.

37. Ibid.

38. Ibid.

39. Ibid., p. 314.

40. Ibid., p. 313.

41. 197 S.E.2d 530 (1973).

42. Ibid., p. 532.

43. Ibid., p. 533.

44. Ibid., p. 533-534.

45. Ibid.

46. Ibid.

47. Ibid.

48. *City of Seattle* v. *Heath,* 520 P.2d 1392 (Wash. State 1974).

49. Ibid., p. 1393.

50. Ibid., p. 1392.

51. Ibid., p. 1395.

52. Ibid.

53. Ibid., p. 1396.

54. Ibid., p. 1395.

55. Ibid., p. 1396.

56. Ibid.

57. 315 N.E.2d 441 (1974).

58. Ibid., p. 446.

59. Ibid.

60. Ibid.

61. Nancy French, "New Jersey Court Disallows NCIC Data as Evidence," *Law & Computer Technology,* January-February 1975, pp. 20, 21.

62. Ibid.

63. Ibid.

64. Ibid.

15

Computer Litigation: Federal Level

A number of Federal courts have recognized, as have some state courts, the realities of a complex and urban business environment. It is almost impossible to identify and obtain the testimony of the many individuals who have personal knowledge of the entries made in a firm's business records. As early as 1927, the Second Federal Circuit Court showed a sensitivity to the needs of a growing business community.

In the case of *Massachusetts Bonding and Insurance Co.* v. *Norwich Pharmaceutical Co.* tabulations of more than 30,000 sale orders were admitted as evidence in order to verify the amount of embezzled stamp money.[1] The proponent had only one clerk testify instead of all those who had worked on the tabulations, as required by the old common-law rule. However, the court noted that the records could be relied on as accurate and trustworthy because they had been routinely prepared.[2] Although many other clerks could have testified, at great expense and trouble to the proponent, such additional testimony would not significantly enhance the credibility given these records.

The court reasoned that even if the other clerks had been called, their memories would have been faded, and they could not have been expected to remember the minute details and the many transactions in which they had been involved.[3] Thus, if the entrant and his superior could testify—as opposed to having all the entrants testify—that the entries were made in the regular course of business, some federal courts would admit the entry without a need to call the entire "chain of entrants."[4]

When the federal government finally adopted the recommendations of the Model Act in 1936, federal courts began to move away from the old common-law rule.[5] However, the first federal case to address the problem of electronically processed data did not arise until 1958. The case was *Sunset Motor Lines* v. *Lu-Tex Packing Co.* and was litigated in the Fifth Circuit (Court of Appeals).[6] An appeal was taken by a truck carrier that had been held liable in a federal district court for the total loss of a shipment of fresh beef.

Among the issues raised by the appellant (truck carrier) was the admissibility of a U.S. Department of Agriculture punch card for machine accounting. The card had been held inadmissible by the lower court. The evidence in question was an IBM punch card that stated that the beef was tainted and denatured and thus unfit for human consumption. It did not show the amount rejected from the truckload in question. The Court of Appeals agreed with the lower court and held the punch card to be hearsay. It was not a record within the federal business records exception, nor was it certified, pursuant to the federal rules.[7]

In 1969 the Fifth Circuit Court faced a similar problem. This case, however, involved computer printouts, and established the principles for all such future cases. In *Olympic Insurance Co.* v. *Harrison, Inc.,* the plaintiff had instituted suit against the H.D. Harrison Company, dba Harrison Insurance Service (defendant).[8] A judgement was sought on insurance premiums on policies that were written by the defendant as the plaintiff's agent.

The plaintiff filed supporting papers that established that, as of October 31, 1968, the defendant was indebted to the plaintiff for insurance premiums in an amount over $300,000. The statement consisted of an itemized IBM printout, annexed to plaintiff's affidavit. The defendant's reply did not deny the accuracy of the statement, nor did it specify any errors. However, the defendant's affidavit stated that, in the past, the plaintiff's IBM statements did contain some errors,[9] although no errors were claimed in the present statement.

The Court of Appeals concluded that it found no merit in defendant's argument that the IBM printouts—which formed the essential proof of the defendant's indebtedness—were unreliable. In fact, the court noted, the printouts were produced in the regular course of business and had, at least, a prima facie aura of reliability.[10] Further, the defendant failed to list any specific objections as to the accuracy of the printouts. Consequently, the lower court did not err in admitting them into evidence.

The defendant's failure here proved to be the failure to attack the accuracy of the printouts at issue, or the requirement that the material be produced in the regular course of business, and the lack of requisite testimony to support the printouts. Defendant could have attacked the lack of a proper foundation, and also the time element involved between the production of the data and their entry in the computer. The Federal Business Records Act was passed with two key elements in mind: (1) accuracy, and (2) reliability. The defendant failed to attack either. Further, he put forth no expert witnesses to attack the plaintiff's computer system and its reliability. Ultimately, there was the failure to take full advantage of discovery tools in order to probe the opponent's weaknesses.

That same year, the Ninth Circuit Court ruled on a case involving printouts, *United States* v. *De Georgia,* which involved criminal violations of the federal laws.[11] It was an appeal by defendant Richard Allen De Georgia from a conviction by a jury for violations of the Dyer Act (18 U.S.C., sec. 2312). The offense involved a 1968 Mustang automobile allegedly stolen from the Hertz Corporation, in New York City, and driven to Arizona.

Defendant had given the police a written confession. However, a confession does not in itself constitute adequate proof of an element of an offense unless, as to that element, it is corroborated by admissible evidence. The prosecution in this case offered no evidence to corroborate the defendant's confession. However, the prosecution called a Hertz security manager for the company's New York zone. He produced documentary evidence that established that the car had been owned by Hertz, and that it had been stolen from the Hertz Kennedy Airport location.[12]

The witness, though, had no personal knowledge of the events; his testimony was based upon information he obtained from the Hertz master computer control in the New York office. According to his statement, Hertz maintains all records of rentals and leases on its computer system. This information is fed into the computer consoles located in each of the Hertz branch offices. These may be retrieved at the master control of the computer.

The witness further testified that information regarding all Hertz' cars could easily be obtained from the center of the system. He stated that sometime in July 1968 he received information that the car in question may have been stolen. He checked with the computer and discovered that the car had not been rented, thus confirming that it had been stolen.

The defense objected to the admission of this information on the ground that it was hearsay. However, the defense made no claim that the records in question were not maintained in a continuous written report of rental and lease transactions, since they had actually been kept in a computer system.

The Court of Appeals disagreed with the defendant. It stated that even if the material were hearsay, there are exceptions to the rule.[13] One of these is the business records exception, which in federal courts has been legislated into 28 U.S.C., section 1732.[14] The court noted that the statute made no requirement that the record be in writing to be admissible. The court also made reference to the proposed Uniform Rules of Evidence, as drafted by the National Conference of Commissioners on Uniform State Laws and approved at its annual conference in 1953.

The court was persuaded to look favorably on the printouts by the proposals of the Committee on Rules of Practice and Procedure of the United States Judicial Conference. It noted that the committee's 1969 draft had a proposed rule (rule 8-03) to deal effectively with hearsay exceptions, which provides that:

A statement is not excluded by the hearsay rule if its nature and the special circumstances under which it is made offer assurances of accuracy. . . .[15]

The proposals set forth in the 1969 draft have since been adopted in the new rules of evidence. It was apparent that, by citing proposed rule 8-13, the court was saying that the defendant had not produced any evidence nor specified any inaccuracies in the testimony or in the printouts offered by the prosecution.

The court declared that regularly maintained business records are admissible as an exception to the hearsay rule because they tend to be more reliable—a company has to rely on its records to assure that business is conducted properly; accurate business records are essential; and the accuracy of the records is not enhanced by the introduction of original documents.

The court, however, failed to consider (and the defense failed to raise) the fact that major frauds are perpetrated with false and misleading data that may be fed into a computer on a regular basis. Data compiled on a day-to-day business will be accurate only if the enterprise has a legitimate objective. If that objective is to defraud the public, say, by creating false earnings and assets, even daily records will not reflect the accurate standing of the firm.

Calling as witnesses all personnel who had the task of entering the daily transactions into the record will not increase the credibility of the data. For example, the court noted, an enormous amount of material would have to be compiled and introduced into evidence. Every Hertz employee who might have consummated a lease or rental agreement regarding the car in question would have to be called. The employees could not be expected to remember whether, out of all the rental and lease agreements they had entered, one involved the defendant. By necessity, recourse must be to the firm's computer.

Although the record is maintained in the computer, procedurally, the opposing party must be protected by the following: (1) he must have the opportunity to inquire into the accuracy of the computer and the input methods that were used; and (2) the trial court must require the party offering the computer data to provide a foundation sufficient to warrant a finding that the data are trustworthy.[16] The same challenges that apply to regularly maintained business records are available here.

In the *De Georgia* case, the testimony of the Hertz employee only corroborated what the defendant had openly confessed to the authorities—that the automobile was stolen. The defendant's argument that the printouts are in violation of the best evidence rule was raised only on appeal. Since no objection had been made at the trial level, the higher court would not consider the point. Appeal courts will only address objections specifically raised at the trial level. Raising an objection for the first time on the appellate level will not suffice.

In a concurring opinion, one of the appellate judges admitted that he would have had more difficulty in allowing the admission of printouts if the defendant had raised the issue of the best evidence rule at the trial level.[17] The judge also noted that, although the Federal Business Act had modified the strict common-law approach to the old shop-book rule, it had not alleviated conformity to the best evidence rule. He pointed out that a number of courts had not allowed summaries of records as evidence, unless the original records were also offered.

However, a criminal case poses serious constitutional questions. These involve the right of confrontation, and, as a result, printouts should be strictly tested. The judge recognized that the *King* decision had relaxed the records exception and had admitted printouts; but he specifically noted that the statute "should never be construed as authorizing carte blanche admission into evidence of any and all information that can be obtained from the records of a business."[18] It should never be interpreted as permitting the introduction of hearsay record evidence (in the nature of opinion or conclusion testimony, as distinguished from recordation of facts).

The judge expressed serious concern that the needs of modern technology could easily displace the rights of the individual. These considerations, it should be noted, have been echoed by many others. There is real fear that relaxing the hearsay rule could allow data in evidence that are not only inaccurate but a threat to basic constitutional rights as well. Printouts involve testimony "by a machine against an accused,"[19] and it is thus essential that the trial court be convinced of the trustworthiness of the records in question.

Had the defendant raised the best evidence rule at the trial, and had he brought forth his own experts to testify on the accuracy of the system, perhaps new issues would have surfaced. Whether the court would have held otherwise remains doubtful. At stake, however, was not only the admission of the printout, but rather the entire computerized record keeping process of a multibillion dollar industry—auto leasing. If the defendant could have evaded prosecution by simply raising the hearsay rule, thousands of other felons like him could have wreaked havoc on the auto leasing industry by simply raising the same objections. The court could not condone this, and this factor must have weighed heavily in its decision.

In 1970 the Second Circuit Court faced the problem of printouts in a criminal prosecution. In *United States* v. *Dioguardi* the defendants had been charged with fraudulently transferring and concealing the property of a bankrupt in contemplation of bankruptcy, and of fraudulently concealing the bankrupt's assets in violation of 18 U.S.C., 152, and conspiring to conceal same in violation of 18 U.S.C., 371.[20] After an 18-day trial, they were found guilty by a U.S. district court jury. They immediately appealed.

Defendant John Dioguardi exercised effective control over the Consumers Kosher Provisions Company (Consumers). Defendant David Perlman was president of the firm. Dioguardi was suspected of being involved in New York organized crime syndicates. In 1964 Consumers faced serious financial difficulties; defendant Dioguardi negotiated a contract with a competing firm to try to salvage it. An agreement was reached whereby the second firm would acquire the first. This deal, though, fell through.

The defendants then began business under the name of a new firm, which made use of the same plant and equipment of the now defunct Consumers firm. The new firm also made use of Consumers entire inventory—at least, what was left of it. On or about January 25, 1965, three creditors filed a petition in bankruptcy against Consumers. The defendants then took some of the firm's equipment and transferred it to another firm in New York. This transfer was discovered by the trustee. At this point, Consumers had debts of over $250,000.

On appeal, several objections were raised by the defendants. The key objection, for present purposes, dealt with the prosecution's failure to produce the "program" by which its witness had instructed a computer to prepare certain statements; these statements showed the dates when the defendants had exhausted, through their new firm, the various items of Consumer's inventory.[21]

The prosecution's computer witness had used as input data Consumer's inventory and various other tabulations that dealt with purchases and sales of material in order to determine when the inventory had been exhausted. A computer had been employed by the government to trace the bankruptcy fraud — to recreate what had happened. The computer was not, as in the cases already discussed, employed to record past events. Rather, it was directly employed to help the prosecutors reconstruct what happened and how it happened. Such roles for computers should expand in the near future, as financial frauds become more sophisticated and the resources of the government remain limited. As a result of its role in *Dioguardi,* the computer has shown significant law enforcement potential.

At the trial, when the prosecution attempted to introduce the printouts, the defense noted that the government's computer expert had not actually made an independent examination of the data fed the computer but had relied on data prepared by others. The defense then moved to strike that testimony and to exclude the computer printouts. However, the defense's motion was denied by the trial judge.

The defense also noted that the program given the computer should have been made available to it under the Jencks Act (18 U.S.C., 3500).[22] The trial judge disagreed. It was further alleged that the prosecution's witness had not participated in the preparation of the underlying documents. The defense made no arguments concerning right of access to the computer programs, save that the programs should have been provided under the Jencks Act.

The defense requested that the prosecution produce the program. The government denied having it. The defense then moved that the government be made to obtain it, which motion was denied. No motion for discovery of the program or other data related to the computer was made. No *Brady* request, as it related to the computer, was ever made.[23] The defense did move, however, to strike the printouts as hearsay, since they had been produced by a computer, outside the courtroom, and since the defendants were denied their right of cross-examination—the very essense of the constitutional protection of confrontation. The judge denied this motion also.

The Court of Appeals affirmed the decision of the trial judge. The defendants had a right to know what operations the computer had been instructed to perform, and to know the precise instruction that it had been given. It is incomprehensible that the government could allow a witness to state the results of a computer operation without making the program available to the defense. The defendant had a right to use it on cross-examination if it so decided.[24] The program and other materials needed for cross-examination of computer witnesses (such as flowcharts) should have been made available to the defense at a reasonable time before the trial. However, the court noted, unless it can be shown that there was an "appreciable risk that prejudice resulted," it would be time-consuming and unfair to order a new trial, simply because there was a failure to compel production of the programs.[25]

Moreover, the operations involved in this case were relatively simple and did not require sophisticated use of the computer. For example, the court noted that defense counsel could have easily checked the results of the computer by simply using an adding machine, or even manually.[26] What the court was saying is that the defense lost little by the judge's denial. Further, the trial went on for some 18 days. The defense neglected, at the trial and on appeal, to identify specific errors in the computer tabulations. The defense had ample opportunity to check the computer's performance and could have renewed its demand for production of the program or reverted to the use of a subpoena. The absence of such motions—even more than two years later, on appeal—represents defense inadequacy, not judicial inflexibility.

Finally, the Appeals Court noted that the computer expert's testimony was really unnecessary. The defendants had never denied making use of Consumer's inventory. The entire controversy centered not around what happened to the inventory, but why it happened—for the benefit of the defendants or that of the firm. The computerized data were never in question, and assumed only peripheral importance.[27]

Thus *Dioguardi* raises some key facts for consideration. For example, how crucial are the printouts to the overall case? Does the case stand or fall on them, or are they really more of a secondary matter? In the above case, the data played a secondary role. Further, what attempts were made by the defense to gain access to the data? Did it make use of its subpoena power? Or discovery? Did it bring its own experts into the case to review and analyze the material? How would this affect the outcome? It is not enough to object to the introduction of data, or to claim lack of access. One must specifically identify defects in that data and explain the negative impact that one has suffered as a result.

In *Dioguardi* the computer was employed to sketch an outline for the prosecutors as to how the fraud was perpetrated. The computer's role in this case can be compared to that of a tabulating machine similarly employed. The data were never challenged by the defense, and the computer only facilitated a process that could have actually been performed manually. The testimony of the prosecution witness was not crucial. The defense stood to gain or lose little, either way. However, if the case had been a complicated one, where the data were in dispute, if the computer had played a key role rather than a secondary one, being employed merely as a tabulator, the outcome of the case might have been different. In this case, the defense made no objection on the grounds of the best evidence rule. The court thus never addressed this critical issue.

In 1973 the Sixth Circuit Court faced a criminal case involving the use of computerized data—*United States* v. *Russo*.[28] In this case, the appellant was a licensed physician in Michigan. He and an associate were charged with 51 counts of mail fraud (18 U.S.C., 1341). Among other things, the defendant had been charged with intending and devising a scheme to defraud Blue Shield of Michigan by "filing claims for services not performed on patients on dates specified and for obtaining money . . . by false and fraudulent pretenses and representations. . . ."[29]

The evidence at trial revealed that during the period of 1966 through 1968 Dr. Joseph Russo, the defendant, leased a group of offices in a blue collar area of Detroit. He practiced from these offices with another physician. Hundreds of patients were seen in any one day. The other defendant testified at trial that he treated an average of 150 persons a day. Blue Shield furnished physicians in Michigan with printed forms that were completed by the doctors and submitted to the company for payment. Each physician in turn was furnished with a code number.

The prosecutors argued, among other things, that the defendants had falsified the types of services provided to their clients. (Not all services are compensable under the Blue Shield program.) Twelve former patients of the defendants also testified for the government; they confirmed the prosecution's charges that the vouchers had been falsified by the defendants, and that the listed medical services had, in fact, never been provided.

The prosecutors also produced the Director of Service Review at Blue Shield as one of their key witnesses. He stated that his office had as its primary duty the integrity of the reporting forms submitted by physicians. His department initiated various audits to ensure compliance with the firm's rules. He testified that each claim form was examined by various firm employees. If it is determined that the claim is proper, the money to be paid and the service provided are both recorded. The forms are then sent to the data recording section of the company, where the information is transferred onto a magnetic tape for processing.

Once the data are stored on magnetic tapes, the claim form is microfilmed and a cross reference is made between the information stored on the tape and the microfilm. The former is used by a computer. The computer retrieves all the payments due each physician under his printed code, and a check is printed for each voucher. The witness testified that the claimants are paid through the mails and that this was the manner by which the defendants were paid.

The witness acknowledged that a computer output is no better than the data fed into it. He also noted that two computer operators are used to screen all claims for errors. The witness testified on statistics gathered by the company concerning the two defendants. The vice president, who is in charge of all Blue Shield computer functions, also testified in support. He described the computer equipment used by the company and its various functions. Further, he informed the court that all new programs are pretested for accuracy.

The first witness also testified that the company keeps a statistical profile of all its physicians, listing all the procedures for which a specific physician has been paid in the last year. Two clerks testified that for the 1967 period, profiles on the defendants had been kept manually. The prosecution attempted to introduce these profiles over the objection of the defense. These profiles, though, had been computerized. However, the trial court ruled that the government had sustained its burden of showing that the computerized data were reliable.

Although the defendants protested their innocence, 10 witnesses identified various claims filed in their cases by the defendants. On appeal, the defendants reiterated their argument that the computerized data did not qualify as a business record under the federal business records statute (28 U.S.C., 1732 (a)).[30] The Court of Appeals acknowledged that computer records are not mentioned in the federal act, but noted that no court could refuse to recognize the developments in the modern business world. The computer provides an opportunity for businesses to store large amounts of data, which can therefore be retrieved on a selective basis.

The high court noted further that the defense had presented no evidence that could cast doubt on the mechanical or electronic capability of the equipment. No questions were raised about the reliability of its output or the procedure used to test the system. The trustworthiness of the system and the data output had not been attacked by the defense, nor put in doubt. The lower court was thus correct in finding it trustworthy.

The defendants also raised the question of time—the printout was not prepared at the time the acts were performed or within a reasonable time thereafter. The court, however, refuted this and noted that testimony had made it amply clear that the opposite was true. A record was made each time a claim was paid. The file consisted of magnetic reels. Since the printout is only a comprehensive form of a mass of individual items, it matters little that the individual accounts were actually prepared later. It would unduly restrict the admissibility of computer records to require that both the output and input be produced at or within a reasonable time after each act or transaction to which it relates.[31]

The business records statute was adopted to facilitate rather than retard the admission of records into evidence. The test is the trustworthiness of the data, and the statute should be liberally construed, according to the court. Judicial interpretation should never be so strict as to deprive courts of the "realities of the business environment."[32] The data prepared by Blue Shield were neither conclusory nor a brief recapitulation of past events, but a record maintained in the regular course of business.

The defendants also argued that no proper foundation had been laid by the prosecutors for the admission of the printouts. The Court of Appeals disagreed. The witnesses were well qualified by training and education, and they were familiar with the operations in question. They each gave a detailed explanation of the mechanics of the system, with a description of the type of information that went into the computer. The court referred to the *De Georgia* decision in support of its conclusion.

The defendants contended that they were not given the opportunity to prepare a defense to the computerized data. It is true, the court noted, that in cases involving sophisticated scientific evidence, the courts must allow the defense adequate time to make similar tests in preparation for trial. However, the record indicates that the defense made no attempt at discovery once it was informed of the government's plans to introduce computerized data at trial. The right of discovery is provided in rule 16(b) of the Federal Rules of Criminal Procedure. Further, both parties and the court discussed the exhibits prior to the trial. The prosecution had provided the defense with statistics in accordance with the court's pretrial order. The defense could have easily obtained a court order providing access to all of Blue Shield's records. Both before and after its opportunity to cross-examine the prosecution's computer-related witnesses, the defense failed to make a request to review the insurance company's computers with one of its own experts.

The defense had adequate time to prepare an analysis of the government's computer evidence. It could have used the existing discovery tools, and failure to do so cannot be held against the government. The defense is solely responsible. The defense had ample opportunity to discredit the evidence prepared by the government. That its challenge came through cross-examination rather than inspection is a question of tactics and strategy, a choice the defense can make; it alone must suffer the consequences. In addition, it should be pointed out that much of the defendants' objections to the introduction of the computerized evidence addressed credibility rather than admissibility.

The defendants had argued that the computerized data did not bear directly on the question of guilt or innocence, but instead had a negative impact on the jury and led it to draw unwarranted inferences.[33] The trial court had ruled that the jury could draw such inferences from the testimony of the computer-related witnesses, that the defendants had not in fact performed all the services for which they had filed claims. However, the trial judge instructed the jury that admission into evidence was not in and of itself proof of any facts, and that *evidence* referred to relevant items that required testing, a generic term used for convenience.

It should be pointed out that many other witnesses also had testified against the defendants. The prosecution's evidence was well presented and explained in detail by expert witnesses. In contrast, the defense failed to raise appropriate objections and failed to take active steps to review and analyze the prosecution's data by one of its own experts. These must rest solely with the defense.

That same year, a federal district court in the Eastern District of New York faced the problem of computer-generated evidence in a civil case—*D & H Auto Parts, Inc.* v. *Ford Marketing Co.*[34] In this case, the plaintiff moved the court to set aside the jury verdict and grant a new trial.

The plaintiff was a wholesaler in auto parts and accessories who had entered into a sales agreement in 1968 with the defendant, the Ford Motor Company. The plaintiff was to act as a warehouse distributor of replacement parts. In turn, the defendant agreed to give the plaintiff various discounts on parts. The contract was signed by the defendant's general sales manager.

During 1969 the plaintiff submitted various inflated claims with the defendant. It received various discounts on the basis of these false claims. The contract provided that a party could terminate the contract if false claims were filed. The plaintiff alleged that the defendant's salesmen had in fact requested that these inflated claims be filed for business reasons. In early December 1970 the defendant terminated its contract with the plaintiff.

The defendant had the burden of showing the amount of the fraudulent claims and the amount of unpaid bills. Three sets of documents were involved. Forms 9375, constituting monthly summaries of sales, were prepared for internal use by the defendant. They were compiled from punch cards prepared each day in the defendant's regional office at Teterboro, New Jersey, which recorded the individual orders received daily. The cards were then double punched to eliminate errors and shipped to Detroit (location of defendant's central office), where they were stored in a computer. Printouts were then checked by the regional depots to ensure conformity with the local records. These forms were provided to the plaintiff during the pretrial discovery period.

The defendant offered forms 9375 into evidence in its affirmative case, in ascertaining damages for breach of contract. The plaintiff objected on the ground that there was insufficient proof of the accuracy of the computers. Nevertheless, the court ruled that they could be received as business records.

The thrust of the plaintiff's argument is that the court erred in admitting forms 9375 in evidence. However, these forms were prepared each month in the regular course of business by the defendant for use by its management. The fact that computers were used in compiling these data should not impair their admissibility. The court, in addressing the federal business records statute, noted that the admission of computer printouts has been approved even in criminal cases.[35]

The plaintiff had an opportunity to cross-examine the defendant's witness, the assistant comptroller in charge of the defendant's accounting department. The court agreed that the defendant had not produced the director of its central data processing department, but the absence of this witness may be "shown to affect its weight, but . . . shall not affect its admissibility."[36] The defendant was not obligated, the court held, under the statute, to produce any other witness. The assistant comptroller sufficed.

Although the plaintiff had the printouts in his possession for over 6 months, he failed to identify any area of inaccuracy; specific objections were listed. The forms were routinely prepared and were not produced specifically for the purpose of litigation. They were prepared from facts supplied by clients similar to the plaintiff, which itself could have easily verified their authenticity. The defendant regarded the forms as accurate and relied on them for business purposes. Consequently, the court did not find the plaintiff's objections sufficient to hold the printouts inadmissible. The court said, in essence, that the hearsay rule would not bar the admission of computer data offered as evidence.

Two years later, the Third Circuit (Court of Appeals), in a criminal case involving the Internal Revenue Service (IRS), faced a somewhat similar problem with computer printouts. In the case of *United States* v. *Greenlee* defendant James W. Greenlee appealed his conviction of willful failure to file an income tax return for the tax years of 1970 and 1971, in violation of 26 U.S.C., 7203 (1970).[37]

The defendant was an attorney employed by an agency of the city of Philadelphia. On December 26, 1972 the defendant met with an agent of the IRS and was informed that the IRS had no tax records for him for the 1970 and 1971 periods.[38] The defendant, however, falsely stated that he had in fact filed both returns and produced copies of both returns the following day.

The major part of the government's case rested on the IRS computer system. The prosecution relied on both a manually prepared text and a computer printout list of nontaxpayers for 1970 to show that the defendant had actually made no tax payment for that period. As to the 1971 filing, the prosecution's case rested on the defendant's request for an extension of time for filing and the IRS's denial of that request. The agent who interviewed the defendant also testified as to statements made to him in the interview. The defense produced a computer expert who testified that computer systems were known for their errors in both the input and output stages.[39]

However, the Court of Appeals held that the IRS had made a sufficient showing to justify admissions of the manually and computer prepared records. The court, apparently, was concerned that the case had more profound repercussions than the surface indicated. At issue was the entire enforcement program of the IRS. Since it relies largely on computerized records for its delegated responsibilities, allowing a defendant to defeat that objective because computer records are held inadmissible, would devastate the IRS. The court must be seen as having recognized the need of the IRS to continue enforcing the laws of the country, rather than the mode by which the material was introduced in evidence.

That same year, in the case of *United States* v. *Liebert,* the Third Circuit faced a similar case involving computer-generated evidence.[40] Defendant Peter P. Liebert, III, had been charged with willful failure to file income tax returns for the period of 1967 through 1969, in violation of the IRS code. Defendant claimed that he had filed a tax return for the years in question.

The prosecution's case rested heavily on the failure of the IRS to find any record in its computers on filing by the defendant. On January 14, 1974, prior to going to trial, the defendant filed motion to gain access to the IRS's computer system for its own expert. The U.S. district court finally granted his motion.

On February 28, 1974, the defendant filed a second discovery motion for production of all records indicating the number of notices the IRS sent to taxpayers in 1967 through 1973 advising that no tax return had been received from them.[41] The district court ordered the prosecutors to furnish the defendant with a mutually agreeable portion of the lists of nonfilers for the years of 1970 and 1971.[42] The government refused, and the judge proceeded to dismiss the charges against the defendant. The government then appealed on the grounds that the lists in question are not subject to disclosure under the IRS code. Further, the information the defendant required could not be made available to him without invading the privacy of numerous taxpayers.

The Court of Appeals agreed with the government, and remanded the case to the district court. Absent any statutory prohibition against the production of nonfiling lists, the district court can order the government to produce such lists under the Federal Rules of Criminal Procedure, rule 16(b).[43] The rule provides that, upon request, the court may order the government to permit the defendant to inspect and copy documents within its possession. However, there must be a showing of materiality to the preparation of its defense, and the request must be reasonable.

The nonfiling lists are material for the defendant's case. A defendant in a criminal proceeding enjoys the Sixth Amendment right of confronting his accusers.[44] There is a constitutional right to cross-examine and challenge the credibility of one's accusers. In this case, a major witness against the defendant will be computer printouts, which will indicate that the IRS had no record of the defendant having filed a return for the years in question.[45]

The introduction of printouts, the court noted, is admissible in a criminal trial. However, the party offering the evidence must lay a proper foundation, sufficient to warrant a finding that such information is trustworthy. Further, the opposing party must be given ample opportunity to test the accuracy of the computer and its input procedures. These are the same rights that are protected when challenging the accuracy of traditional written records.[46]

A party seeking to impeach the reliability of computer records should have sufficient opportunity through pretrial motions to review and analyze the machine and the data fed into it. He must inspect to see if in fact those who supply it with the data have performed their tasks accurately. The nonfiling lists here in dispute are important since they list a variety of nonfilers. If the computer has a pattern of errors, then these lists could be crucial in testing the accuracy and reliability of the system, or in attempting to impeach the reliability of the computer.

However, rule 16(b)—the discovery rule in criminal cases—requires that a discovery request be reasonable, which means a balancing of interests. The decision will lie with the most compelling need. The interests opposing the defendant's request are considerable: the privacy of many taxpayers. The defendant's purpose is to communicate with those on the list. These disclosures, however, may result in an invasion of privacy and could prove very disturbing to those involved.[47] Further, these individuals may be in violation of the IRS code and may themselves be under investigation; such files are thus confidential.

The government, the Court of Appeals noted, had complied with the lower court's order to make its computers available to the defendant, allow his experts to study all IRS computer procedures, machine operations, and other relevant data. The defendant should have had access to statistical analysis of the system's ability to identify nonfilers and to a government expert who was familiar with all aspects of the processing phase.[48] Studies on the reliability of the system should have been made available. The government, however, did volunteer to conduct tests to demonstrate the retrieval ability of the system.

The court held that such access should suffice to enable the defendant to examine the system's reliability and accuracy, and to cross-examine the computer's testimony.[49] These procedures would ensure the defendant his safeguards and would also protect the right of privacy of the many other taxpayers here involved.

The Court of Appeals reached a compromise and vacated the judgment of the district court, but recommended that the lower court order the government to produce the material and experts necessary to conduct a test of the system. Each party, however, would bear its own costs.

The above decision analyzed in great detail the problems associated with discovery of computer data and the system itself. It also reviewed the problems the IRS would face if open-ended discovery were allowed. The Court of Appeals conceded that the defendant had a right to confront and examine his accuser, even when the latter is a computer. However, the process to test the accuracy and reliability of that testimony must be contained within the realities of the various interests at work. There must be a balancing of the competing interests. The right to access is not unlimited.

However, the Court of Appeals fell short by its holding that each party should bear its own costs. Discovery and testing of computer systems can be an expensive proposition. Many experts charge an average of $50 to $100 per hour. Obviously, one is limited by resources. Further, a thorough review can be complicated and time consuming, possibly requiring several experts. It may even require another computer for testing purposes. Such review is an expensive proposition, and one that the courts have not yet addressed. The right to confront one's accusers means little if the ability to test their accuracy and reliability is lacking because of high costs.

The majority of the cases already discussed, both state and federal, have dealt with the issue of whether a printout is admissible under the hearsay exception accorded business records. The cases have thus been restricted to printouts that only store input and consolidate items at the output phase. None of the cases has addressed the difficulty of laying a proper foundation in a highly sophisticated computer system, such as a system that arrives at complex and independently contrived conclusions not verifiable by examination of the input data.

In highly sophisticated systems, computers may also be called upon to make interpretive evaluations. The reliability of these value judgments will pose a difficult problem when tested. To date, no case has completely eliminated, although many have relaxed, the personal knowledge requirement. Further, with the exception of the *Lievert* case, the other cases have not addressed the issue of whether the admission of printouts may in fact violate the confrontation or due process clause of the Constitution.

Two recent cases involving the use of computers to perpetrate crimes have come up in Maryland—*United States* v. *Jones*[50] and *United States* v. *Seidlitz.*[51] However, neither of these cases has resolved the preceding problems. There are other crucial issues yet to be resolved. Further, the congestion and backlog in our large urban courts only add to the problem of litigating computer crime cases. The cases discussed have only dealt in a peripheral fashion with the problem of printouts. The majority of our courts have yet to take a position.

References

1. 18 F.2d 934 (2nd Cir. 1927).
2. Ibid., pp. 937-938.
3. Ibid.
4. Note, "Revised Business Entry Statute: Theory and Practice," 48 Colum. L. Rev. 920, 921 (1948).
5. 5 Wigmore, *Evidence,* sec. 1520, p. 365 (3d ed. 1940).
6. 256 F.2d 495 (1958).
7. Ibid.; see also 28 U.S.C.A., secs. 1731-1745.
8. 418 F.2d 669 (1969).
9. Ibid., p. 672.
10. Ibid., p. 670.
11. 420 F.2d 889 (9th Cir. 1969).
12. Ibid., pp. 890-891.
13. Ibid., p. 891.
14. Ibid.
15. Ibid., p. 892.
16. Ibid., p. 893.
17. Ibid., p. 894.
18. Ibid., p. 895.
19. Ibid.
20. 428 F.2d 1033 (2nd Cir. 1970), cert. denied, 400 U.S. 825.
21. Ibid., p. 1037.
22. 18 U.S.C., 3500.
23. *Brady* v. *Maryland,* 373 U.S. 83.
24. 428 F.2d 1033 (2nd Cir. 1970).
25. Ibid.
26. Ibid., p. 1038.
27. Ibid.
28. 480 F.2d 1228 (6th Cir. 1973), cert. denied, 414 U.S. 1157.

29. Ibid., p. 1230.
30. Ibid., p. 1236.
31. Ibid., p. 1237.
32. Ibid.
33. Ibid., p. 1240.
34. 57 F.R.D., 548 (1973).
35. Ibid., pp. 550, 551.
36. Ibid., p. 551.
37. 517 F.2d 890 (3rd Cir. 1975).
38. Ibid., p. 891.
39. Ibid.
40. 519 F.2d 542 (3rd Cir. 1975).
41. Ibid., p. 543.
42. Ibid.
43. Ibid., pp. 546-547.
44. Ibid.
45. Ibid.
46. Ibid.
47. Ibid., pp. 548-549.
48. Ibid., p. 550.
49. Ibid.
50. 414 F.Supp. 964 (1976).
51. U.S. District Court for the District of Maryland, Crim. No. H-76-079.

16 Crimes of the Future: EFTS

In the near future you may live in a world where paper money is a rarity. You may soon find that paying bills can be done simply by dialing a number and instructing your bank's computer to transfer funds from your account to that of your creditor. While shopping, if you find that you bought too many items, there is no cause for alarm; just give the clerk your plastic card. After he inserts it in a terminal, you may push a series of numbers—a secret code known only to you—and instantaneously, electronic signals will be relayed back to a computer. If you have sufficient credit with the bank, the computer will signal the clerk. Funds are then transferred, electronically, from your account to that of the store.

This is a prediction of how our economic system will operate in the not too distant future. The necessary technology is already here. The foundations have been laid, and electronic fund transfers, admittedly in simple forms, are presently in operation. This is the world of the Electronic Funds Transfer System (EFTS). It is a world that will facilitate our daily transactions. It may do away with much of crime as we know it today. In a cashless society, armed robbery will have little meaning; muggings may become a thing of the past. Unfortunately, in this world the computer felon will emerge as the replacement for the common hoodlum. The world of EFTS may open up a Pandora's box unless preparations, born from understanding, are made. It is a world full of promise, and yet, one that holds serious challenges for our justice system.

Defining the New World

EFTS is the transfer of data relating to financial transactions over a series of communication networks. It begins with the input at the point of sale and culminates in computerized bookkeeping at a bank many miles away. EFTS represents the movement of funds from the account of the buyer to that of the seller, or from that of an employer to that of the employee. Unlike our present cash society, where transfers are by paper, under EFTS the movement will be electronic: impulses transmitted from terminal to terminal, computer to computer, and utilizing thousands of miles of wire. The system will create a network of many computers and terminals that will be used to relay data of all types.

However, many ask why have EFTS? A debate rages, and the outcome may have ramifications that are neither understood nor even foreseeable. In an EFTS

181

society, electronic terminals will be found everywhere—in stores, gasoline stations, places of entertainment, and possibly even places of worship. Our present paper exchange system may be reaching the point where it can no longer handle the added influx of checks, cash, and other paperwork. For example, in 1970 more than 22 billion checks were written in the United States.[1] The growth of check volume is in the area of 7 percent per year.[2] By 1980, experts estimate that it may reach more than 40 billion per year.[3] The total cost of operating our paper society is high—more than $8 billion.[4] A change in this paper system is both necessary and inevitable.

The Argument for EFTS

At present, it costs banks about 30 cents to process each check.[5] An EFTS system could reduce the cost by as much as 80 percent.[6] Alternately, the paper problem is also serious, and constantly growing. This year alone some 27 billion checks will be processed.[7] There is fear that our banking system may eventually follow in the footsteps of our postal service and be overcome by the mountains of paper that are generated annually.

In addition, proponents of EFTS also argue that the system will make it easier for the elderly and the infirm to bank and pay their bills from the convenience of their homes. Crimes against the elderly, common in our large cities today, may become a thing of the past, as criminals realize that attacking them will produce no benefits; thus EFTS further ensures the security and convenience of the elderly, as well as the disabled or disadvantaged. Lines at the bank on cold days will also become a thing of the past.

Traditional crimes will become less remunerative and, consequently, less frequent under EFTS. For example, robberies will not bring the felon any money. The victim will probably be carrying an EFTS identification card and will have committed to memory a secret code that only she or he knows. Even stealing the identification card will do the felon little good since the card alone, without the secret code, will not gain entry for the felon into the computer system. Also, even if the victim is forced to divulge the code, there is no guarantee the code given will be the correct one. Robbers are not prone to call on their victims for the correct code.

An EFTS will indirectly assist our present postal system by making it unnecessary to conduct most of our financial transactions through the mails. For example, there will be no need to mail checks, to forward bills or other forms of payment. Most payments can be handled from the convenience of the living room or, in the case of professionals or businessmen, from places of business. A large percentage of our present mail may be eliminated. Use of computers in the brokerage industry has already assisted that industry in eliminating part of the glut caused by large volumes of paperwork.

An EFTS may also cut down political bribery. Since all transactions will be recorded in a system of computers, and since paper funds may be totally replaced by electronic record keeping, it will become very difficult for government officials to "hide" bribes. Further, since checks will be replaced by EFTS, forgery may also become a crime of the past, along with counterfeiting and "fencing" operations. Paying a thief will be difficult, since all transactions will be recorded; even assassins may have to find other employment, since the funds they receive will be recorded by EFTS.

EFTS will affect every facet of our lives. It will make some activities less difficult and less time consuming; it will certainly bring with it the blessings of a sophisticated technology. The requisite computer technology is now available with which to construct a national EFTS. Steps have already been made toward that goal.[8] However, EFTS will also give rise to other crimes. It may, in fact, enable a small group of individuals to review any transfer or decision that occurs. These are some of the crimes of the immediate future.

The Technology Is Here

In late 1974 the U.S. Congress provided funds for the creation of a National Commission of EFTS, composed of 26 members who represent all the major federal agencies and departments.[9] However, the Commission started its work late. Not until 1976 did it begin to fully study the problem of EFTS.[10] By this time, many of the key decisions in the area of EFTS had already been made. The requisite technology had begun to take hold. At present, there exists a fragmented EFTS in many areas of the country, and more than $5 billion has already been put into the system.[11]

In the early 1970s the first operational Automated Clearing Houses (ACHs) made their appearance in this country. The ACH is the most fundamental element in the development of an EFTS. The ACH replaces the standard check-clearing facility with paperless entry facilities that clear electronically. Data are stored on magnetic tapes, and computers are employed to transfer the necessary payment information between participating institutions.[12] The expense of processing the large volume of paper checks has prompted this electronic substitute.[13]

The ACH has been employed as a substitute for checks in areas involving regular payments, such as wages, dividends, and utility payments.[14] ACHs have been established in San Francisco, Boston, Atlanta, Pittsburgh, Dallas, Minneapolis, and numerous other cities.[15] The ACH movement began first in California when about a dozen banks in that state formed a Special Committee on Paperless Entries (SCOPE) in the late 1960s. The objective of the committee was to find alternatives to the paper transfer system. The California SCOPE made recommendations that led to the implementation of ACHs in that state. In

1974, as other states followed the California example, a National ACH Association (NACHA) was formed, with members from all parts of the country.

The ACH offered certain key advantages not found in traditional banking, such as a variable debit service that allowed the customer to preapprove bills for automated debit.[16] Further, it enabled a single savings-and-loan association to handle the entire financial services of a family.[17] A client could pay all his fixed regular monthly payments through this service, doing away with the need to make monthly mortgage, insurance, utility, and other family-related payments.[18] Another advantage of the ACH is its ability to handle large volumes of orders. Also, the Federal Reserve System supports the program because it complements the federal wire and other clearing networks. There is even a trend to integrate the ACH into an international payments network.[19] The ACH has laid the foundations for a more sophisticated, national electronic payments system.

While the ACH developed, a parallel electronic revolution took place in the banking industry. This was the establishment in the late 1960s of Automated Teller Machines (ATMs). ATMs have now become an indispensable part of the business world. At present, there are more than 5000 of them in operation.[20] The ATM is an automated "branch office" of the local bank. It provides most of the banking services traditionally provided by nonautomated banks. For example, one can make cash withdrawals, interaccount transfers, and even credit card withdrawals from the ATM. The advantage of the ATM is convenience for the customer and an ability by the bank to extend itself into many other areas of the customer's life. Although ATMs face legal problems, they have proven satisfactory. One of the more successful ATM systems is found in Atlanta. The First National Bank of Atlanta embarked on an aggressive promotional campaign.[21] It named its machines "Tillie the Alltime Teller(s),"[22] and installed more than 20 "Tillies" in Atlanta.[23] By 1980 it is estimated that there may be more than 30,000 ATMs around the country.[24] The full potential of the ATM has not yet been realized, partially because of federal regulations that have posed a problem. For example, the McFadden Act, passed in 1927, prevents banks from operating branches outside their home states.[25] Although the Comptroller of the Currency ruled in 1974 that customer bank communication terminals were not branches, many state courts have ruled otherwise.[26] At least one United States Court of Appeals has upheld state branching laws.[27] The United States Department of Justice has also expressed concern that these terminals may be in violation of the federal antitrust laws.[28] However, the Federal Home Loan Bank Board has indicated that it will take a liberal approach in this area. ATMs, despite some of the present legal problems, have played a key role in the development of a national EFTS. The requisite technology has undergone rigorous and practical testing situations.

In 1971 a major, albeit unknown, pilot project was begun by the Hempstead Bank of Long Island, New York. A 14-month experiment was implemented to determine customer reaction to an electronic funds transfer system.[29] A number of select customers, one of its branches, and 35 stores participated in this experiment.[30] Initially, each customer was given a card. When a purchase was made at one of these preselected 35 stores, the customer handed the clerk his card, which was then inserted into a terminal linked to the bank. At this point, the computer either approved or disapproved the transaction. If the transaction was approved, the computer then automatically credited the store's account and debited that of the buyer.

Similar operations were tested in other parts of the country. For example, the City National Bank of Columbus conducted a test not unlike the New York model. However, the system began to assume the structure of a sophisticated EFTS in the Nebraska test.[31] The Nebraska Electronic Transfer System (NETS) began in late 1973. The First Federal Savings and Loan Association of Lincoln (federal) began the experiment in two supermarket outlets.[32] Terminals were installed in each. Federal customers could make their purchases by simply presenting the store clerk with their identification cards. They could also make either deposits or withdrawals at these stores when the bank was closed.[33]

In Iowa the Iowa-Des Moines National Bank became involved in a similar project. The system is called the Iowa Transfer System (ITS).[34] In the first month of operation, the Iowa system handled more than 60,000 transactions.[35] Another system has been implemented in Minneapolis. The latter system is run by the Farmers and Mechanics Savings Bank and has more than 1000 participating businesses.[36] The service costs customers 10 cents per bill paid.[37]

The preceding examples illustrate the Point of Sale System (POSS). This system consists of one or more banks, participating stores, and customers of the member banks. Terminals are set up in each store, and customers are given identification cards. When purchases are made, the cards can be used instead of cash for payment and can also be used to make deposits and withdrawals. The store terminals include a check verification capability. Like the ATMs, critics charge the POSS is a violation of the McFadden Act when out of state banks are involved. The federal authorities have noted that possible antitrust violations might be involved. However, to date no formal action has been taken.

The POSS presents a means to curtail the large volume of paper presently used in our monetary system. It enables the user to verify the buyer's account instantaneously. Transfers are also immediate. There is no time lag between the purchase and the final transfer of funds from the account of the buyer to that of the seller. One or more computer systems may be involved, and under a more sophisticated and larger POSS, complex computer switching centers could easily handle the transfers. This system, more than any other, approximates the true EFTS.

Unfortunately, the POSS has suffered some setbacks. For example, the Glendale Federal Savings and Loan Association of California shut down its POSS.[38] The system was hooked into 20 Food King supermarkets. However, after spending more than $400,000 in two years to implement the system, the bank gave up.[39] The Los Angeles-based California Federal Savings and Loan Association also gave up its POSS experiment.[40] Its system involved 17 supermarkets in the San Fernando Valley.[41] Like other POSS systems that have failed, this one suffered from low usage. The reason for failure by the smaller financial institutions is that large sums of money are needed to begin a successful POSS operation. For example, the average terminal costs $3000 to install.[42] The staff that operates the system must also be well trained; consumers must be taught how to use it properly. These are all operations that call for substantial investments in both funds and training.

On the other hand, some systems have shown promise. The First National City Bank of New York (Citibank) began its entry in the POSS field in 1973. It issued terminal cards, Citicards, to more than 500,000 personal checking account customers. By 1977 Citibank had invested more than $100 million in the system. It is now examining the foreign market, where the system may hold great promise. International transactions could be facilitated by an EFTS.

In 1976 the Washington Mutual Savings Bank (State of Washington) began its own POSS operations.[43] The system involved 23 of the bank's branches, more than 1000 merchants, and an equal number of customers.[44] Each user paid a monthly fee of $2. The user calls the bank, gives a secret code that activates the computer, and then gives his payment code.[45] He can do all this either from his home or office. If he catches a mistake, he informs the computer. If he does not, then the error will be recorded as an entry.[46] Errors have been entered and have posed a problem.

A more recent example involves the St. Louis system. The experiment involves 8 local banks and 42 supermarkets.[47] The system also allows customers to make deposits or withdrawals at these stores when the banks are closed. The banks are hoping to add other merchants, including a large hardware chain, in that area.[48] The system seems to be meeting with relative success. Some problems have arisen, especially cases involving customers who forget their secret codes.[49] However, adequate time has not passed to determine the type, extent, and frequency of other problems. However, the St. Louis experiment does demonstrate that POSS is attractive to many in the banking industry, and that, as the cost of the technology is lowered and some of the "bugs" are worked out, POSS may come to dominate our lives in the near future. Presently, there are more than 10,000 POSS terminals working in numerous stores across the country.[50] These are the bases of a true EFTS.

An assortment of other systems are currently at work that further reinforce the move toward a true EFTS. For example, the U.S. Treasury Department and the Social Security System have agreed to employ ACHs. It is hoped that loss, theft, and forgery of Social Security checks will be eliminated. The Treasury hopes to switch from a check to an EFTS system for about 40 percent of its transactions by 1980.[51] At present, more than 5 million federal transactions a month are handled electronically. The U.S. Air Force and the Federal Reserve System have also worked out a similar agreement. This system makes wide use of ACHs.

The Federal Reserve Wire System (FRWS) is another factor that lends support to a true EFTS. The system allows participating banks to clear interbank payments through a teletype communications system, through their respective Regional Reserve Banks.[52] This system allows all 12 Federal Reserve Banks and their 24 branches to communicate with each other and with the U.S. Treasury Department. The center of this system is in Culpepper, Virginia. It has been described as a "vault," capable of withstanding an atomic blast.[53] A direct computer-to-computer linkup is now being worked out between the various members of this system. Although not a true EFTS, it is a step in that direction. The Culpepper system employs four computers (each costing several million dollars) and can handle an average of 25,000 messages per hour.[54] The designers hope to increase its capability dramatically in the future.

Another electronic transfer system is the Bank Wire System (BWR). This system had its beginnings in the early 1950s and was first established to facilitate payment transfers between New York and Chicago-based banks. It now includes banks from other areas of the country and makes use of computers to transfer messages from one financial institution to another.[55]

Another system that parallels both FRWS and BWR is the Mutual Institutions National Transfer System (MINTS). It was developed to accommodate the needs of the smaller banks; and like the other systems, it employs computers to transfer data on financial transactions from one bank to another. It enables customers of any member bank to make withdrawals or deposits at any other member bank. A plastic card is issued to all clients of MINTS member banks; both the number of clients and the number of member banks are rapidly increasing.

At present the requisite technology to construct a national EFTS exists. Forces are at work that may in fact make this a reality in the near future. The true EFTS may assume the shape of a fragmented system of regional EFTSs all linked together. There is opposition, however; and there is also fear that access to this system may be limited to a handful of large banks. This consideration is not unfounded, since large sums of money have already been invested both by the private sector and the federal government in an EFTS technology. Ultimately, it is only a matter of time before the cashless society, with all its problems and promises, will be upon us.

Problems for the Consumer

The backbone of any true EFTS will be the computer. Without it, an EFTS is not possible. The ACHs, POSSs, ATMs, and other related systems have also become realities because of the computer. The present problems of crime and abuse connected with the computer will only be augmented and magnified by EFTS. The latter will also require an investigatory and prosecutorial apparatus that can meet its needs. The present apparatus cannot possibly meet the challenge. Evidentiary rules will also have to be modified and brought up to par with the EFTS challenge. A judicial system that takes three years to decide a present noncomputer case may find itself outmoded by the needs of the cashless society. Other problems, difficult and unforeseeable, will also arise.

The potential for error, already shown to be great under our present limited computerized record-keeping systems, will increase dramatically under an EFTS that will make use of thousands of computers, millions of terminals, and billions of wires.[56] POSS tests have shown that error is a real danger. If a bank's computer errs under an EFTS, it could cause serious difficulties for the individual.[57] Thus the consumer will have to maintain accurate and daily records of his transactions. Proof of payment may be difficult. At present, when questioned, the individual can present his cancelled check. The check is used in both civil and criminal litigations to show that payment was made.

Errors in the computer system can cause serious difficulties for the citizen of the cashless society. For example, if you instruct the bank's computer to pay some of your store bills and the computer, by error, pays someone else's bills, how do you prove that in fact you did make payment or at least instructed the computer to do so? In our present system, the buyer can present his cancelled check as proof of payment. In cases involving the IRS, what if X instructs the computer to pay the IRS funds owed for last year's taxes and the computer fails to do so because of some error, can X be prosecuted for failure to pay his income taxes? How can he prove that he did order the computer to make payment and it failed to do so because of its own error? In the alternative, could not an individual raise as a defense of "computer error" for his willful failure to pay his taxes? These are some serious problems presented by the EFTS.

There is also the problem of crime. Traditional crimes may only be replaced by more sophisticated frauds. The computerized EFTS may open vast areas to the felon of the cashless society. Paper trails may be nonexistent, and errors rampant. The prosecution of a felon who raises the defense of simple error is very difficult. Further, EFTS will open up as yet untouched economic areas to organized crime. Banking frauds may become highly lucrative for the felons of the future. With the assistance of a handful of insiders, criminals will be able to loot banks. Further, will stores with terminals in them be defined as bank branches? If not, then criminals may attack banks simply by making use of store terminals and thus evading prosecution under many of the present federal bank statutes. Many recent studies have shown that the majority of computer systems, even when provided with security, are still open to attack and can be penetrated by sophisticated criminals.

There is also the problem of stopping payment. If a consumer discovers that he or she has been defrauded, presently he or she has the opportunity of stopping payment. The bank is simply ordered to stop payment on the check. Under EFTS, transactions are instantaneous. It is difficult to stop payment when transfers occur in a matter of seconds. Felons will thus be able to bank the victim's money, and the victim has lost his stop payment leverage. Even if prosecuted, there is no assurance that the felon will be forced to return the funds to his victims. The latter may have civil recourse; but without proof of payment, it will be difficult. Thus the consumer will lose his ability to control his finances.[58] A loss of this control can only result in easier manipulation by felons. It may take some time before the consumer discovers that he was "taken." The present system, although somewhat cumbersome, does offer the consumer some protections the EFTS does not offer.

Privacy Problems

EFTS will also give rise to serious privacy problems. The individual's private life, his daily affairs, and even his more intimate contacts may become a public matter. At the touch of a button, both government and private groups will have access to an individual's private life. He can become the object of surveillance or blackmail. Criminals may be able to manipulate the computer's records and thus place him in an unfavorable light. For example, three officials of a national labor union were arrested in Virginia and charged with bribery after they allegedly paid the employee of a large drug store chain $1000 in exchange for a list of names and addresses of the chain's employees. The information was listed on a computer printout. The example illustrates how simple it is to find a black market for valuable data.

An individual's political opponents may also "tap" a computer system for embarassing data on their opponent. The potential for criminal abuse is serious. One federal study has listed several safeguards that, at the minimum, are needed, and are presently lacking, to safeguard the individual's privacy:[59]

1. The individual must have access to his own records.
2. He must be able to prevent the abuse of data about him.
3. He must be able to correct erroneous data about him.
4. Organizations that maintain data must take steps to prevent misuse.

Under our system of government, the right to privacy is a cherished one. The United States Constitution guarantees the citizen these related rights: right to free speech, assembly, and worship. The Fifth Amendment prohibits the government from forcing the individual to be a witness against himself in a criminal case. There is also concern for the personal nature of the individual's privacy. For example, the Fourth Amendment prohibits unreasonable searches and seizure of the home, effects, papers, and person of the individual. However, these guarantees apply only to the arm of government. They do not apply to private groups. The courts, however, and legal scholars, have extended some of these rights into the private sector.

In the late nineteenth century the doctrine of privacy began to take hold. In 1890 the noted legal scholar, Louis Brandeis, wrote his now famous article, "The Right to Privacy."[60] The doctrine soon took shape, and presently covers four major areas dealing with privacy. First, an individual has a right to the privacy of his name and likeness; these cannot be used by another for private gain without the individual's consent. In at least one case, *Grant* v. *Esquire, Inc.,* the courts have addressed this issue.[61] In the *Grant* case the defendant published the photo of the plaintiff, a Hollywood star, for private gain without the plaintiff's authorization. The court awarded damages to the plaintiff and held that one cannot use the photograph of another, whether the latter is famous or not, without obtaining his consent first. The court laid the following test: (1) the likeness must be used without the individual's authority; and (2) the defendant must benefit from it materially. This area of law is clearly delineated and could easily be employed to safeguard the individual's privacy under EFTS.

A second area of privacy protected by the doctrine is the individual's reputation: he cannot be placed in a false light. In the case of *Cantrell* v. *Forest City Publishing Company* the U.S. Supreme Court held that if one prints information about an individual, knowing that information to be false, one is liable for civil damages.[62] The key, however, is "knowing" it to be false. Thus, under EFTS, the knowing publication of false information about an individual can open a private group to civil suit. There is the problem of error in computer systems, and the plaintiff will have to demonstrate that in fact the publication was not an error, but rather the product of an intentional act.

A third protected area concerns the disclosure of private facts about an individual. There have been numerous cases in this area, including many in the credit-related field. In *Vogel* v. *W.T. Grant Company* an employee of the defendant firm telephoned friends and relatives of the plaintiff in an attempt to embarass him and force him to pay money owed the company.[63] The plaintiff sued, and the court held for him. The judge laid down the following test: (1) there must be publicity; (2) it must be unreasonable; and (3) it must deal with private matters. In a similar case, *Briscoe* v. *Readers Digest,* the U.S. Supreme Court held for the plaintiff, lending further support for the privacy doctrine.[64] There is every reason to believe that this protected area will continue to remain so even under EFTS.

A fourth area of protection under the doctrine addresses itself to the threat of electronic surveillance by the private sector—wire-tapping or bugging. Many local jurisdictions have their own statutes, which in some instances make such electronic surveillance a criminal offense. In the now classic case of *Nader* v. *General Motors Corporation,* the famous consumer advocate (plaintiff) filed suit against the large automaker (defendant), alleging that his telephone had been tapped.[65] The court found for the plaintiff. The threat of electronic surveillance will be real under EFTS. An individual whose privacy has been invaded by either tapping or bugging will have a right to file suit under the doctrine.

The federal government has passed added legislation to protect the individual against invasions of his privacy from the private sector. For example, in 1970 the U.S. Congress passed the Fair Credit Reporting Act (FCRA).[66] The act primarily addresses itself to credit-type activities. It attempts to regulate the content, updating, and accuracy of data collected and stored by consumer reporting agencies. The act delegates to the Federal Trade Commission (FTC) the duty of ensuring that its provisions are properly implemented. The act, however, does suffer from several drawbacks. The FTC has shown itself to be lax in its enforcement, and thus this provision is really a "paper tiger." Further, the act relies on private enforcement by the consuming public. This may be difficult since very few consumers have the requisite funds to engage in prolonged litigation with large firms. The act also provides for certain exemptions for credit firms from suits for defamation, negligence, and invasion of one's privacy. The act may, however, prove of some limited value in an EFTS environment. However, further legislation in this area may be needed.

In 1967 the U.S. Congress passed the Freedom of Information Act (FOIA), and later amended it in 1974.[67] This act is directed at the executive branch of the federal government. The act has as its objective keeping that branch of government open and honest to the people. Upon request, an executive agency must provide the requestor with the information requested. There are exemptions under the FOIA, and if material falls within these, it will not be made available. The FOIA, however, like the Privacy Act of 1974 (PA),[68] suffers from a similar drawback—found in all privacy-oriented federal statutes—the individual must do the ultimate enforcing. It is the individual who must finally go to court and enforce the act if the government fails to honor his request. Needless to say, this places limited value on these statutes. Few individuals can afford prolonged litigation. These statutes, however, may prove of some limited value under EFTS.

EFTS, however, will pose a serious test for the individual's privacy. Challenges will come from both the private and governmental sectors. In 1976 the U.S. Supreme Court, in the case of *United States* v. *Miller,*[69] ruled that an individual's financial records belong to the financial institution and not to him, even though they deal with his financial transactions. The Federal Home Loan Bank has recently informed the Privacy Protection Study Commission that it sees no need for further legislation in the privacy area. There is fear that, with increased computerization, a small handful of large financial institutions will capture the banking-related market. There is concern that the nation's more than 14,300 banks and 7000 thrift institutions may become compressed into fewer than 100 national institutions under EFTS.[70] There is real basis to fear that privacy may become a thing of the past. Legislation is needed to protect the individual from both the governmental and private sector.

EFTS is upon us. The requisite technology exists, and the needed foundations have already been laid. EFTS crimes will take on new forms and pose serious problems for present law enforcement. The individual will become an "open book," for government, credit firms, and also criminal elements to open when necessary. It will be a new and interesting era. Whether our legal system will be able to meet the challenge remains to be seen.

References

1. Mark G. Bender, *EFTS* (Port Washington, N.Y.: Kennikat, 1975), p. 10.
2. Ibid.
3. Ibid.
4. Ibid.
5. "Electronic Banking—A Retreat from the Cashless Society," *Business Week,* April 18, 1977, p. 81.
6. Ibid.
7. Ibid.
8. Sylvia Porter, "EFTS Commission Urges Safeguards," *Washington Star,* March 24, 1977, p. D-8.
9. Ibid.
10. Ibid.
11. "Electronic Banking—A Retreat from the Cashless Society," *Business Week,* p. 81.
12. William M. Adams, "Time to Automate the Clearing House?" *Banking,* May 1973, pp. 74, 119.
13. Federal Reserve Board of Governors, *The Purposes and Functions of the Federal Reserve System,* Washington, D.C., September 1974.
14. Paul E. Homrighausen, "One Large Step Toward Less-Check: the California Automated Clearing House System," *The Business Lawyer,* July 1973, p. 1143.
15. "Electronic Banking—A Retreat from the Cashless Society," *Business Week,* p. 81.
16. R.R. Campbell, "New England's Automated Clearing House," *FHLBB Journal,* July 1974, p. 20.
17. Ibid.
18. Ibid.
19. William Hall, "SWIFT: the Revolution Round the Corner," *The Banker,* June 1973.
20. "Electronic Banking—A Retreat from the Cashless Society," *Business Week,* p. 80.
21. Ibid., p. 82.
22. Ibid.

23. Ibid.

24. Roy A. Skoba, "The Impact of Marketing on Electronic Funds Transfers," *U.S. Investors/Eastern Banker,* September 23, 1974, p. 17.

25. "Electronic Banking—A Retreat from the Cashless Society," *Business Week,* p. 86.

26. Ibid.

27. "Bank Terminals Curbs Upheld," *Washington Star,* March 24, 1976, p. F-1.

28. "U.S. Opposes Plan of Nebraska Banks on Transfer System," *Wall Street Journal,* March 8, 1977, p. 10.

29. Robert E. Knight, "The Changing Payments Mechanisms: Electronic Funds Transfer Arrangements," *Monthly Review,* Federal Reserve Bank of Kansas City, July-August 1974, p. 16.

30. Ibid.

31. "Electronic Banking—A Retreat from the Cashless Society," *Business Week,* p. 83.

32. Ibid.

33. Ibid.

34. Ibid.

35. Ibid.

36. "Those Buck Passing Machines," *Money Magazine,* February 1976, pp. 47-48.

37. Ibid., p. 48.

38. "Electronic Banking—A Retreat from the Cashless Society," *Business Week,* p. 86.

39. Ibid.

40. Ibid.

41. Ibid.

42. Ibid., pp. 81-82.

43. Harriet King, "Let Your Fingers Do the Paying," *New York Times,* July 19, 1976, p. F-1.

44. Ibid.

45. Ibid.

46. Ibid.

47. Pamela Meyer, "St. Louisians Like Saving at the Grocery Store," *St. Louis Post-Dispatch,* June 7, 1977, p. 10B.

48. Ibid.

49. Ibid.

50. "Electronic Banking—A Retreat from the Cashless Society," *Business Week,* p. 80.

51. Ibid., p. 91.

52. Charles R. Babcok, "Feds Keep Hillside Vault," *Washington Post,* February 26, 1976, pp. A-1, A-4.

53. Ibid.

54. Ibid., p. A-4.

55. Richard M. McConnell, "The Payments System: How It Works Now and Why It Is Changing," *Banking,* May 1974, pp. 35-36.

56. Jane B. Quinn, "Watch for Electronic Banking," *Washington Post,* October 25, 1976, p. C-12.

57. Ibid.

58. Ibid.

59. Mark G. Bender, *EFTS,* p. 66.

60. Samuel Warren and Louis Brandeis, "The Right to Privacy," 4 Harv. L. Rev. 193 (1890).

61. 367 F.Supp. 876 (1973).

62. 419 U.S. 245 (1974).

63. 327 A.2d 133 (1974).

64. 43 U.S.L.W. 4343 (1975).

65. 255 N.E.2d 765 (1970).

66. 15 U.S.C., secs. 1681-1681t (1970).

67. 5 U.S.C., sec. 552(b) (1974).

68. 5 U.S.C., sec. 552(a) (1974).

69. 96 S.Ct. 1619 (1976).

70. "Electronic Banking—A Retreat from the Cashless Society," *Business Week,* p. 87.

Conclusion

In June 1971 Army Lt. Col. Lindsay L. Baird, Jr., was assigned to the 2nd Infantry Division at Camp Caseys, South Korea. Mr. Baird was given the job of Provost Marshall and told to reduce the "incidents of larceny." Soon afterward, he came across a sophisticated computer fraud that involved the South Korean government itself, as well as members of that country's underworld, and even some members of our armed forces. The computer center was located at Taegu. The facility was staffed primarily by South Koreans, supervised by a handful of Americans. A key figure in the fraud was a South Korean by the name of Ooh.

Mr. Baird, who has been called a first-rate investigator, soon uncovered an elaborate scheme. The South Koreans were using the computer center to "store, and move to desired locations, materials they were going to steal for their own use." Once the material was moved to a desired location, all records of its existence were destroyed. For example, more than $100,000 worth of American field uniforms were diverted into this illegal market in one instance alone. The material was diverted every Monday, Wednesday, and Friday from the Camp Edwards supply center. On the average, more than $10 million in food and material were stolen by the South Koreans, yearly, with the assistance of our computers.

Recently, Army witnesses told the House (Congressional) Armed Services Investigations Subcommittee that fictitious names and dates were fed into Army computers to fill the weekly recruiting quotas. These "phantom recruits" were not detected by the Army and came to light only when a recruiting sergeant "blew the whistle."

Computer crime is growing daily. One Congressional study has found that the federal government has been unable to secure its own computers against fraud and physical assault. There is also serious concern that the growing threat of terrorism may find its way into the computer area. Well-armed zealots could easily destroy many of our computers and cripple the economy of this country. Computers can also be employed by both criminal and political elements to "eavesdrop" on telephone conversations that use microwave communications. Our very physical and personal security is presently threatened by an un-harnessed technology.

The Federal Computer Systems Protection Act of 1977 is a beginning. It attempts to address itself to the problems of computer crime and makes acts that have criminal objectives involving the computer punishable by up to 15 years imprisonment and/or $50,000 in fines. However, the problem is more subtle and complex than first meets our eye. The act alone will not suffice.

Our present investigatory apparatus, both at the local and federal level, is ill-prepared for this new era. Overburdened with red tape and open to political pressure, the investigatory apparatus finds itself unable to move with the requisite flexibility and speed. It may take several years before an investigation is finally completed. However, by that time, the computer felon may have made off with his "loot" and may have erased his "tracks" in the process. Many federal cases are usually turned down by the Justice Department and never make their appearance in court. It makes little sense to give this Department such vast prosecutorial powers. There is little or no excuse for not allowing some of the regulatory agencies and nonagencies to prosecute their own criminal cases.

Further, the entire process itself must be opened to the public so as to rid it of political corruption. The computer frauds that have surfaced at present, save for the Equity Funding scandal, have involved unimportant individuals and relatively small amounts of money. In the overall scheme of white collar crime, a theft of $500,000 is not "big money." However, should important and influential elements make use of computers to bilk the public of large sums of money, the present investigatory and prosecutorial machinery might easily lend itself to political manipulation. In fact, given the present confidential nature of federal investigations, it is difficult to know if and when such pressures are applied.

The investigatory apparatus is also in need of training and developing programs to secure, as well as to combat, computer crimes. The present prosecutorial machinery is also in need of training in this area. Save for a small number of fraud units assigned to federal prosecutors in our large cities, few prosecutors, local or federal, have had any experience with this type of crime.

Our present rules of evidence must also be amended to adapt to this new era of technological crimes. The hearsay rule poses serious problems. It is the product of a feudal system. Admittedly, the rule does provide certain safeguards. However, there are other tools available to litigants to ensure the reliability and authenticity of the data presented at trial. A party can employ his own experts; present his own rebuttal evidence; as well as make use of cross-examination to ensure the data are accurate and credible.

There is also need for legislation at the state level, similar to the New Federal Rules of Evidence, which specifically addresses itself to the problem of computer-related litigation. For example, the South Australia Evidence Act of 1972 addresses the problem of computer-related litigation. Section 59(a) of the act defines a *computer output* as any statement or representation of fact produced by a computer. *Input data* are defined as any statement that has been transcribed by appropriate methods and fed into the computer. Section 59(b) gives the courts great latitude in admitting computerized data. The court must be satisfied that the data were programmed correctly and are free of error or manipulation. The act, far from perfect, is a beginning and merits study.

At present, our courts have shown great laxity when sentencing computer felons. In early August 1977 a deaf-mute was sentenced, by an Ohio court to 1 to 10 years in prison for stealing a bottle of beer. Several months before, a Maryland court sentenced a computer felon to three years probation. The latter had been involved in a fraud that exceeded $100,000. Computer felons are a serious threat, not only to society, but also to the confidence of the public in our system of justice. A legal system that sentences one individual to a long term of imprisonment for stealing several dollars worth of goods and places one who steals millions on probation invites disrespect and scorn. It invites felons to change their techniques, rather than their ways. I recently visited a felon in a prison. We discussed his case, and then he asked me if it was true that computer criminals received only probation. I responded that it was so. He smiled, and said, "That's the way to steal."

The problem of computer crime is, in great part, the failure of our laws, jurists, lawyers, and law schools to adapt to the needs of a changing environment. The legal establishment has shown a reluctance to meet change. Our law schools prepare students for an era that has long since passed, and offer no courses in the area of technological crimes. The courts, too, must bear their share of criticism. They operate in a manner that is more reminiscent of eighteenth century England rather than modern America.

The business world must also bear part of the burden. Whenever firms are "raped" by computer, instead of informing the authorities, they "sweep" the episode under the rug. This kind of behavior only invites further attack. Legislation may be needed to make it mandatory for such crimes to be reported to the authorities. At present, by law, banks must report crimes against them to the authorities. This experience has proven successful in the investigation and prosecution of felons who prey on banks. A similar requirement involving computer crimes might also be of some assistance.

The computer has its blessings. For example, computers are presently employed to assist X-ray scanners in constructing a cross-section or "slice" of the human body. In Virginia Beach, Virginia, computers are presently employed to assist the dispatch of police cars to scenes of crimes. The computer analyzes the more than 3400 daily complaints received over the telephone by the police and instructs the police dispatcher to send one or more units to the scenes. It also identifies which units should be sent to the crime scene.

Computer technology is still in its infancy. Its benefits have already been felt. It guides air travel, ships at sea; the banking industry relies on it. However, it opens doors to a new world. Criminals, especially organized crime types, will attempt to use it for their ends. We must ensure that it is used only in the best interest of society. Time is still with us. We need only the will to adapt the spirit of the common law to the needs of the electronic age.

Index

199

About the Author

August Bequai is a practicing attorney in Washington, D.C., specializing in legal aspects of technology. A former federal prosecutor and chairman of the Federal Bar Association's Subcommittee on White-Collar Crime, he also has been vice-chairman of the Federal Bar Committee on Criminal Law and presently chairs the Subcommittee on Computer Legislation for the American Society for Industrial Security.

Bequai holds the J.D. from The American University Law School and the L.L.M. from the National Law Center of The George Washington University. He is an adjunct professor of criminal law at The American University and has lectured widely before numerous law-enforcement and business groups such as the FBI Academy, The George Washington University, the Institute on Organized Crime, and others. He is the author of more than thirty articles dealing with various aspects of the law as well as a contributor to the *Maryland Jury Instructions In Criminal Cases.*

DATE DUE

MAR 3

MAR 3/11 92

MY 01 92

NY 8 92

OCT 2 3 1980

APR 2 2

AUG 5 1982

JUN 7 1983

MAR 0 8 09

DEC 02

DEC 1 8 1983

FEB 27 1984

APR. O 2 1984

NOV 0 1 1984

JUN 1 3 1985

SEP 3 0 1985

OCT 2 4 1985

NOV 1 3 1985

MAR 1 1 1986

OCT 1 3 1986

OCT 2 7 1986

NOV 3 1986

NOV 2 4

GAYLORD

About the Author

August Bequai is a practicing attorney in Washington, D.C., specializing in legal aspects of technology. A former federal prosecutor and chairman of the Federal Bar Association's Subcommittee on White-Collar Crime, he also has been vice-chairman of the Federal Bar Committee on Criminal Law and presently chairs the Subcommittee on Computer Legislation for the American Society for Industrial Security.

Bequai holds the J.D. from The American University Law School and the L.L.M. from the National Law Center of The George Washington University. He is an adjunct professor of criminal law at The American University and has lectured widely before numerous law-enforcement and business groups such as the FBI Academy, The George Washington University, the Institute on Organized Crime, and others. He is the author of more than thirty articles dealing with various aspects of the law as well as a contributor to the *Maryland Jury Instructions In Criminal Cases.*

DATE DUE

	MAR 3 3 1987	
OCT 2 3 1980	3/11 88	
APR 2 2 198	MY 01 '92	
AUG 5 1982	MY 8 '92	
JU 7 1983		
DEC 0 2 198	MR 0 8 '09	
DEC 1 6 1983		
FEB. 2 7 1984		
APR. 0 2 1984		
NOV 0 1 1984		
JUN. 1 3 1985		
SEP. 3 0 1985		
OCT. 2 4 1985		
NOV 1 3 1985		
MAR 1 1 1986		
OCT 1 3 1986		
OCT 2 7 1986		
NOV 0 3 1986		
NOV 2 4 1986		
GAYLORD		PRINTED IN U.S.A.